GUIDE
TO THE
CONTINENTAL
DIVIDE
TRAIL

GUIDE TO THE CONTINENTAL DIVIDE TRAIL

Volume 3: Wyoming

James R. Wolf

CONTINENTAL DIVIDE TRAIL SOCIETY
WASHINGTON, D.C.   20014

Library of Congress
Cataloging in Publication Data (Revised)

Wolf, James R.
Guide to the Continental Divide Trail

Vols. 2- published by Continental Divide
Trail Society, Washington, D.C.
Includes bibliographies.

CONTENTS: v. 1. Northern Montana.
v. 2. Southern Montana and Idaho.
v. 3. Wyoming.
1. Continental Divide Trail — Guide-books — Collected works.
2. Hiking — Wyoming — Guide-books — Collected works.
3. Wyoming — Description and travel — Guide-books — Collected works.
4. Natural history — Continental Divide — Collected works.
I. Title.
GV199.42.C84W64   917.8604'33   76-17632

ISBN 0-87842-054-1 (v.1)
ISBN 0-934326-02-9 (v.2)
ISBN 0-934326-03-7 (v.3)

Guides to the Continental Divide Trail
are published by
CONTINENTAL DIVIDE TRAIL SOCIETY
P.O. Box 30002
Washington, D.C.   20014

Would you cultivate walking as a fine art, learn to see and to hear what the world, which man has not made nor has entirely marred, is telling you of the wonders of that life which she kindly nourishes upon her bosom.

W. J. Holland

Contents

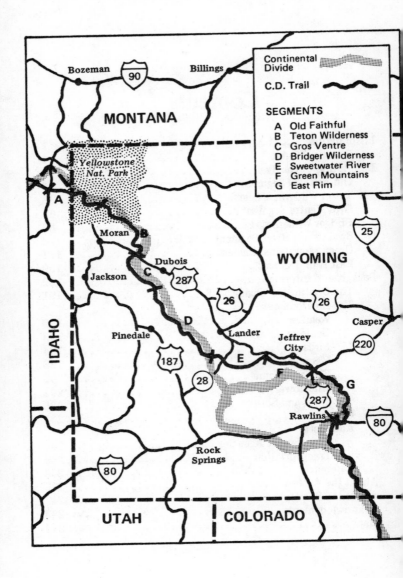

Introduction

This volume describes a route for the Continental Divide Trail from Macks Inn, Idaho to Rawlins, Wyoming, a distance of 496 miles. Elevations range from 6,250 to 11,500 feet, providing a variety of hiking experiences. Excellent scenery, abundant wildlife, and frequent historic points of interest should satisfy every taste.

The route through Yellowstone National Park offers some fine backcountry travel, as well as a visit to Old Faithful. Shoshone and Heart Lakes are particularly memorable. Next comes the Teton Wilderness, a land of high plateaus separated by cliff-lined glacial valleys. The Trail generally follows the bottoms through green meadows, but at one point climbs to the high country for a grand panorama.

Beyond the highway crossing at Togwotee Pass, the Trail scrambles over several lightly forested ridges, then continues with a long gradual ascent of the South Fork of Fish Creek. The old fire trail system has deteriorated and a hiker, unlikely to see other people for days, must be prepared to rely occasionally upon map and compass in addition to the guidebook.

The highest and grandest parts of the Trail in Wyoming, and the most popular for backpackers, are found in the Bridger Wilderness, along the west slope of the Wind River Range. Much of the Trail here is around timberline, with splendid lakes and mountain scenery.

The character of the Trail changes abruptly as it leaves the Wind Rivers. It circles the north and east rims of the Great Divide Basin, at places following the tracks of the old Oregon Trail. This is predominantly grassland, with a great deal of sagebrush. Even here there is much to cherish — the rugged and remote canyon of the Sweetwater River, several ghost towns, the fine vistas from the forested plateau of Green Mountain, pothole country full of ducks, and antelope and sage grouse too numerous to count. This part of Wyoming receives little precipitation, and the need for reliable water sources dictates a detour to the North Platte River, largely along paved road, for the last twenty miles approaching Rawlins.

INTRODUCTION

The table on pages 4 and 5 provides additional general information regarding the Trail. The figures for "auto road" (passable by car as well as jeep) and "cross-country" involve sometimes-arbitrary judgments; they are intended merely to suggest the kind of hiking to be expected in a section. Mileages are primarily based upon use of a map-measurer (a calibrated wheeled device); they are conservative and may not allow completely for minor shifts of direction or for extra length resulting from elevation changes.

Old Faithful Segment (61.6 Miles)

Yellowstone National Park — the world's first such reservation — was set aside in 1872 "as a public park or pleasuring ground for the benefit and enjoyment of the people," with provision for its "curiosities or wonders" to be retained in their natural condition.

Those wonders of Yellowstone can be traced to eruptions of incredible force. The last of the great explosions, some 600,000 years ago, was accompanied by an enormous outpouring of gas, steam, and ash. With the sudden release of pressure, the surface of the ground collapsed, forming a huge depression or caldera. Thereafter, volcanic action continued, though less dramatically, with repeated flows of sticky lava, which cooled to form the rhyolite that is the characteristic surface rock of the national-park's core.

Park visitors must observe certain precautions. The first is to recognize that the ground around thermal features may be weakened by invisible underground pools or voids; many people have been seriously injured by dropping unexpectedly into scalding hot springs. Remain on the established trails and boardwalks. Second, remember that the animals in the park are wild. Bison, moose, bear, and elk should be viewed with circumspection. Grizzly bear, though numbering only in the hundreds and tending to stay out of sight, are a particularly serious potential hazard. No one should enter the backcountry without studying the Park Service's brochure on bears. Trails may at times be closed because of grizzly activity.

Park regulations, while necessary because of heavy visitor

2

use, complicate the planning of a hike. Camping is restricted to designated locations, which must be reserved on a first-come basis when setting out, or up to two days in advance. Hunting is prohibited, and fishing requires a permit, obtainable from rangers without charge. It is of course unlawful to damage natural features.

The Segment is notable for beautiful Shoshone Lake, magnificent geysers and hot springs, and meadows with plentiful wildlife. It begins with a long ascending road walk from Macks Inn, Idaho, in the valley of the Henrys Fork, to the Yellowstone boundary at 16.5. The Trail continues through forest across the flat and dry Madison Plateau to some hot springs near the Continental Divide just before Summit Lake, at 26.4. The route drops to the Biscuit Basin, a thermal area along the loop road in the Park, at 34.0. A walk through the Upper Geyser Basin, passing Old Faithful and several other major geysers, leads to the visitor center at 36.8. The Trail returns to backcountry, mostly in forest, to the remote Shoshone Geyser Basin at 46.6 and the west end of placid Shoshone Lake at 48.2. Some meadows break up the hike as it heads to a ford of the Lewis River, at the lake's southeast tip, at 56.4. Dense forest continues to the roadhead at 60.0, where an alternate route from Delmoe Lake (near Butte, Montana) converges with the Trail. The Segment ends by the South Entrance Road, at 61.6.

Teton Wilderness Segment (78.9 Miles)

Compared to Yellowstone and the Wind Rivers, few hikers have discovered the heart of the Teton Wilderness. Perhaps the reason is that the trails for the most part follow the valleys instead of the skyline. But these are very handsome valleys, deep steep-walled canyons scoured by glaciers.

This portion of Trail offers much in addition to its impressive cliffs. The Two Ocean Plateau, a patch of high country with outstanding views, is inspirational. Nearby is the Parting of the Waters, where a creek splits into branches destined to flow into the Pacific Ocean and the Gulf of Mexico. Elsewhere, a large stream, hemmed in   chasm barely six feet wide, makes an abrupt 80-foot plunge. Near the beginning of the Segment, in

SUMMARY TABLE

From	To	Miles Total	Auto Road	Cross-Country	Elev. Gain
Old Faithful Segment					
Section 1 Macks Inn	Park Boundary	16.5	16.3	0.2	1850
Section 2 Park Boundary	Biscuit Basin	17.5	0.0	0.0	650
Section 3 Biscuit Basin	Old Faithful	3.0	0.1	0.0	100
Section 4 Old Faithful	Shoshone Geyser Basin	10.2	0.0	0.0	1000
Section 5 Shoshone Geyser Basin	South Entrance Road	14.4	1.6	0.3	1350
	Subtotal	61.6	18.0	0.5	4950
Teton Wilderness Segment					
Section 1 South Entrance Road	Snake River	15.0	0.0	0.0	600
Section 2 Snake River	Mink Creek	15.5	0.0	0.0	2250
Section 3 Mink Creek	Two Ocean Pass	8.3	0.0	0.0	1450
Section 4 Two Ocean Pass	Buffalo Fork	14.6	0.0	0.0	850
Section 5 Buffalo Fork	Cub Creek Pass	18.0	0.0	0.0	4200
Section 6 Cub Creek Pass	Togwotee Pass	7.5	0.6	1.2	1200
	Subtotal	78.9	0.6	1.2	10550
Gros Ventre Segment					
Section 1 Togwotee Pass	North Fork, Fish Creek	11.6	0.0	2.5	600
Section 2 North Fork, Fish Creek	South Fork, Fish Creek	12.1	0.0	6.2	2000
Section 3 South Fork, Fish Creek	Fish Creek Park	10.7	0.6	1.8	1050
Section 4 Fish Creek Park	Green River Lakes	16.8	0.8	8.1	1500
	Subtotal	51.2	1.4	18.6	5150
Bridger Wilderness Segment					
Section 1 Green River Lakes	Green River Pass	16.0	0.0	0.0	2750
Section 2 Green River Pass	Pole Creek	17.7	0.0	0.0	2600
Section 3 Pole Creek	North Fork Lake	14.8	0.0	0.0	1400
Section 4 North Fork Lake	East Fork River	16.3	0.0	0.0	1900

Section	From	To				
Section 5	East Fork River	Big Sandy Entrance	8.2	0.0	0.0	650
Section 6	Big Sandy Entrance	Temple Peaks	9.9	0.0	0.0	2450
Section 7	Temple Peaks	Sweetwater Guard Station	13.6	0.0	0.0	1150
Subtotal			96.5	0.0	0.0	12900
Sweetwater River Segment						
Section 1	Sweetwater Guard Station	East Sweetwater River	10.4	2.2	0.0	1150
Section 2	East Sweetwater River	Wyoming Highway 28	10.9	0.0	0.5	1700
Section 3	Wyoming Highway 28	Lewiston	17.9	4.2	1.6	300
Section 4	Lewiston	St. Mary Station	13.0	0.0	4.1	0
Section 5	St. Mary Station	Sweetwater Station	12.2	2.3	0.0	50
Subtotal			64.4	8.7	6.2	3200
Green Mountains Segment						
Section 1	Sweetwater Station	Happy Spring	8.6	1.5	0.0	600
Section 2	Happy Spring	Cottonwood Creek	11.5	0.0	0.0	900
Section 3	Cottonwood Creek	Crooks Creek	8.8	7.2	0.0	900
Section 4	Crooks Creek	Sheep Creek	3.0	2.2	0.0	550
Section 5	Sheep Creek	Willow Creek	13.3	1.4	2.2	2350
Section 6	Willow Creek	Muddy Gap	12.1	0.6	1.2	400
Subtotal			57.3	12.9	3.4	5700
East Rim Segment						
Section 1	Muddy Gap	Ferris Mountain Ranch	10.8	3.5	0.9	1600
Section 2	Ferris Mountain Ranch	Sand Creek	15.2	0.0	0.5	1200
Section 3	Sand Creek	Deweese Creek	9.2	2.7	0.0	950
Section 4	Deweese Creek	Saltiel Creek	9.1	0.0	0.0	900
Section 5	Saltiel Creek	Seminoe Road	15.1	0.0	0.4	800
Section 6	Seminoe Road	Sinclair	20.6	16.5	0.0	500
Section 7	Sinclair	Rawlins	6.9	6.9	0.0	150
Subtotal			86.9	29.6	1.8	6100
Continental Divide Trail in Wyoming			496.8	71.2	31.7	48550

Yellowstone Park, the Trail passes geysers and hot springs along scenic Heart Lake. Elk, moose, and black and grizzly bears all occur, and fishing is said to be exceptionally good. (See the comments under the Old Faithful Segment, above, with respect to hiking in Yellowstone National Park.)

This is well-watered country, with snowfields persisting at higher elevations into July. Travel in the early part of summer may be complicated by high water, especially at fords on the Heart River and Snake River (which can be avoided by a detour). Park rangers can provide current information.

From the South Entrance Road in Yellowstone National Park, the Trail crosses a low ridge and drops to Heart Lake, and nearby thermal features, at 7.1. It continues around the north side of the lake and descends to the Heart River at 15.0. The next several miles require numerous fords as the Trail proceeds up the Snake's forested valley. Meadows predominate around the remote entrance to the Teton Wilderness at 26.1. After crossing a burned ridge, the Trail heads on up Mink Creek from 30.5 to 31.9, then climbs to the Two Ocean Plateau. Excellent panoramic views are available from the 10,000-foot crest from 34.5 to 35.1. The descent leads to the Parting of the Waters, at 38.2, the point where North Two Ocean Creek divides into eastward- and westward-flowing streams.

Cliffs overlook the Trail as it proceeds along the edge of spacious North Fork Meadows. There is a forested ridge on the way to the Buffalo Fork (of the Snake) at 53.4. The Trail swings up the South Buffalo Fork, largely in meadow again, to a ford at 64.6. (South Fork Falls, a short detour, should not be missed.) A ridge at 68.3 provides more fine views. The Trail leaves the Teton Wilderness at Cub Creek Pass at 71.4, but some of the most impressive scenery of the entire Segment occurs as the route continues down a cliff-lined valley past Upper Brooks Lake at 71.7 to Brooks Lake Lodge at 74.9. A climb over a notch at the base of Sublette Peak's summit pyramid, followed by a cross-country descent in forest, leads to the end of the Segment at Togwotee Pass — where U.S. 26-U.S. 287 crosses the Continental Divide — at 78.9.

Gros Ventre Segment (51.2 Miles)

The heart of this Segment is the valley of the South Fork of

Fish Creek, a stream of varied moods. Both its rushing portions and its calm meanders through meadows are very attractive. Aside from gravel roads near Union Pass, which may unwisely be upgraded to a high-standard auto route across the mountains, the wilderness character has generally been preserved. The occasional high places on the Segment offer some splendid views. Moose and elk are common.

The hiking season extends from July into October. Snow will linger into early summer around Togwotee Pass, and several fords can be challenging so long as the water levels remain high. The trail system has received little maintenance over the years, so one should be prepared to rely upon map and compass.

As the Trail proceeds from Togwotee Pass through Squaw Basin to a ridge at 5.0, steep-walled mountains dominate the scene. The route then drops in forest interspersed with meadows, past Beauty Park at 7.8, to the sagebrush-lined North Fork of Fish Creek, which is forded at 11.6. A hike over a couple of ridges, rewarded by good vistas, leads to a difficult ford of the South Fork of Fish Creek at 23.7. The Trail follows this creek upstream to the vast upland meadows of Fish Creek Park, near historic Union Pass, from 34.4 to 38.4. The remainder of the Segment follows the general route of the old Highline Trail, now apparently abandoned. After a climb to Gunsight Pass at 43.2, with its magnificent view of the nearby gateway to the Bridger Wilderness, the route drops down to the glaciated Roaring Fork Basin. The ford of Roaring Fork, at 45.6, can be tricky. The final stretch is a hike down the open slopes to the outlet of the Green River Lakes, at a roadhead at 51.2.

Bridger Wilderness Segment (96.5 Miles)

The Bridger Wilderness extends about 80 miles along the Continental Divide on the west slope of the Wind River Range. Several glaciers remain at the highest elevations, and throughout much of the Wilderness past glaciation has left its mark in a rugged terrain of steep slopes, high cirques with beautiful lakes, and deep valleys. An excellent trail system is available for travel from one end of the area to the other, though some of the greatest rewards await the visitor who explores the high country off the beaten track.

INTRODUCTION

Vegetation includes dense stands of lodgepole pine, areas of stunted timber, and high alpine meadows above timberline. Black bear and mountain sheep are present, but are not likely to be seen along the main travel corridors. Fishing is very popular.

The earliest commercial ventures into the area were beaver trapping and trading expeditions in the 1820's and 1830's. By the turn of the century, grazing of domestic sheep had become an important activity. in the high meadows — and even now seasonal movements of livestock may be encountered along the Trail between North Fork Lake and the Big Sandy Entrance.

The season for hiking the high country is brief. Snow at upper elevations and high water in some streams may cause problems until mid-July. And with the arrival of September, there is a chance that new snows can once again obscure the route. Be sure to inquire in advance regarding current regulations, including possible restrictions on camping.

A walk along the shore of Green River Lakes past the imposing monolith of Squaretop Mountain is the introduction to the Bridger Wilderness. The Trail then crosses the Green River at 9.4 and climbs through forest to Green River Pass at 16.0. Outstanding alpine scenery marks the route as it rims several high lakes, including Island Lake, which sits in the shadow of lofty peaks along the Continental Divide at 27.4. After climbing over Lester Pass at 30.6, the Trail drops to ford broad Pole Creek at 33.7.

The Trail continues on easy grades to Horseshoe Lake at 41.5 and then climbs in dense forest to North Fork Lake at 48.5. A delightful hike on a high open plateau, often in sight of the towering ramparts of Mt. Bonneville, marks the next several miles. After the ford of the East Fork River at 64.8, the Trail descends past more lakes to a trail junction at 73.0 close to the Big Sandy roadhead. Beautiful Big Sandy Lake, at 77.8, is a good base to explore the impressive Cirque of the Towers. The Trail then covers an especially rugged stretch as it ascends to its highest elevation in Wyoming, a 11,500-foot pass on the shoulder of Temple Peak at 82.9. It drops quickly, soon entering forest. Route-finding may be difficult near Little Sandy Lake. After Little Sandy Creek at 89.9, the Trail crosses to the Atlantic side of the Continental Divide at 90.9 and descends in forest to the head of a jeep road at 94.6 and proceeds down to the end

8

of the Segment, near the site of the former Sweetwater Guard Station, at 96.5.

Sweetwater River Segment (64.4 Miles)
Green Mountains Segment (57.3 Miles)
East Rim Segment (86.9 Miles)

The great mountain chain of the Rockies is interrupted in central Wyoming. In the gap between the Wind Rivers to the north and the Sierra Madres to the south lies the Great Divide Basin, over two million acres of rolling grassland and sagebrush embraced by two arms of the Continental Divide.

It is dry country, some portions receiving only six to eight inches of precipitation annually. Wildlife thrives nevertheless. Pronghorn antelope are abundant. Wild horses, mule deer, badger, coyotes, and jackrabbits are among the other prominent mammals. Moose and elk also occur at places.

There is a way to enjoy the country on foot, with assured water supplies, and with a generous sampling of scenic and historic points of interest. To do so, one need only follow the perimeter of the Basin along its northern and eastern sides. The route traces the path of the Oregon Trail, approaches gold-mining ghost towns and present-day uranium mines, and passes by other archaeological and historic sites. The varied landscape includes a remote river canyon, a high forested plateau with fine vistas, sand dunes, and an isolated cluster of ponds crowded with waterfowl.

Since this portion of the Trail is relatively low-lying, it should be possible to traverse nearly all of it from May through October. There might be some difficulty with high water along the Sweetwater and its tributaries in early season, but serious problems seem unlikely.

Note that a number of places, described in the detailed text, are on private property. * *It is imperative that a visitor respect the landowner and his property. Avoid litter, disturb livestock as little as possible, and crawl under any gate that might be difficult to close after passage. Use a portable stove instead of an open fire; be careful with any flame, because with wind and dry vegetation a fire can get out of control very quickly.*

---

* Landowners are invited to to advise the Society with respect to the use of their land by hikers. (Anyone planning to hike in these Segments should check in advance with the Society; please enclose self-addressed stamped envelope.)

INTRODUCTION

The *Sweetwater River Segment* follows jeep roads, over low grassy ridges, to the East Sweetwater River at 10.4. The Trail next proceeds up a secluded valley, then (on unmaintained footway) crosses the timbered southernmost ridge of the Wind River Range at 15.5. There are good views toward South Pass, the broad level gap where hundreds of thousands of pioneers surmounted the Continental Divide on their westward travels. Passing Wyoming Highway 28 at 21.3, the Trail reaches South Pass City at 24.0. Once a thriving gold-mining town, it is now being restored as a historic site.

The Trail continues, largely on jeepways, down the virtually treeless valley of Willow Creek until it intersects the Oregon Trail at 32.4. It follows the Oregon Trail past dredged Rock Creek at 34.7, and then on gravel road to the ghost town of Lewiston at 39.2. A detour from the emigrants' route starts out with a hike down Strawberry Creek to its confluence with the Sweetwater River at 43.3.

The scenic highlight of the Segment is the wild canyon where the Sweetwater River flows swiftly between 500-foot bluffs. At 48.5, the valley opens up enough for a jeep road to gain access. This soon rejoins the Oregon Trail. One of the historic route's landmarks, St. Mary Station at 52.2, was a rest stop for stagecoaches and for riders on the Pony Express. After following the river through the open valley to 58.7, the Continental Divide Trail veers north to intercept U S. 287 at 62.1. The Segment ends at the settlement of Sweetwater Station, at 64.4, where the highway crosses the Sweetwater River.

In the *Green Mountains Segment*, the Trail tracks the long ridge to the north of the Great Divide Basin. The first part is a hike across rolling high plains. At Happy Spring, at 8.6, the Trail swings eastward and follows the base of Crooks Mountain on jeep roads. The colorful quicksand-like springs of the Soap Holes are an interesting feature at 15.2. There are a couple of oil fields along the improved road that the Trail uses between Cottonwood Creek at 20.1 and a junction at 28.9, near Crooks Creek.

The route climbs past active uranium mining operations on Sheep Mountain. (A short detour may be necessary, because of access restrictions.) It then continues, in part cross-country, to the edge of the plateau atop Green Mountain at 34.6. There are roads, mostly poor, along the rim of the tablelands. The terrain is forested, but interrupted by grassy parks. Several points offer exceptional views, especially looking southwest over the Great Divide Basin. The Trail descends fairly quickly from Wild Horse Point Overlook at 42.7 to Willow Creek at 45.2, then much more gradually through sagebrush country to the end of the Segment at the hamlet of Muddy Gap on U.S. 287 at 57.3.

The only portion of the Trail that lies within the Great Divide Basin is in the *East Rim Segment.* The hike through the uninhabited desert landscape of the first two-thirds of the Segment is fascinating, with picturesque mountains, abundant wildlife, and several points of historic interest.

From Muddy Gap, the Trail rises over a low ridge on its way to the narrow defile of Whiskey Gap, at 2.8, where in 1862 barrels of prohibited whiskey were condemned and destroyed by a conscientious cavalry commander. Secluded Black Canyon is a pretty feature on the way to Ferris Mountain Ranch at 10.8. The Trail then contours on jeep road along the base of Ferris Mountain, a wild and high ridge with massive free-standing rock flakes on its slopes; elk have a small range here. A curious spot is a small pond surrounded by sand dunes near the Larsen Place at 19.6.

The Trail turns south at Sand Creek at 26.0. The next stretch traverses an isolated corner of the Great Divide Basin. The terrain is broken by ponds which provide habitat for myriad ducks and other birds. Some cross-country travel may be necessary, but conspicuous landforms mark the way. From Boot Ranch at 32.4, the Trail climbs over the East Rim and descends to Deweese Creek at 35.2. The highest elevation in the Segment is reached as the Trail passes Bradley Peak at a gap at 38.0. The ruins of an old stage station can be explored at 42.0. The Trail then proceeds down tiny Saltiel Creek; Bradley Peak continues to provide a scenic backdrop.

Beyond the crossing of Saltiel Creek at 44.3, access to water becomes an important consideration. Therefore, after climbing over low Cheyenne Ridge at 46.4, the Trail cuts eastward through sandy sagebrush country to trickling O'Brien Spring at 54.0. Ancient Indians employed a rock-rimmed amphitheatre at 58.3 to corral and capture stampeded bison. The route turns south on paved road at 59.4. It follows the bank of the North Platte River through a steep-walled gorge from 67.4 to 70.2, then continues close to the winding river on jeep road to 74.3.

Hardtop surface, once again, is the route to the oil-refining town of Sinclair at 80.0. The final stretch is on a secondary paved road that parallels I-80 to the city of Rawlins, where the Segment ends at 86.9.

Logistics

Public transportation provides seasonal access to the Trail at Macks Inn, Idaho and at several places in Yellowstone National Park. The only other regular bus service is on U.S. 287 (at Sweetwater Station and Muddy Gap) and at Rawlins. Rawlins is also accessible by train and plane.

Post offices on the Trail are at Macks Inn (ZIP 83433), several stations in Yellowstone National Park (all 82190), South Pass City (82520), Sinclair (82334), and Rawlins (82301). Groceries can be purchased at Macks Inn, Yellowstone, Sweetwater Station and Muddy Gap (both with limited variety), Sinclair, and Rawlins. Public accommodations include a wide range of facilities in Yellowstone, Brooks Lake Lodge near the end of the Teton Wilderness Segment, Big Sandy Lodge in the southern part of the Bridger Wilderness Segment, the River Campground (with shower) at Sweetwater Station, an old hotel in Sinclair, and motels in Rawlins.

Description of the Trail

An itinerary as long and varied as the Continental Divide Trail is difficult to appreciate unless its parts are brought into focus. These volumes therefore break the route into large *segments*, which are marked by their physiographic or other distinctive characteristics, and into small *sections* that are typically bounded by road crossings or other access points. Just as the Introduction presents an overview of the segments, this Description concerns itself with the individual sections.

The account for each section begins with an introduction that sets the mood — summarizing the scenic attributes, trail conditions, water and camping opportunities, and some historic or wildlife highlights. It also calls attention to routing options that will need to be examined as the work of developing the Trail proceeds in the years ahead. Information on land status is included as well, because any effort to improve the Trail should emphasize cooperation with the private landowners. When appropriate, the discussion indicates points of access (including means of public transportation) and places to resupply, and gives the name of the Forest Service ranger districts to whom inquiries may be addressed. The introduction ends with references to applicable maps — both the U.S. Geological Survey topographic maps and the ones bound in this volume. The scale of the topographic maps is stated — 1:24000 for 7½-minute quadrangles, and 1:62500 for 15-minute quadrangles.

The principal part of the text is written with extensive detail. It is not necessary, or even desirable, to refer to it for every creek and trail junction. But it should be remembered that the Trail at this time is not the well-blazed and worn footway that it may some day become. Where the route is cross-country, especially, even small features such as outcrops or clumps of trees are important landmarks that a guide should identify if it is to be understood.

The section description ends with a listing of distances and elevations (rounded to the nearest 50 feet). This has two purposed: first, to assist in relating the text to the topographic maps and, second, to provide a convenient tool for preparing a hiking schedule. (The key to this is to know one's own pace —

for example, estimating one hour for each two miles and an additional hour for each 700 feet of elevation gain.)

The information is reported on the basis of single observations, which accounts for the liberal use of such qualifiers as "probably" or "should be." Further research, and the benefit of readers' observations, will result in more definite statements in future editions.

A few terms merit a special word. The *Trail* (capitalized) means the Continental Divide Trail, as described in this series. The term *trail* (uncapitalized) is employed in its normal sense. A *jeep road* is well-worn, sometimes marginally passable by car. A *jeep trail*, definitely for four-wheel-drive vehicles only, has a well-worn surface. A *jeep track* shows signs of vehicle travel, but lacks regular use.

References to the *left bank* or *right bank* of a creek are natural for a downstream hike. When the route goes up the creek, however, it must be remembered that the left bank is to the traveler's right (and, in these cases, the trail description usually includes the compass direction as well). In addition to the term *pass*, the text uses *saddle* or *notch*, especially if the feature is relatively broad or narrow, respectively. A *park* is a meadow or other open area surrounded by forest. Some alpine terms are *cirque* (a steep-walled feature resembling an amphitheatre) and *couloir* (a steep gully). *Talus* is the large broken rock at the foot and on the gentler slopes of a mountain; *scree* is finer rubble.

A notation such as *T14N, R6E* identifies a *township* in the conventional terminology which appears on topographic and Forest Service maps. Each township is divided into *sections*, which must be distinguished from sections of Trail description. Bearings and directions are always given as true values (i.e., as a compass reading that has been corrected for declination).

The natural history emphasizes the birds and flowers. The references merely suggest likely places for observing the mentioned species; the flowers, in particular, are sure to change over a period of weeks.

And, now, on to the Trail. Happy hiking!

OLD FAITHFUL SEGMENT

Section 1

Macks Inn to Park Boundary

Distance 16.5 Miles

The modest charms of this Section, a long but easy climb from the Henrys Fork to the edge of the Madison Plateau, are views westward to the Centennial and Henrys Lake Mountains. The route is on road, through lodgepole forest that is being actively logged.

From Macks Inn, the Trail follows paved Idaho Highway 84 eastward to 3.2. Continuing on forest road, it rises only slightly to about 5.3, than begins a thousand-foot climb to Latham Spring at 12.2. There are small elevation changes as the Trail picks a way through a maze of logging roads before climbing an escarpment to reach the edge of the Madison Plateau, on the boundary of Yellowstone National Park, at 16.5.

This Section should eventually be relocated to foot trail, which could be constructed along any of several ridges or drainages in the national forest land east of Macks Inn. One possibility would be to pass close to Big Springs and then ascend Black Canyon; another option is to come up Moose Creek to Latham Spring.

Motels, groceries, and meals are available at Macks Inn. There is also a post office (ZIP 83433). Greyhound provides daily bus service during the summer months from Macks Inn—northbound to West Yellowstone, Montana and southbound to Idaho Falls. (Backpacking equipment and food can be purchased in West Yellowstone.)

Forest Service regulations prohibit camping at undesignated sites in the Henrys Fork valley—i.e. from Macks Inn to Lucky Dog Creek at 3.4. There is a public campground at Macks Inn, but it is very likely to be filled early in the day. Latham Spring, at 12.2, is the only publicly-owned campsite with water after Lucky Dog Creek. Carry water for the climb to Latham Spring and then load up with it, as the next 13 miles, across porous rhyolite flows, are completely dry. Arrangements should be made for camping in Yellowstone National Park before leaving Macks Inn. (See introduction to Section 2 for details.)

Nearly all of the Section is on public land in the Island Park Ranger District of the Targhee National Forest, and the remainder uses public right-of-way. The first part appears on the 1:24000 *Island Park* quadrangle (Idaho) of the U.S. Geological Survey. This is all good road, and the map is not needed. The outdated 1:62500 *Buffalo Lake* quadrangle covers the rest of the Section. (Many roads have been put in since it was issued. The description here, which may be somewhat inexact, is based upon use of compass and other personal observations. Revised U.S.G.S. maps are scheduled for early publication and should be obtained, if available. Additional changes may be expected if proposals to tap geothermal resources in the area are approved.) See also Maps 1 and 2 in this volume.

Detailed Trail data are:

Macks Inn, at the start of the Section, is on the south side of the highway bridge crossing Henrys Fork of the Snake River. A grocery, cafe, and lodging are available here.

Follow U.S. 191 south a short distance, turning left at 0.1 on Idaho Highway 84 toward Big Springs. (Continuing another couple of hundred yards on U.S. 191, one comes to the Forest Service's Flatrock Campground, a short way off the highway to the right.)

The Macks Inn post office (ZIP 83433) is on the left at 0.2. Remain on the paved highway, passing a number of side streets and private summer homes. Enter national forest land at 1.3. Cross the Union Pacific railroad tracks at 2.6. Remain on the highway at 2.8 where a gravel road turns right into a meadow. Cross Moose Creek at 3.0 A spur road at 3.1 leads to a parking area adjacent to the creek; kokanee (sockeye) salmon are netted here in September and their fertilized eggs removed to a hatchery.

Turn right at 3.2 at a signed junction in an open spot. Proceed on a graded dirt road toward the Moose Creek Plateau. At 3.4, cross a bridge over crystal-clear Lucky Dog Creek, which flows from ample springs just a mile upstream. Take water here for the climb to Latham Spring. Camping on public land is authorized past this point. Moose Creek is accessible, though apparently on private property, to the right at 5.3. Pass a summer home development and begin climbing.

16

The well-signed Chick Creek Flat Road turns right at 5.9; keep climbing to the left here. The graded and signed Lucky Dog Road turns off to the left at about 6.9. Continue straight, climbing on auto route, with some views over the valleys to the south.

Pass by the signed Moose Creek Breaks Road, which turns right at 9.1. A clearcut at 9.3 affords an opportunity for a sweeping view from the Henrys Lake Mountains to the north, past Island Park Reservoir to the west, and on to the plateaus to the south. Reach another clearcut at 10.3. Stay on the main road here where a logging road turns right. At the forks at 11.6, take the ascending left fork along the Black Canyon Road. There are good views south as the road climbs.

Latham Spring is reached by a jeep road to the right at 12.2. (A sign by the road notes this location.) The spring, fenced and piped, is about 200 yards from the main road, below the ruins of a log cabin. Fill up on water, as there are no other springs or creeks for the next 13 miles.

Come to the junction with signed and graded Park Line Road at a leveling-out spot at 12.9. Here turn right, continuing generally southeast to south. Much of the country has been clearcut. Make a swing to the left at 13.5 (A graded logging road joins from the right here.) Follow the best road, passable by car, at all times. Going over a rise at 13.7, the wooded escarpment of the Madison Plateau is visible close at hand. Bend right at 13.9, heading due south and dipping slightly.

Reach a T-intersection, with clearcuts in three quadrants, at 14.2. Turn left, traveling northeast for a bit; then make a sharp swing to the right, dropping to cross the gully of the North Fork of Split Creek at 14.4 and continuing down the left bank. There is no water here or at other culverts along the way to Yellowstone Park. Climb again, bending gently left and angling toward the escarpment further to the south.

Go straight as a series of logging roads lead off to the right between 14.7 and 14.9. Swing east and then northeast, climbing easily and crossing culverts at 15.1 and 15.3. Bend left after the latter and begin to climb more steeply along the side of the escarpment. Good views of the Centennial Range and the Henrys Lake Mountains are obtained at 15.6. Make a sweep to the right at 15.9 and continue southwest at an easier grade, and then southeast.

OLD FAITHFUL SEGMENT

A turnaround at the dead end of the road, which is still passable by car, is at 16.3. From the turnaround, angle left and head about 100°, rising slightly through forest with much fallen timber. Reach the boundary of Yellowstone National Park, marked with white metal signs, at 16.5. Along the boundary is the well-defined West Boundary Trail, a cleared path with orange metal blazes that cannot be missed. This is the end of the Section, the route continuing by turning right and heading due south on the West Boundary Trail.

Distances and elevations are:

0.0	Macks Inn	6400
0.1	Idaho Highway 84	6400
1.3	Forest boundary	6400
2.6	Railroad tracks	6400
3.2	Road junction	6400
3.4	Lucky Dog Creek	6400
5.6	Enter Buffalo Lake Quadrangle	6400
5.9	Road junction	6450
6.9	Road junction	6700
9.1	Road junction	7300
10.3	Clearcut	7350
11.6	Road junction	7450
12.2	Latham Spring	7650
12.9	Road junction	7700
13.7	Rise	7850
14.2	T-intersection	7800
15.1	Culvert	7900
16.3	Roadhead	8200
16.5	Park boundary	8200

OLD FAITHFUL SEGMENT

Section 2

Park Boundary to Biscuit Basin

Distance 17.5 Miles

A small thermal area and an unspoiled lake are features of this unpretentious section.

The initial stretch follows the West Boundary Trail due south to 2.3. The route then swings east on the Summit Lake Trail, rising imperceptibly on the level Madison Plateau to cross the Continental Divide at 9.3, just after passing between a pond and some interesting hot springs. Circuiting Summit Lake at 9.9, it then descends gradually to reach the developed area of the Park at the Biscuit Basin at 17.5. Nearly all of the Section is in forest, on the rhyolite that is the characteristic rock of the Yellowstone caldera.

Yellowstone National Park regulations require all visitors to obtain permits for overnight camping in backcountry areas. The rangers wish to issue permits in person; this gives them an opportunity to give advice with regard to protection of Park features and precautions against bears. Hikers should therefore expect to detour to visit the ranger station at West Yellowstone before leaving Macks Inn.

Water is available at Summit Lake (which may still be the only authorized campsite) and for about a mile in either direction, and also at the very end of the Section. Most of the way is bone-dry, however, and water should be carried.

Although the trails are marked with orange metal rectangles, the markings along the west boundary may be obscure. This part of the Section is on the 1:62500 U.S.G.S *Buffalo Lake* quadrangle. For the remainder, the 1:62500 U.S.G.S. *Old Faithful* quadrangle (or the 1:125000 U.S.G.S. map of *Yellowstone National Park*) should be consulted. Refer also to Maps 2, 3, and 4.

Detailed Trail data are:

The Section begins at the boundary of Yellowstone National Park, at the midpoint of the eastern edge of T13N R45E, section 23. Take the well-worn West Boundary Trail, heading due south along the west edge of the Madison Plateau. There are several rises and dips. After descending to a low point with a stand of young firs to the right, at 2.1, the Trail bends left and climbs to the southeast; the route may be a little hard to follow at spots, but should present no serious problem.

Reach a T-junction at 2.4. Turn left on the Summit Lake Trail. (The West Boundary Trail continues to the right, ascending, toward Buffalo Lake.) Soon the Trail, with quite a gravelly tread, begins to travel due east with a very slight and steady upgrade. Look for the rose-colored pygmy bitterroot among the rocks; some lanceleaf springbeauty may also be found well into July. Pass through a small open patch of young lodgepole at 3.2.

The Trail is flat and featureless as it crosses into Wyoming at the unsigned boundary at 4.4. (This is 826.1 miles from the international border in Glacier National Park.) Head due east on faint travelway through a large park from 5.7 to 6.0. It is level, with the trees on all sides blocking any more distant view.

Pass a gravelly depression with young lodgepole at 6.4. The smooth and shiny rocks, flecked with white, are rhyolite. After climbing a bit, go through a small grassy opening at 7.0. Cross a wide and dry gravel runoff channel at 8.2. Walk on the left side of an opening at 8.6, crossing a creekbed that may have a trickle of water at its far end.

There is a pond about a hundred yards to the left of the Trail at 9.1. A thermal basin to the right of the Trail at 9.1 is also worth a visit; one particularly nice feature consists of three connected pools of boiling emerald water with a sulfur-yellow fringe. (Use caution when approaching any hot springs. Also, remember that it is unlawful to throw anything into them, or to disturb them in any manner.)

A very slight rise leads at 9.3 to the unmarked Continental Divide. The Trail remains level for a bit, then drops to touch the southern edge of Summit Lake at 9.9. The round lake, with conifers backing its narrow marshy fringe, is quite attractive. The water is warm enough, but at least on the south side it is too shallow to swim. There will probably be a Barrow's goldeneye on the lake, along with pine grosbeaks in the nearby trees. Bistort and plantainleaf buttercup grow on the grassy bank, while marshmarigolds decorate the wetter spots.

Continue eastward around the lake. Note the heaths, including red mountain-heather and alpine laurel, on the landward side.

Summit Lake.

There is easy access to the lake at a trail sign at 10.1. Follow the right bank of the outlet creek, with nearly imperceptible drop, in meadow to 10.5 and then in forest. The flow in the creek completely disappears by the time the Trail crosses to its left bank at 10.8. Return to the right bank from 11.0 to 11.3, then descend fairly steeply to 11.6.

Walk through a meadow at 12.0; bistort, pussytoes, cinquefoil, aster, and daisies provide plenty of color. Step to the right bank of a creek at 12.2 (This may be a permanent source of good water, but the flow disappears a short way downstream.) The Trail is almost level to and beyond the next meadow, which is to the left at 13.0. The very gentle descent continues, with several crossings of the gully.

Drop a bit more steeply from 15.2 to 15.5, then bend left away from the gully. At 15.8, leave the edge of a bluff, double back to the right, and descend. Steam from the Biscuit Basin ahead is soon visible and the drop is steep for a couple of hundred yards. There are other short steep pitches on the way down to the valley, but for the most part it is fairly gradual.

Reach a meadow at 16.8. Turn left here, at a junction that may be obscure. Remain at contour, crossing several creeks and the Little Firehole River, whose two branches may be crossed on bridges or downed tree trunks. Intercept the Mystic Falls Trail at 17.1 and turn right. Climb to a junction with the Fairy Creek Trail at 17.2. Turn right and reach the edge of the Biscuit Basin boardwalk at a trail register at the end of the Section at 17.5.

Distances and elevations are:

0.0	Park boundary	8200
0.8		8300
1.3		8200
1.9		8250
2.1		8150
2.3	Summit Lake Trail junction	8250
4.4	Idaho-Wyoming boundary	8400
5.7	Park	8450
6.9	Enter Old Faithful Quadrangle	8500
8.2	Creekbed	8550
9.3	Continental Divide	8600
9,9	Summit Lake	8550
12.2	Creek	8250
15.8	Bluff	7900
16.8	Meadow	7300
17.1	Mystic Falls Trail junction	7250
17.2	Fairy Creek Trail junction	7300
17.5	Biscuit Basin	7250

OLD FAITHFUL SEGMENT
Section 3
Biscuit Basin to Old Faithful
Distance 3.0 Miles

The Trail cuts through the heart of the spectacular Upper Geyser Basin, passing several of the world's largest and most famous geysers and ending at Old Faithful.

Several exceptional hot springs are found in Biscuit Basin at the beginning of the Section. The Trail crosses the Grand Loop Road at 0.4. It passes the cone of Giant Geyser at 1.6, Grand Geyser at 1.9, and reaches Old Faithful at 2.7. The end of the Section is the Old Faithful Ranger Station at 3.0.

No overnight camping is allowed in the Old Faithful area. There are cabins and hotel rooms ranging from plain to elegant, but reservations should be made in advance.

Scenic coach service connects Old Faithful to various access points, including Mammoth, West Yellowstone, and Jackson Lake Lodge as well as to principal tourist points of interest in the Park. Service is relatively infrequent, however.

Besides the ranger station and visitor center, there are restaurants, snack bars, grocery stores, public showers, and branch post office at Old Faithful. Mail will be directed here only if marked for Old Faithful Station. Backpacking supplies and foods may not be be available for purchase, so it would be wise to forward items needed for further travel by parcel post. (As an alternative, consider detouring from the Trail at the end of this Segment to buy supplies at West Thumb if the store there is still in service, and to pick up mail at the Grant Village branch post office.)

The U.S. Geological Survey 1:62500 *Old Faithful* quadrangle (as well as the 1:125000 map of the Park) is out-of-date, as new parkway has been built and the old road has become a visitor footpath. No map is needed, but a Park publication entitled "Guide to the Upper Geyser Basin" contains interesting geological information as well as showing the network of walkways. The Section also appears on Map 4 in this volume.

Detailed Trail data are:

Before proceeding, pay a visit to the springs of the Biscuit Basin. Stay on the boardwalk loop, beginning and ending at Avoca Spring, a vigorous boiler that works its way to an overflowing erupting climax. A particularly attractive feature is Sapphire Pool, a blue-white seething deep caldron. To continue on the Trail, keep well to the right, to the footbridge (south southeast) across the Little Firehole River. (A foot trail supposedly begins about 100 yards back in the woods, but it was not observed.) Look for migrating shorebirds, such as the solitary sandpiper, in the moist ground to the left of the Trail.

Cross the bridge at 0.3 and continue past the Grand Loop Road at 0.4. Keep going on the bike trail on the opposite side of the road, generally paralleling the Firehole River. Turn left at the first junction, at 1.4. (To the right 0.1 mile is the Daisy Geyser Group. Daisy and Splendid Geysers may be bubbling, but the impressive eruptions for which they are noted are unpredictable and infrequent.)

Reach the Upper Geyser Basin walkway at 1.5 and turn left for 50 yards to Grotto Geyser. Its contorted shape, with numerous arched side vents, is the result of the deposition of geyserite on tree trunks. It plays about half the time, for several hours per eruption, mostly not exceeding 10 feet.

The Trail turns right here, but a detour to the left is recommended (0.3 mile each way) to visit Morning Glory Pool and Riverside Geyser. The latter, set in the bank of the Firehole, shoots a jet of water over the river at regular intervals of about 5½ hours, reaching a height of 75 feet.

Giant Geyser, on the Trail at 1.6, was one of the mightiest of all the thermal features. Though dormant since 1955, it continues to show boiling from the open side of its throat-like dome. Its eruptions, reaching 250 feet and lasting a couple of hours, could discharge 1,000,000 gallons of hot water.

After crossing a bridge over the Firehole River at 1.7, the Trail passes Chromatic Spring and the especially lovely many-colored Beauty Pool. The pool to the left at 1.9 is the vent of the largest active feature in the Upper Geyser Basin, Grand Geyser. It plays at intervals of about 8 hours, the eruption consisting of a series of bursts attaining a height of 200 feet.

Riverside Geyser.

NPS

Keep going straight at the junction at 2.0. (The path leading to the right and crossing the river goes to Castle Geyser, notable for its turret-like dome. Detour to visit it if it is erupting. It shoots a column of water about 90 feet high every nine hours or so, then continues with a steam phase that an early observer compared to "a gigantic boiling pot with a thunderstorm in its stomach.")

Take the right fork at 2.3 and immediately pass the Lion Group; its largest member, the Lion, plays irregularly to a height of 60 feet, accompanying the eruptions with steam phases that sound like the lion's roar. Next comes Beehive Geyser, named for the shape of its cone, which shoots a jet up to 200 feet high about twice a day. Giantess can be observed to the left the few times a year when it is active; rising from a large pool, the eruptions reach 200 feet, repeating themselves at frequent intervals until the geyser subsides into another quiet phase.

OLD FAITHFUL SEGMENT

Turn right at the junction at 2.5 and drop down to cross the bridge over the Firehole River. Reach the path around Old Faithful Geyser at 2.7 and follow it to the left. Old Faithful is remarkable for the frequency and predictability of its eruptions, which occur on the average of once every 68 minutes; a typical eruption has a height of 130 feet, with a discharge of 5,000 to 7,000 gallons of hot water.

Old Faithful Lodge is to the left at 2.7. Rental cabins are available here; there is also a restaurant. Come next to the visitor center, where publications and up-to-the-moment information regarding geyser activity can be obtained. Apply here for backcountry permits for the continuation of the trip through Yellowstone National Park. (Post office and grocery store are across the roadway to the rear of the visitor center.) The next large building, the rustic Old Faithful Inn, provides hotel rooms, restaurant, and bus service. Turn left just before reaching the Inn and follow the edge of the parking lot to the ranger station at its lower end, at 3.0.

Distances and elevations are:

0.0	Biscuit Basin	7250
0.4	Grand Loop Road	7250
1.7	Firehole River	7300
2.3	Lion Group	7350
2.6	Firehole River	7350
2.8	Old Faithful Visitor Center	7350
3.0	Old Faithful Ranger Station	7350

OLD FAITHFUL SEGMENT

Section 4

Old Faithful to Shoshone Geyser Basin

Distance 10.2 Miles

An easy hike through forest leads to the Shoshone Geyser Basin, one of the finest backcountry thermal areas in Yellowstone National Park.

After crossing a minor ridge, the Trail drops to the Firehole River at 3.7. It parallels the river to 5.1, passing some hot springs on the way. A gentle climb takes the Trail over the Continental Divide at viewless Grants Pass at 6.8. At 7.8, the route picks up Shoshone Creek and follows it through the Shoshone Geyser Basin, just before the end of the Section at 10.2.

There are several authorized campsites along the upper Firehole River and near the Shoshone Geyser Basin, but exact locations are subject to change. A backcountry permit allowing overnight use must be obtained at the visitor center at Old Faithful. Water is available at frequent intervals.

See the introduction to Section 3 for comments regarding transportation and resupply opportunities at Old Faithful.

The Trail is well marked and signed. Either of the U.S.G.S. maps — the 1:62500 *Old Faithful* quadrangle or the 1:125000 *Yellowstone National Park*—may be used to supplement Map 4.

Detailed Trail data are:

From the Old Faithful ranger station, head away from the geyser area and toward the entrance road. Cross both traffic lanes and continue straight on the fire road, reaching the Grand Loop at 0.2. Cross the highway to the trail marker and enter the woods, reaching a signed junction in 40 yards. Turn left and parallel the road. Come to a trail junction and register box at 0.5. Continue straight, crossing Myriad Creek on a footbridge in 60 yards. (To the right is the loop trail to Fern Cascades.)

At 0.7, opposite the "Old Faithful — 1 Mile" sign on the road, bend right and start climbing in forest. It is gradual to 1.3, then fairly steep to 1.8, after which the Trail levels out. A swamp pond is to the right at 2.1. Reach the edge of the plateau at 2.5 and then descend gradually in forest.

Intersect a gravel road at a signed trail junction at 3.4. Keep to the right, on the gravel road. (The trail angling left leads in 0.2 mile to Lone Star Geyser, which spurts a jet of water up to 40 feet above its tall dome; the main phase of each eruption, occurring at about three-hour intervals, lasts nearly half an hour.) A campsite may be located in the flat area to the right at 3.6.

Come to the Firehole River at 3.7 and cross it on a plank and beam bridge. Pass through a stretch with numerous small hot springs on both sides of the Trail. Hooded ladies-tresses grow near the creek at 3.9. Climb well above the east bank of the Firehole River before returning to its banks, near some more hot springs at 4.7. Blue-eyed grass and self heal may be observed nearby. There may be another designated campsite just to the right of the Trail at 4.8.

Cross meadows to 5.1, passing about half a dozen small creeks on plank bridges. Pine grosbeaks and their smaller look-alikes, Cassin's finches, may be seen; there may also be some moose. Enter forest and climb gradually. Level out at 6.1 and reach Grants Pass at 6.8. The Continental Divide here is a broad flat ridgetop; a sign marks the exact location of the crest.

Just beyond Grants Pass, drop gradually in mixed forest. At 7.3, reach a junction with the Bechler River Trail, which bears right (eventually leading to some exquisite waterfalls). Take the left fork, the Shoshone Lake Trail. Enter meadow, passing a small creek at 7.4. Cross another creek on a bridge of logs at 7.7 and reach Shoshone Creek at 7.8.

The Trail crosses Shoshone Creek on secured logs and continues just above its left bank, in meadow or open woods. Continue straight at 8.2 on the Geyser Basin Trail. (A horse trail crosses Shoshone Creek and proceeds to Shoshone Lake by a more westerly route that misses the geyser basin, the foot trail is to be preferred because of the geologic interest of the thermal area, though it does require crossing a very wet marsh thereafter.) Climb a few feet to go above a washout at 8.6. The Trail continues at contour, slightly higher above the left bank, crossing a couple of minor side creeks about 8.9 and 9.1.

Go straight at 9.4 where the North Shoshone Trail turns left. (If the route beyond the thermal area is impassable, return to this point and follow the North Shoshone Trail to the Shoshone Lake ranger station by way of DeLacy Creek.) Drop down out of woods to meadow, reaching the north end of the Shoshone

A pool in Shoshone Geyser Basin.

Geyser Basin at 9.6. A side trail leads back to the left out of the thermal area to Basin Bay, a small cove on Shoshone Lake, where there may be a campsite.

At 9.7, cross poles over the outlet for some periodically boiling crystal-clear pools. Next, note the small bubbling pools next to Shoshone Creek. Just before going over a rise at 9.8, a pool on the right boils periodically and then disappears into a hole. After the high point, there is a lovely blue-green pool just to the right; behind it is domed Minuteman Geyser (which erupts every minute or so to a height of about 10 feet) and a couple of bubbling rimmed pools, one of which occasionally plays to a height of five feet. Beyond this, on the left, is a belching air vent. The dome on the right, before the Trail leaves the Basin at 10.0, is Union Geyser, which is among the largest in the Park; it is active about once each three days, usually with two separate eruptions spaced about two or three hours apart.

OLD FAITHFUL SEGMENT

Leave the active thermal area and drop down to the flats extending out to Shoshone Lake. An authorized campsite may be on the right at 10.2. The Section ends here as the Trail crosses Shoshone Creek. (It may be possible to use a downed trunk for a bridge; otherwise ford the knee-deep stream, which is about 15 feet wide.)

Distances and elevations are:

0.0	Old Faithful Ranger Station	7350
0.5	Myriad Creek	7400
2.5	Plateau	7850
3.4	Junction	7650
3.7	Firehole River	7650
4.4		7800
5.1	Meadow	7700
6.8	Grants Pass	8000
7.3	Bechler River Trail junction	7900
7.8	Shoshone Creek	7850
8.2	Geyser Basin Trail junction	7850
8.9	Creek	7900
9.4	North Shoshone Trail junction	7850
9.6	Shoshone Geyser Basin (north end)	7800
10.0	Shoshone Geyser Basin (south end)	7800
10.2	Shoshone Creek	7800

OLD FAITHFUL SEGMENT
Section 5
Shoshone Geyser Basin to South Entrance Road
Distance 14.4 Miles

The Trail in this Section swings around the south side of Shoshone Lake, second largest in Yellowstone Park. The lake, nestled in a shallow basin of conifer-covered hills, is a pristine spot with attractive campsites.

The first part of the Section crosses a very wet marsh, reaching a sandy beach at 1.0. The Trail then climbs over a ridge and proceeds, at places through inviting meadows, along Moose Creek. It approaches Shoshone Lake again at 7.7 and fords the Lewis River (which drains the lake) at 9.2. After following the scenic shore north to the Shoshone Lake ranger station at 9.5, it heads southeast to an access road at Lewis Junction (where it joins the alternate route from near Butte, Montana) and continues on level gravel road across the South Entrance Road at 14.3 to the end of the Section in the parking lot at the head of the Heart Lake Trail, at 14.4.

The lovely setting of Shoshone Lake makes it a deservedly popular place for camping. Authorized sites are at both ends of the lake, but exact locations are subject to change. Water is available at frequent intervals until 9.5, where the Trail leaves Shoshone Lake for the last time. If hiking straight through to Heart Lake in a dry summer, carry water from here as the most likely source of drinking water (a creek in the parking lot at the Heart Lake trailhead) might be dry.

The bus connecting Old Faithful with Jackson Lake Lodge travels the South Entrance Road, but will not ordinarily stop to pick up passengers except at designated places, the closest being at Grant Village, nearly six miles north of the end of the Section. The bus will drop passengers here, however. Hikers continuing south on the Trail should either pick up supplies before setting out from Old Faithful or make a detour to West Thumb and Grant Village, as described in the introduction to Section 1 of the Teton Wilderness Segment.

U.S. Geological Survey topographic maps—either the 1:125000 map of *Yellowstone National Park* or two 1:62500 maps (the *Old Faithful* and *West Thumb* quadrangles) — can be used in addition to Maps 4 and 5.

Detailed Trail data are:

The Section starts at Shoshone Creek, a short distance south of the Shoshone Geyser Basin. The first part, which may lack trail markings, can be difficult. The route southeast across the neck of the large marsh is exceedingly wet, so you may have to plow through several inches of standing water. (If it proves to be impassable, backtrack through the Shoshone Geyser Basin and take the North Shoshone Trail around the north shore of the lake.) Nevertheless, it is excellent territory for bird study; look, for example, for Wilson's phalarope, common snipe, redwing, and yellow-headed blackbird. Large concentrations of Canada geese may also be found at times.

Thermal features continue until the steaming hot creek at 0.3. The Trail is then in forest to 0.6. It continues in marsh, with numerous bridges to get over creeks and wet spots, though there are still places where wet feet are unavoidable. Emerge on the sandy beach of Shoshone Lake at 1.0.

The view out over Shoshone Lake is inspiring; set in its shallow forested basin, it is more reminiscent of Maine or Minnesota than the Rocky Mountains. There will surely be waterfowl, such as Barrow's goldeneye, bufflehead, Canada goose, and the uncommon and formerly-endangered trumpeter swan. Spotted sandpipers and white-crowned sparrows feed along the beach, while tree swallows may swirl all about in swift flight.

This spot — no doubt still a designated campsite — is an excellent place to spend a night. From here, continue to the right along the beach. At 1.2, climb up the grassy break between the trees. Going over a high point at 1.4, drop down to a meadow and a plank bridge over a creek. Continue with minor elevation changes, in forest, dipping to step across small creeks at 2.0 and 2.1.

The Trail then climbs steeply to 2.4, where the lake, obscured by trees, can be seen below. Hike over a further rise, dip to cross a pebbled gully at 2.7, and then proceed with small ups and downs along a ridge. At 3.7, drop down from the ridge to the meadows along Moose Creek in the valley to the right. The Trail flattens out in the bottomland, which is quite open. A clear view to the right at 4.8 may reveal the tall and retiring sandhill crane. After another patch of woods, approach Moose Creek itself very closely at 5.0. This would be a satisfactory campsite if lakeshore sites are unavailable, but special arrangements would be necessary if the area has not been designated for this purpose.

Leave the meadows here and climb gradually into forest. The Trail quickly loses sight of Moose Creek, though generally paralleling its left bank. There are minor elevation changes. Approaching the creek again at 6.3, the Trail goes over another rise and then descends steeply to Moose Creek at 6.7.

Ford Moose Creek, only about 10 feet wide. (A wider, but shallower — ankle-deep — ford is a few yards downstream.) Beyond the willows, start downstream in forest for about 20 yards. At the junction here, turn right and begin climbing the hillside. (The path straight ahead leads to a campsite for horse parties.)

After a ridge at 7.0, the Trail drops down to circle around extensive marshes along the south shore of Shoshone Lake, which is seen off to the left. Passing these flats from 7.7 to 8.1, the Trail rises over another fairly flat-topped wooded ridge, with steep spots on both the climb and descent.

Reach Shoshone Lake at its outlet at 9.2. This is the head of the Lewis River, which must be forded. The stream is about 50 feet wide, thigh-deep. In summer the current is not too strong, and the water is a pleasant 60°.

Follow the shore northward toward the Shoshone Lake ranger station. The Lewis Lake Trail leads off to the right through a wet meadow at 9.3. Remain on the shore. At 9.5, just before the ranger station, turn into the Outlet Campground, crossing a wet patch on some parallel logs. (The alternate route on the north side of Shoshone Lake rejoins the Trail here.) The campground, set among the trees and equipped with tables, fire grates, and outhouses, accommodates several parties.

The Trail swings sharply to the right, away from Shoshone Lake. (Fill a canteen from the lake, particularly if you plan to hike straight through to Heart Lake.) At 9.7, the Trail crosses

Shoshone Lake, viewed from the ford of the Lewis River.

Summit Creek, likely to be no more than pools of stagnant water. Climb easily through lodgepole woods sprinkled with the yellow blossoms of heartleaf arnica. Lupine, strawberry, and violets are present, too. Mosquitoes may be a notable nuisance for the rest of the Section.

After reaching a high spot around 10.8, drop briefly to a depression with a meadow and a waterlily-speckled pond, to the left of the Trail. Northern three-toed woodpeckers, along with gray jays and dark-eyed juncos, are resident in the forest. At 11.6, some poles have been laid to provide footing across a wet meadow; elephantshead is abundant. There are a number of small ponds and swamps as the Trail descends.

Hike up and over a small rise, with a register box at the top, dropping to cross Dogshead Creek, another stagnant stream. In 50 feet, at 12.8, come to the trailhead at the end of a spur automobile road. This is Lewis Junction, where an alternate route from Delmoe Junction (near Butte, Montana) rejoins the Continental Divide Trail. The former is much more direct and cuts about 220 miles off the distance.

Follow the graded dirt road, with little elevation change. (The obscure path leading up the hill out of the parking lot goes to the abandoned South Entrance Trail, which can no longer be followed.) A sweep to the right at 13.8 is succeeded by a long straight stretch southward. Keep going in this direction where the road curves left to meet the highway and, again, at the end of a small turnaround. Intersect and cross the South Entrance Road at 14.3, entering the Heart Lake trailhead parking lot at the same oblique angle. The Section ends in the parking lot at 14.4 at the beginning of the Heart Lake Trail.

Distances and elevations are:

0.0	Shoshone Creek	7800
1.0	Shoshone Lake	7800
1.4		7950
1.5	Creek	7900
1.8		7950
2.1	Creek	7900
2.6		8250
3.7		8150
3.9	Enter West Thumb Quadrangle	8000
5.0	Meadow	7900
5.6		8000
6.3		7900
6.5	Rise	7950
6.7	Moose Creek	7800
7.0	Ridge	8000
7.7	Marsh	7800
8.8	Ridge	8050
9.2	Lewis River	7800
9.5	Shoshone Lake Ranger Station	7800
9.7	Summit Creek	7800
10.8		8000
12.8	Lewis Junction	7800
14.3	South Entrance Road	7800
14.4	Heart Lake Trail parking lot	7800

TETON WILDERNESS SEGMENT
Section 1
South Entrance Road to Snake River
Distance 15.0 Miles

Heart Lake is the focus of this Section. It is an especially scenic place, with the slopes of Mount Sheridan rising directly from the water and climbing nearly 3000 feet. Near the lake is a thermal area with hot springs and geyser.

The Section begins with a slight and gradual climb, mostly in forest, to 4.3. Crossing a ridge, the route drops through the Heart Lake Geyser Basin along the hot waters of Witch Creek. The Trail reaches Heart Lake at 7.1, then swings around its north side, in forest and wet meadow, well back from the shore. From a junction at 11.4, it descends the Heart River — fording it twice — and reaches the banks of the Snake at 15.0.

Supplies will be needed for several days of travel (to Brooks Lake Lodge in Section 6 or to Togwotee Pass at the end of the Segment). The grocery stores in Yellowstone National Park are not a reliable source for backpacking specialties, so mail shipments may be desired. The post office closest to the Heart Lake Trail is at Grant Village. Mail should be addressed to oneself, General Delivery, Yellowstone National Park, Wyoming 82190 and conspicuously marked with the branch — for example, Old Faithful or Grant Village — at which it is to be held.

The Old Faithful - Jackson Lodge scenic coach will make a stop to leave hikers off at the start of the Section.

Start out with a canteen, as the only reliable running water before Heart Lake comes from the hot springs of the geyser basin; further on, however, there is plenty to drink. Several campsites have been designated around 7.1 where the Trail reaches the lake; others are near the Trail at 11.9 (at the southeast corner of Heart Lake) and in a meadow by the Snake River at the end of the Section. Exact campsite locations are subject to change from year to year; obtain current information from the Park rangers, who issue permits.

The U.S. Geological Survey 1:125000 topographic map of *Yellowstone National Park* is at about the same scale as Map 6.

The Trail appears in greater detail on the 1:62500 *West Thumb*, *Frank Island*, and *Mount Hancock* quadrangles.

Detailed Trail data are:

The Section begins in the large parking lot at the Heart Lake Trailhead, just off the South Entrance Road. Take the trail at the far end of the circle, obtaining good water from the creek just to the left. Sign in at the register at 0.1 and follow the red metal blazes. Follow the right fork at 0.2. (The left fork apparently rejoins the Trail at 0.3.) Walk through level lodgepole forest. Stay to the left of a deadwater as the Trail passes through a small meadow at 0.5. Meadow and forest alternate to 1.0, where the Trail begins to climb easily through woods.

Follow the north bank of a gravelly ravine uphill at 1.7. The Trail at 2.4 is routed on short bridges over some wet spots. Take the blazed right fork at 3.1 and hike to the right of a small meadow. (The left fork seems to rejoin just beyond the meadow.) Factory Hill is seen to the south beyond a meadow on the right at 3.6 and again at the high point of the Section at 4.3.

Break out of forest at 4.4, with Heart Lake ahead. Small boiling springs, the first thermal features of the Heart Lake Geyser Basin, are on the right of the Trail here. Come to an exceptional view of the entire expanse of Heart Lake at a bend in the Trail at 4.6. The prominent mountains beyond the lake are Chicken Ridge and Mount Hancock; to the left are high mountains on the eastern side of the Park, including the especially prominent dome of Turret Mountain.

A bridge at 5.3 crosses the steaming hot water of Witch Creek. There are a couple of hot pools on the left at 5.4 and some small pretty ones on the right in a grassy area just before the Trail returns to the left bank of Witch Creek on another bridge at 5.7. Mount Sheridan is in view on the right. Continue in spruce forest, crossing several bridges over wet spots and side creeks.

Approaching Heart Lake, the Trail comes to the Heart Lake patrol cabin at 7.1 and, in 50 yards, reaches the junction of the Heart Lake Trail (to the right) and the Trail Creek Trail (to the left). There are several campsites in the area — 0.2 mile to the right at the mouth of Witch Creek and another 0.2 mile to the

Mt. Sheridan and Heart Lake. NPS

right, by the lakeshore below Rustic Geyser. A visit to Rustic Geyser is recommended, in particular for a look at Columbia Spring, a large pool of bright blue water. The fringed gentian, official Park flower, can be found there. The lakeshore around Witch Creek attracts shorebirds, common mergansers, and gulls. (The Park Service has special regulations aimed at helping the cutthroats to repopulate. Swimming in the Witch Creek area may be prohibited during spawning season. The rangers stress that soap should not be used here at any time.)

From the trail junction, turn left on the Trail Creek Trail and walk eastward along Heart Lake. Progress along the sandy beach is slow, though logs along the shore provide some good footing. Enter forest at 7.4, rising slightly. There are small ups and downs and several little creeks, often with bridges. Small meadows at 8.3 and 8.5 afford glimpses of Mount Sheridan and Heart Lake to the right.

Beaver Creek, just after the Trail enters meadow at 8.8, may be well over a foot deep and too wide to jump across. Try to find a log already in place for use as a bridge; otherwise it will be necessary to ford. The path that joins acutely from the right on the east side of Beaver Creek presumably leads to the shore. Follow the Trail along the line of trees at the left edge of extensive, wet meadows.

Leave the meadow at 9.2 and hike in lodgepole forest, well back from the lake, but only slightly above it. The Trail remains very close to contour, occasionally dipping to cross a small creek. Grouse whortleberry is the common ground cover; some flowers of the late season include monkshood, arrowleaf groundsel, white hawkweed, and goldenrod.

Bear right at the prominently signed junction at 11.4, following the Heart River Trail. (Straight ahead, the Trail Creek Trail continues to Yellowstone Lake.) Enter meadows at 11.7; Outlet Creek is to the left. At 11.9, approach the confluence of the Heart River and Outlet Creek, where there may be a designated campsite; there are also campsites upstream along the Heart River.

Cross Outlet Creek and then proceed to the right bank of the Heart River at 12.0. Both must be forded. (The former is about 25 feet wide and calf-deep; the Heart River is 50 feet wide and knee-deep.) Follow the swift river closely for about 300 yards, ignoring the blazes on the left bank. Remain about at contour until 12.7. Then, from a point overlooking the river toward cliffs on the far side, there is a short descent. Take the obvious right fork and cross the lower end of a small meadow at 13.6. Drop down to the level of the river and follow the right bank closely.

Walk through tall grass for about a quarter of a mile approaching a narrow swift-current ford of the Heart River. (Look about 50 yards upstream where a logjam may provide an easier way across.) Swing left and cut through flat meadow. Reach the Snake River at a trail junction at 15.0. This is a lovely open spot, with a good view northwest toward Mt. Sheridan. There should still be a designated campsite nearby.

Distances and elevations are:

0.0 Heart Lake Trail parking lot   7800

TETON WILDERNESS SEGMENT

1.7	Ravine	7950
3.1	Meadow	8000
4.3		8150
5.3	Witch Creek	7600
5.7	Witch Creek	7500
7.0	Enter Frank Island Quadrangle	7450
7.1	Heart Lake patrol cabin	7450
7.8		7550
8.5		7450
8.6		7500
8.8	Beaver Creek	7450
9.5		7500
11.4	Heart River Trail junction	7450
11.7	Enter Mount Hancock Quadrangle	7450
12.0	Heart River	7450
14.2	Heart River	7250
15.0	Snake River Trail junction	7300

TETON WILDERNESS SEGMENT

Section 2

Snake River to Mink Creek

Distance 15.5 Miles

The Trail gradually climbs the upper reaches of the Snake River — at first through a narrow forested canyon and then in broad and verdant meadows. Several fords may be impassable during periods of high water. The Section is very satisfying, both in Yellowstone National Park and in the smaller portion that lies in the Teton Wilderness.

The Trail, mostly in forest, remains close to the river for the first few miles. There are a number of pretty places where tall summits can be seen behind the graceful bends of the stream. Steep slopes crowding the river force the Trail to zigzag, with six fords between 1.1 and 3.9. From there, it contours above the right (north) bank to another river crossing at 7.5. The valley then opens up, with delightful meadows, on the way to an easy ford at 10.6. The Trail leaves Yellowstone National Park at 11.1, at the Fox Creek patrol cabin. Entering the Teton Wilderness, the route continues up meadows along the headwaters of the Snake River, which is crossed for the last time at 13.3. After climbing over a burnt ridge at 14.7, the Trail drops to Mink Creek at the end of the Section at 15.5.

Camping is unrestricted in the Teton Wilderness (Buffalo Ranger District, Bridger-Teton National Forest) and several good campsites are available. However, unless additional sites are hereafter designated along the Snake River, or unless special arrangements are made, the only places where an overnight stop in Yellowstone National Park may be authorized are at the start of the Section and at 10.8, close to the Fox Creek patrol cabin. Water is plentiful.

The Snake River may be impossible to ford safely in early summer. The water will usually have receded by mid-July, but current information should be obtained from a ranger station in the Park. (The difficult crossings can be bypassed by making the following detour: from the junction at 11.4 in Section 1, continue on the Trail Creek Trail past the South Arm of Yellowstone Lake, then turn south on the Two Ocean Plateau Trail and follow it to the South Boundary Trail and the Fox Creek patrol cabin, where the regular route is resumed. The detour is seven miles longer and adds about 1000 feet of climbing.)

The route appears on the U.S.G.S. 1:125000 map of *Yellowstone National Park* and on Maps 6, 7, and 8 in this volume. These should be supplemented by the 1:62500 *Mount Hancock* and *Two Ocean Pass* quadrangles, the latter for a small bit only.

Detailed Trail data are:

The starting point of the Section is the pretty meadow by the Snake River at the junction of the Heart River Trail and the Snake River Trail; the prospect northwest toward Mount Sheridan is especially fine. Hike up the right (north) bank of the Snake River, in forest. Ford a side channel of the river, at 0.7, possibly boulder-hopping, and promptly return to the right bank.

The Trail crosses the Snake River two times in close succession, at 1.1 and 1.3. Both are knee-deep fords — the second, only about 30 feet wide, has a notably strong current. There are views of Mt. Hancock to the south and Mt. Sheridan to the northwest as the Trail continues, quite level, up the right bank. Step over a small side creek as it meets the river at 1.9. Walk in forest from 2.5, soon passing a little side creek and returning to the riverbank at 2.8.

There are four fords of the Snake River in the next mile or so. The first crossing, at 3.0, is the narrowest and probably the most difficult, but all have calf- to knee-deep water. The next ford, at 3.4, is followed by small Sickle Creek, which flows past a bare shale ledge at 3.6. After a small rise, return to the river for fords at 3.8 and 3.9 to avoid a steep highwall that drops down to the water's edge. Red willowherb (sometimes called riverbeauty) may be found at these crossings. Go over another rise, returning to the right bank of the Snake River at 4.1.

The Trail continues from here by climbing in forest, well above the river, along the flank of Mt. Barlow. There is a brief dip at 4.8. From a high point at 5.0, observe a waterfall beneath a narrow chute in the river; Mt. Hancock sticks up directly across the canyon to the right. Dip to a meadow, at 5.1, rich in harebell, goldenrod, coneflower, yarrow, lupine, and sticky purple geranium. There may be a confusing blaze here, located too far above the well-worn path of the Trail.

Orange agoseris grows near a creek which drops steeply down an open hillside at 6.2, opposite a creek on the other side of the valley. Pass a nice overlook, with low cliffs abutting the river below, at 6.7. Climb to 7.1, then drop into the valley, following the Snake River upstream to a ford at 7.5. The stream is much reduced in volume, with water just above boot level on the 50-foot crossing.

Continue in meadow and light woods, often with pleasant views left toward the meandering course of the river. Cross a ridge at 8.0 and boulder hop a creek at 8.2. After another ridge at 8.7, followed by a gully and a short rise, emerge into completely open valley. Several paths may be visible: take the one, which should be blazed, that angles down to (but does not cross) the river. Walk along the left (west) bank from 9.1, crossing over a low ridge that meets the bank at 9.4 and then continuing close to the stream. Elephantshead and fringed gentian are abundant. Stay right by the river where a trail climbs up a ridge to the right at 9.6. The Trail does not make a ford at the location shown on the topographic map; remain on the left bank, angling slightly away from the river.

The South Boundary Trail joins acutely from the right at 10.5. At this junction, keep going straight for a few yards, then bend left across a small creek and go over the side of a knoll to reach the Snake River at 10.6. Ford the ankle-deep stream. Boulder hop a creek without difficulty at 10.8. (This may be the location of a designated campsite.) Continue climbing, passing by an unmarked trail that leads to a pasture on the right.

Reach a trail junction at a meadow at 11.1. The Fox Creek patrol cabin sits back about 50 yards to the left from here. On the right side of the meadow is a register box and, just beyond it, an entrance sign for the Teton Wilderness. Turning south, sign the register and leave Yellowstone National Park.

Follow the path through meadow and light woods, passing a lovely overlook over the Snake River to the right at 11.4. Continue straight on good tread in meadow at 11.7, toward Phelps Pass, at a signed junction where an obscure route turns right toward Big Game Ridge. Ravens may serenade with their croaking call.

The vast flat area to the right is Fox Park. Ford Plateau

Creek at 11.9. (The shallowest place is probably at the bend downstream, where the creek does not reach over boot tops.) Ignore a cross-trail at 12.0. Bend left at 12.6 at the junction near the far end of Fox Park. (A trail joins acutely from the right.) The Forest Service Fox Park patrol cabin can be seen across the Snake River, to the right. Hop across a small, but deep, creek in willow thickets next to the river. (Owing to recent beaver activity, a minor detour may be necessary.) The cross-trail at 12.8 leads to the cabin to the right.

Climb over a ridge, passing through young lodgepole forest at 13.0 and dropping to another large meadow where the Snake River is forded, for the last time, at 13.3. Here it is barely a large creek, only a few inches deep. Rosecrown is found along the bank. After the ford, proceed toward the low burnt ridge ahead. Plunge across a small creek at 13.7; again, beavers may have flooded the area.

Leave the pretty valley around 14.0 and climb in light woods. Watch for moose or their track. The burnt standing timber may also attract a hairy woodpecker and western wood pewees. Pearly-everlasting is common on the slopes between the young spruces. Except for a bit of Mt. Barlow to the northwest, there are no high mountains to be seen as the Trail goes over a ridge at 14.7. Dip slightly, then bend left. Leave the old burn at 14.9 and climb a bit, passing a small creek at 15.1 and a high point at 15.2.

Angle down the slope, aiming to meet Mink Creek upstream. The Section ends at 15.5, where the Mink Creek Trail joins from the right at a signed junction.

Distances and elevations are:

0.0	Trail junction	7300
1.1	Snake River	7300
1.3	Snake River	7350
1.9	Creek	7350
3.0	Snake River	7450
3.4	Snake River	7450
3.6	Sickle Creek	7500
3.7		7550
3.8	Snake River	7500
3.9	Snake River	7500

4.0		7550
4.1		7500
4.6		7750
4.8		7700
5.0		7800
5.1	Meadow	7700
6.2	Creek	7850
6.4		7900
6.7	Overlook	7850
7.1		8000
7.5	Snake River	7850
8.0	Ridge	8000
8.2	Creek	7950
8.7	Ridge	8100
9.1		8000
9.4	Ridge	8050
9.6		8000
10.5	South Boundary Trail junction	8050
10.6	Snake River	8050
10.8	Creek	8100
11.1	Fox Creek patrol cabin (Park boundary)	8200
11.7	Trail junction	8200
11.9	Plateau Creek	8200
12.6	Creek	8200
13.0		8300
13.3	Snake River	8250
13.7	Creek	8350
14.7	Ridge	8800
15.1	Enter Two Ocean Pass Quadrangle	8750
15.2		8800
15.5	Mink Creek Trail junction	8600

TETON WILDERNESS SEGMENT

Section 3

Mink Creek to Two Ocean Pass

Distance 8.3 Miles

Superlative scenery awaits the hiker climbing to alpine elevations in this Section. Here, too, is the remarkable Parting of the Waters, where a creek divides into branches flowing toward the Atlantic and Pacific.

The Trail starts out with a gradual climb up the meadows along Mink Creek, beneath cliffs of breccia (broken and re-cemented volcanic rock). Approaching a low pass on the Continental Divide, the route turns south at a junction at 1.4. A climb of over a thousand feet in forest, broken only by a stretch of level meadow past 2.4, leads to a high plateau on the Divide. The panorama is splendid from the 10,000-foot heights from 4.0 to 4.6. A long and fairly steep descent ends at the Parting of the Waters, at 7.7, with North Two Ocean Creek forking into the Yellowstone and Snake River drainages. The Section soon ends, in Two Ocean Pass, where the Trail crosses Pacific Creek at 8.3.

There are several good campsites. If weather conditions are favorable, the plateau is a choice place to spend the night; water collected in high basins on the mountain top, though stagnant and rich in invertebrates, is evidently good to drink. Water is regularly available all along the way.

The Section is in the Teton Wilderness (Buffalo Ranger District, Bridger-Teton National Forest). The Trail is marked on the U.S. Geological Survey 1:62500 *Two Ocean Pass* quadrangle as well as Map 8.

Detailed Trail data are:

Start at the junction of the Snake River and Mink Creek Trails. Climb very gradually in meadows along the right (north) bank of Mink Creek. Breccia cliffs, to the left of the Trail beginning at 0.4, are pocked with numerous cavities.

Reach a signed junction at 1.4, toward the end of the high

46

cliffs. Bear right on the less-traveled fork leading to Two Ocean Pass. (The Trail straight ahead crosses the Continental Divide in a mile at Phelps Pass.) Within 100 yards, ford inches-deep Mink Creek. Immediately past a hunters' camp and fire circle, take the right fork. In another 50 yards or so, a trail joins acutely from the right, from the bank of Mink Creek; and a few yards beyond that, take the right fork up the hill instead of the left fork bending closer to contour. Climb through a forest of tall spruces and firs. A side trail joins from the right at 1.7; ignore two more side trails which drop left at 1.9. Climb steeply at times. The sheer-walled Trident can be seen to the left, beyond the valley of Falcon Creek, from an overlook at 2.1.

The Trail levels out as it enters a high meadow at 2.4. Look for ducks in the three ponds to the left of the Trail. Leave the meadow at 2.9 and continue climbing steeply toward the Continental Divide, which is the ridge ahead. As the Trail at 3.3 makes a sharp switchback to the left above another, smaller, meadow, glance back to the southwest for a first view of the Tetons. From 3.6, climb in open country with scattered clumps of trees.

Reach the Divide at 4.0, at the edge of the Two Ocean basin, which is embraced by parallel ridges marking the Continental Divide. There is a half-acre pond to the right of the Trail at 4.1; with favorable weather conditions, a beautiful high camp can be made here.

There are a number of knolls on the tableland, so it is necessary to make short detours from the Trail in order to get the best views. But it is well worth the effort. The 13,766-foot Grand Teton, 40 miles to the southwest, towers over Jackson Lake. Continuing clockwise, follow the canyon of the Snake River in the northwest toward Barlow Peak. Mt. Washburn and Specimen Ridge, gateposts for the Grand Canyon of the Yellowstone River, are visible beyond the flat expanses of Yellowstone Lake and the Hayden Valley. The northeast offers noteworthy views of the Absaroka Range and the Thorofare country. Most prominent, beyond the canyon of Falcon Creek, is Turret Mountain; it is flanked on the left by Colter Peak and on the right by northern peaks of The Trident. Pinnacle Mountain (11,485 feet) is the high summit in the mid-distance between Turret and Trident. The skyline to the east — consisting of the Thorofare Plateau and Thunder Mountain — is quite flat; beyond the latter, east southeast, is 12,165-foot Younts Peak (highest in the Wilderness), from whose slopes the Yellowstone River rises. Completing the impressive panorama is Soda Mountain, its sheer cliffs forming a razoredge to the south southeast.

A very small pond is to the right of the Trail at 4.3. Pipits fly from boulder to boulder in the grassy upland, which is laced profusely with lupine, bistort and alpine avens. Reach a high point, marked by cairn and tall pole, at 4.6; the Tetons are handsome from here. Immediately turn left on indistinct tread and follow cairns down to the draw at 4.7; then descend to the south. The Trail is briefly on a ridge, with cliff-sided valleys on both sides. Continue by dropping down along the slope on the right side, first with occasional limber pine and then some spruce and fir. Cross a dry creekbed at 5.4 and 5.5.

Descend steeply, bending left at 5.8 toward North Two Ocean Creek and switchbacking down to boulder hop it at 6.2. A 30-foot waterfall, possibly home for a dipper, is a few yards below the stream crossing. The rich moist soil supports a garden of red monkeyflower, mertensia, brook saxifrage, willowherb, cow parsnip, veronica, elephantshead, aster, yellow columbine, white bog-orchid, fringed grass-of-Parnassus, and sharptooth angelica.

A Steller's jay might call out from the large spruces and firs along the forest trail, which descends well above the left bank of the creek. Beyond 6.7, the route is again open, the slopes in early summer full of arrowleaf balsamroot. Views overlooking Two Ocean Pass are quite pretty.

At 7.7 reach the Parting of the Waters, where one branch of North Two Ocean Creek begins a 3488-mile journey to the Atlantic Ocean, while a slightly smaller one starts out for 1353 miles to the Pacific. Boulder hop Atlantic Creek and step across Pacific Creek, continuing downhill. Sidebells pyrola grows inconspicuously in the forest at the forks of the creek.

There are a number of confusing trails beyond the Parting of the Waters. The proper route, though it may be obscure, remains on the right bank of Pacific Creek. At 7.9, while hiking within 30 yards of the creek, come to a junction with the Atlantic-Pacific Trail. Just beyond this, enter open Two Ocean Pass, remaining on its right edge and soon crossing long plank bridges through thickets. Boulder hop across Evermann Creek at 8.1.

Two Ocean Pass.

There are pleasant views of the flats in the pass before the Trail swings away, crossing to the left bank of Pacific Creek on a sturdy bridge at 8.3, the end of this exceptional section.

Distances and elevations are:

0.0	Trail junction	8600
1.4	Trail junction	8700
2.4	Meadow	9350
3.3	Switchback	9650
4.0	Continental Divide	10000
4.6	Continental Divide	10050
5.4	Creekbed	9450
6.2	North Two Ocean Creek	8950
7.7	Parting of the Waters	8150
7.9	Atlantic-Pacific Trail junction	8150
8.1	Evermann Creek	8100
8.3	Pacific Creek	8100

49

TETON WILDERNESS SEGMENT

Section 4

Two Ocean Pass to Buffalo Fork

Distance 14.6 Miles

The heart of this Section is an easy walk, in meadows, down-stream along the North Buffalo Fork. Cliffs dramatize the scenery, especially up the glacial valleys to the east of the Trail.

From Two Ocean Pass, the route ascends the valley of Trail Creek to 3.2, where it crosses a low ridge. It descends, with good views of the upper North Fork valley and precipitous Soda Mountain, to 5.6. The Trail is level as it proceeds south through the North Fork Meadows, following the river's right bank closely to 8.2. It climbs a bit and, while contouring, overlooks the Soda Fork valley, which is ringed by rugged towering mountains. Swinging away from the North Fork at 11.7, there is a rise over a forested ridge before the Trail drops to the end of the Section on Buffalo Fork (below the confluence of its north and south branches) outside the Teton Wilderness boundary. The Buffalo Fork Road is accessible from here, a mile to the west in Turpin Meadow.

Fine campsites and water sources are plentiful. The Section can be approached by car on the road to Turpin Meadow. This is so lightly traveled that hitch-hiking may be difficult. (From Turpin Meadow, it is about 10 miles downhill on the road in the Buffalo valley to U.S. 287 and another three miles to Moran Junction.)

The Section is entirely in the Buffalo Ranger District of the Bridger-Teton National Forest. The principal U.S. Geological Survey topographic maps are the 1:62500 *Two Ocean Pass* quadrangle and the 1:24000 *Joy Peak* and *Angle Mountain* quadrangles. (A small bit appears on the 1:24000 *Rosies Ridge* quadrangle, which is not needed.) Refer also to Maps 8 and 9.

Detailed Trail data are:

The Section begins in Two Ocean Pass, where the Trail crosses Pacific Creek. A good unmarked path joins from the left at 0.2 as the Trail reaches the south edge of the wide meadows and bends right. The treadway is heavily chewed up by stock, with some mucky spots. Keep straight at 0.7, taking the North Fork Trail. (The Pacific Creek Trail bears right.)

Soon begin climbing, gradually, passing through a meadow that stretches back to the valley. Cross a creek in a narrow band of trees at 1.2. Bear right, leaving the heavily-used main route at 1.4 in order to visit a 25-foot waterfall, where Trail Creek drops over a black, moss-covered ledge down to a small pool. There is a good campsite here.

Fifty yards beyond the waterfall, at 1.5, return to the main route. Immediately take a right fork and continue a prettier route along the creek, hitting the main trail once again at 1.6. Walk through meadow from 1.7 to 2.1, crossing a couple of minor creeks. Then climb gently along the right (east) bank of Trail Creek, in forest followed by meadow again, with fair-sized side creeks at 2.3 and 2.4. The steep-walled mountain straight ahead is Joy Peak. Boulder hop the main stem of Trail Creek at 2.5 and continue straight in the open valley along the right bank of a tributary. Cross this creek on a bridge at 2.6. Approaching the ridge between Trail Creek and the North Fork, there are fine views, especially toward the cliffs of flat-topped Soda Mountain to the southeast.

The Trail descends from 3.2. Scarlet gilia occurs on the well-drained slopes, along with lupine, yarrow, and umbrella plant. Observe the glacier-carved upper valley of the North Buffalo Fork, steep-walled on all sides and including several peaks of Soda Mountain, from a fine overlook at 3.8; then drop abruptly toward the more gentle contours of the North Fork Meadows straight ahead. After a patch of forest, emerge on open slopes at 4.7, with the white-water North Fork to the left. Continue straight at a junction at 4.9. (Joining from the left is a dead-end trail to North Fork Falls.) Level out and walk through mixed forest and meadow above and well back from the river.

After crossing several side creeks, drop to the North Fork Meadows, a flat jumble of willow thickets at this point. Follow the right edge of the meadows from 5.6. Cross gushing side creeks at 5.8 and 5.9, and a smaller one opposite a pretty ox-bow pond at 6.0. Both directions, back to cliffs and forward over the meadows, offer photogenic views, especially by the gravel bar at 6.2. Bedstraw and clover are among the abundant flowers, along with harebell, asters, goldenrod and cinquefoil.

The Trail is in forest at 6.4, where a small pond can be seen to its left. Cross a small creek at 6.7. Leave the forest at 7.0, opposite Joy Peak, and continue in open sagebrush. Cross a small side creek at 7.2. There is a regularly used campsite, with light tree cover, immediately before the little creek at 7.4. This is a good place to find harriers, quartering low to the ground in search of rodents. The Divide Lake Trail joins from the right at 8.0.

After passing through a small stand of trees, leave North Fork Meadows at 8.2 and climb the forested knoll above the right bank of the river. Pass the high point at 8.5. Cross a small creek, at 9.0, just before entering a meadow. Obtain a clear view of the North Fork and bare Terrace Mountain from the Trail at 9.2. As the Soda Fork canyon opens up to the left, Smokehouse Mountain's bold contours are prominent.

A very fine campsite is on the right just beyond the small creek at 10.1. Camprobbers (gray jays) keep an eye out for visitors; Steller's jays, western tanagers, and chattering red squirrels may add to the interest.

The junction with the Soda Fork Trail is at 10.2. Continue straight on the North Fork Trail. (The Soda Fork route might be a superior alternate way to the South Fork, except for early summer when Nowlin Meadow may be too wet to cross without difficulty.) Take either fork where the tread divides at 10.5, and then rejoins after crossing a small creek. (The right fork, along the edge of meadow and passing a campsite, is the nicer.) Continue on level wide footway, dipping slightly at 11.1 to cross a gully. The trail joining acutely from the left at 11.3 is another route connecting with Soda Fork.

Start to climb gently at 11.7, in a meadow with Angle Mountain ahead and to the left. Veer away from the North Fork, crossing a little creek in a willow thicket at 12.2 and another near the top of the forested saddle at 12.4. After descending, fairly steeply at places, cross a small tributary of Clear Creek at 13.4 just after leaving the Teton Wilderness.

The Trail rises slightly to an opening at 13.9 and then, as it proceeds downhill, the summit of the Grand Teton is seen off to the right. Western kingbirds may be spotted darting off a perch to grab some unlucky insect. Reach the end of the Section at a T-junction at 14.6, above the right bank of the

Buffalo Fork. The Trail continues by turning left on the South Fork Trail. (To the right it is a mile up and over a hillside to Turpin Meadow.)

Distances and elevations are:

0.0	Pacific Creek	8100
0.7	North Fork Trail junction	8100
1.5	Waterfall	8300
2.5	Trail Creek	8450
2.8	Enter Joy Peak Quadrangle	8500
3.2	Ridge	8600
3.8	Overlook	8400
4.9	Trail junction	7800
5.6	North Fork Meadows	7650
7.2	Creek	7650
8.0	Divide Lake Trail junction	7650
8.5	Knoll	7800
9.0	Creek	7550
10.2	Soda Fork Trail junction	7400
11.3	Trail junction	7400
12.4	Saddle	7550
13.0	Enter Angle Mountain Quadrangle	7450
13.3	Wilderness boundary	7250
13.4	Clear Creek	7200
13.9		7250
14.5	Enter Rosies Ridge Quadrangle	7000
14.6	South Fork Trail junction	6950

TETON WILDERNESS SEGMENT
Section 5
Buffalo Fork to Cub Creek Pass
Distance 18.0 Miles

This is an uphill hike to the Continental Divide. The Section starts with a gradual rise through forest and meadows along the South Buffalo Fork, then climbs to vantage points overlooking the Tetons and other mountains. The South Fork Falls, about midway, are of special interest.

After crossing a ridge, the Trail reaches the confluence of North Buffalo and South Buffalo at 3.1. A pleasant hike close to the South Fork proceeds upstream, largely through meadow, to a ford of the river at 11.2. (A short detour from here leads to South Fork Falls.) The route climbs over high ridges before descending to Cub Creek at 16.1 and ascending once again to Cub Creek Pass on the Continental Divide, where the Trail leaves the Teton Wilderness and the Section ends.

The Section lies within the Buffalo Ranger District of the Bridger-Teton National Forest, virtually all of it in the Teton Wilderness. There are plenty of good campsites, and water is regularly available.

The U.S.G.S. 1:24000 topographic maps are *Rosies Ridge*, *Angle Mountain*, and *Togwotee Pass*; the last of these is unreliable as to fine details of the Trail's alignment. Refer also to Maps 9 and 10.

Detailed Trail data are:

Begin the Section by turning left at the junction of the North Fork and South Fork Trails. Cross a creek on a small horse bridge at 0.2. Along the bank are currants, roses, and leafy asters — and possibly a wandering garter snake beneath them. Look back toward the Tetons as the Trail begins to climb above the north bank of the Buffalo Fork. Follow a narrow ridge at 0.5. The Grand Teton and Mt. Moran are especially prominent, beyond the twisting course of the Buffalo Fork, from a high overlook at 0.8.

Returning to the Teton Wilderness at 1.1, the Trail levels out in forest. Shinyleaf spirea and showy aster brighten the shaded understory. As the Trail climbs gradually, pass through an occasional opening with abundant flowers — some daisies, Engelmann asters, hawkweed, goldenrod, balsamroot, yarrow, umbrella plant, and scarlet gilia among them. Besides the gray and Steller's jays, chickadees, and juncos, there is a chance to find Williamson's sapsucker in the forest.

There are glimpses of the Tetons about 300 yards before the Trail crosses a ridge at 2.1. Descend steadily and easily. Look out over the valley of the South Fork, with Terrace Mountain on the left and Angle Mountain to the right, from a meadow at 2.7. The meandering of the Buffalo through gravel bars to the right is a nice feature at 2.9, as is the valley of the North Fork to the left at 3.0.

Drop and swing left to cross the North Buffalo Fork on a steel arch bridge at 3.1. (There are excellent campsites to the right, on the bank above the gravel bar.) Go over a rise at 3.2 and then dip slightly, continuing in flat meadow to a signed trail junction at 3.4. Proceed straight on the South Fork Trail toward South Fork Falls. (The path bearing right is the Angles Trail, which promptly crosses the South Fork on another steel bridge, by a good campsite.) Keep straight again at 3.5 where another path from the South Buffalo Bridge joins from the right.

The Trail climbs, reaching a flat ridge at 4.0. Continue north along it, with little elevation change. Canada buffaloberry and common juniper are prominent shrubs beneath the canopy of lodgepole pines, many of which are dead or dying. Take the right fork at 4.5, dipping briefly as the Trail swings eastward. Descend to a small creek and boulder hop across it at 5.1 near its confluence with the South Fork. Look for ducks in the quiet oxbow to the right as the Trail crosses a rise at 5.4. Drop down to pass a little creek at 5.5.

The Trail is next to the South Fork from 5.7 to 5.8, where there is a very fine shaded flat campsite. After an opening with sagebrush at 5.9, bend left away from the river, climbing fairly steeply in forest to go over a pass at 6.2; pikas may be heard or seen in the rock slide above the raspberry-lined footway before it tops out.

The South Fork rushes over ledges through a narrow channel at 6.4. A side trail joining from the right connects with the Angles Trail. Just beyond, an outcrop on the right overlooks the frothing water dropping through a chute. Switchback left and climb. Ignore an unblazed pack trail joining from the left at 6.6. Walk through a shaded rock-lined ravine to a high point at 6.8, then drop back down to the South Fork at 7.0.

The insipid thimbleberry and the toxic baneberry are abundant in the next, level, stretch in the forest; there may also be some twistedstalk in the moist and shaded woods. Jump or ford a shallow creek at 7.4 and return to the riverside at 7.6. Unnamed cliff-topped summits tower above the opposite bank of the South Fork, which winds through gravel bars. Cross a little creek at 7.9. A camp could be made at 8.1, where the South Fork is 50 yards to the right through a clearing.

Break into the open again at 8.2 and follow the streambank beneath a cliff. There is another stretch of open forest, well back from the South Fork, starting at 8.6. A secondary trail joins from the right at 8.7. Keep straight and level, with the Gibraltar-like summit of Smokehouse Mountain soon appearing ahead and to the left. Take the blazed right fork in a small meadow at 8.9. (The left fork would apparently be all right, as it rejoins the recommended route at 9.1.) A side trail at 9.2 leads to a campsite used by large parties; continue straight.

Start across the extensive treeless Lower Pendergraft Meadow (Terrace Meadows on the topographic map), remaining left of its center and aiming east northeast for the cliffband on Pendergraft Peak, far up the valley; some stakes point the way. Jump across a fairly deep creek at 9.5, as the shallow ford is quite muddy. Leave the meadow at 10.0 and continue in lodgepole forest. Poor trails join from the right at 10.2 and from the left, after an open spot, at 10.4.

Pick up the Cub Creek Trail, which bears right at the junction at 10.7. (The South Fork Trail, which bears left, provides a blazed route to South Fork Falls.) Hit the bank of the South Fork again at 11.0 and follow it, past its confluence with Cub Creek, to a ford at 11.2.

(A side trip should be made to South Fork Falls, where the river drops more than 80 feet through a couple of two-foot-wide channels separated by a jutting rock prow; from the base of the falls, the stream churns through a narrow canyon with walls so perpendicular or even overhung that at places the rims are barely a yard apart.)

Ford the South Buffalo Fork, which is about ten yards wide. The water may be knee-deep at first, but the current is not excessively strong. Check the river for about 50 yards above the horse ford for a crossing that may appear slightly easier. There is a good campsite just beyond the ford. Follow the river upstream at first and then gradually swing away from it. An unblazed trail cuts off to the left at 11.4. Keep straight and then bend right, ascending. A faint trail turns left to the falls, at a signed junction at an opening overlooking the South Fork valley from 11.5. As the Trail climbs, largely in meadow, sheer cliffs of Smokehouse Mountain jut up to the north.

The Trail is close to the rim of a cliff at 11.7, with an outstanding view of the winding course of the South Fork. Continue to climb, far above the right (east) bank of Cub Creek, in fairly open spruce-fir forest. Look for black-headed grosbeaks in the forest and for blue grouse on the meadow slopes, which are adorned with balsamroot, yarrow, asters, cinquefoil, yampa, sticky geranium, scarlet gilia, goldenrod, harebell, umbrella plant, cow parsnip, and lupine.

From 12.4, climb close to a trickling creek, which is on the right. Beyond 12.6, this is likely to be a dry gully. Cross the gully at 12.8 at the bottom of a small meadow. Ascend in forest, passing a few mammoth spruces, to go over a ridge at 13.3. The only visible peak is unnamed summit 10794, a pyramid to the southeast. Outfitters' trails join acutely from the left at 13.5 and 13.6 (the latter, connecting with the South Fork several miles above the falls, being particularly clear) as the route descends a grassy draw.

Boulder hop Trail Creek at 13.8. Add still more flowers — columbine, Indian paintbrush, arnica, and parrotsbeak — as the Trail climbs in forest. The route forks and rejoins while descending at 14.4; either fork can be used. Begin to climb again at 14.6, with Soda Mountain becoming visible as the line of sight crosses above a closer ridge; a good view can be obtained by going up the slope to open meadow.

Level out at 14.9, just after passing a knoll to the right of the Trail. Breccia Peak and its massif loom up to the southwest.

Break through a patch of timber at 15.3, suddenly coming upon the first view of the great band of gray cliffs along the Continental Divide to the southeast. Reach a trail junction in less than 50 yards and take the left fork at contour. (The fork descending to the right is a good alternate.) Come to a second junction at 15.4 and here turn right, descending fairly steeply on the left side of a grassy hollow. Cross to the left bank and back to the right bank of a creek before the alternate trail rejoins from the right at 15.8. Descending through sagebrush, cross the creek again at 15.9, and another small one at 16.0, and reach Cub Creek at 16.1.

Cub Creek, which is a little more than ankle deep, must be forded. Pick any likely spot upstream from the confluence of Clear Creek, which enters on the south side. Then take the worn path on the right (east) bank of Clear Creek and proceed south. A trail joining from the right at 16.2 comes from a ford downstream from Clear Creek. Step over a little stream and climb along its east bank.

The Trail passes just to the west of a small rise at 16.6 and enters a meadow. Stay right, along the edge of the meadow; at its high point, at 16.7, two other paths converge upon the Trail from the left. Ascend through forest, boulder hopping a creek at 17.1. Climb up the east bank and follow it upstream above the creek. At 17.3, an abandoned trail (the one shown on the topographic map) descends to the left. Walk next to the creek, again in a meadow after the Trail levels out at 17.5. Climb gently up the side of the creek, passing its source spring at 17.9. Reach the Continental Divide in Cub Creek Pass (Bear Cub Pass on the topo map) at 18.0. The Section ends here, on the Continental Divide, as the Trail leaves the Bridger-Teton National Forest and the Teton Wilderness.

Distances and elevations are:

0.0	Trail junction	6950
0.2	Enter Angle Mountain Quadrangle	7000
1.1	Wilderness boundary	7300
2.1	Ridge	7650
3.1	North Buffalo Fork	7050
3.4	Angles Trail junction	7100

4.5	Trail junction	7300
5.1	Creek	7200
5.4	Rise	7300
5.8	Campsite	7250
6.2	Pass	7400
6.4	Trail junction	7300
6.8		7550
7.4	Creek	7450
8.8	Enter Togwotee Pass Quadrangle	7450
9.5	Creek	7500
10.7	Cub Creek Trail junction	7550
11.2	South Buffalo Fork	7550
12.4	Creek	8300
12.8	Meadow	8550
13.3	Ridge	8900
13.8	Trail Creek	8650
14.3		9000
14.6		8950
14.9	Meadow	9100
15.4	Trail junction	9050
16.1	Cub Creek	8400
16.7	Meadow	8700
17.1	Creek	8900
17.5	Meadow	9100
18.0	Cub Creek Pass	9200

TETON WILDERNESS SEGMENT

Section 6

Cub Creek to Togwotee Pass

Distance 7.5 Miles

Subalpine meadows beneath towering cliffs, along with a couple of lakes, provide outstanding scenic rewards. Although the Section lies outside the Teton Wilderness, the route is almost entirely free of human intrusions. A small portion requires cross-country travel in forest.

The Trail descends from Cub Creek Pass to Upper Brooks Lake at 0.3. It follows meadows down to Brooks Lake, passing close to Brooks Lake Lodge at 3.5. The Trail climbs to a high grassy plateau just below the precipitous glacier-carved east wall of Brooks Mountain, then continues up to a splendid viewpoint in a notch between that mountain and Sublette Peak at 5.7. It descends cross-country in forest, at 6.9 reaching U.S. 26-U.S. 287 just after circling Wind River Lake. It follows the highway to the end of the Section, Togwotee Pass on the Continental Divide, at 7.5.

Brooks Lake Lodge (Box 333, Dubois, Wyoming 82513) is a rustic guest ranch founded in 1922. It is the most convenient resupply point between Yellowstone Park and the Bridger Wilderness. Through hikers who plan to visit the Lodge as overnight guests may be able to arrange to have food parcels held for their arrival.

There are post offices to the west (at Moran, ZIP 83013) and to the east (at Dubois, a larger town), but these are each about 30 miles from the Trail. Public transportation is not available.

Water is in good supply. There are fine campsites on Upper Brooks Lake and below Brooks Mountain. The Section is in the Wind River District of the Shoshone National Forest.

See Map 10 as well as the U.S.G.S. 1:24000 *Togwotee Pass* and *Lava Mountain* quadrangles.

Detailed Trail data are:

The Trail, leaving the Teton Wilderness, enters the Shoshone National Forest at Cub Creek Pass on the Continental Divide.

Descend to the larger of the Upper Brooks Lakes, spread out just ahead in a flat and open basin. Follow the left edge of the lake, passing by side trails. At 0.5, after the third creek and near the far end of the lake, there is a fine campsite on a grassy bench up the slope to the left; towering cliffs rise up beyond the water. You may have the company of gray and Steller's jays, Clark's nutcrackers, and flickers as you admire the scene.

Rise slightly to 0.7, where the Trail goes through the edge of forest above a narrow part of the meadow. Take any of the paths on the left of the meadow as it widens out again. At 1.2, just before Brooks Lake Creek meanders close to the east edge of the valley, ascend the path climbing the bank into forest; at the top of the rise, take the right fork and drop down to Brooks Lake Creek at 1.5. (It is probably possible to remain on the valley floor from 1.2, at least in fairly dry weather.) Although the creek is nearly 15 feet wide, it can be boulder-hopped.

Pick up a jeep trail and follow it south, rising a bit in dry meadow. More jeep tracks join from the right just before a small creek at 1.6 and again at 1.7. There is an exceptional panorama at 2.0, just before the Trail passes to the right of a forested knoll. Glaciers in recent time (about 15,000 years ago) carved the cliffs all about. Particularly noteworthy are the spires and gargoyles of Pinnacle Buttes to the southeast, Sublette Peak standing by itself in the southwest, and Smokehouse Mountain far off to the north beyond the head of the valley at Cub Creek Pass.

Keep straight at 2.4, where a trail angles off to the right and doubles back to a cabin. Downs Peak (13,344 feet) in the Wind River Range, glistening with snowfields near its summit, is seen 40 miles distant, to the south southeast beyond Brooks Lake. Descend the main path toward the lake, passing a junction with the Dunoir Trail, which joins from the left at 2.5. Watch for moose near the north shore.

Circle around the west side of Brooks Lake, using the best paths. At the far end of the lake, at 3.5, head for the narrow gate in the pole fence just to the left of the slope. (From here Brooks Lake Lodge is 0.2 mile past the fence and up the hill; the Forest Service campground, accessible by car, is 0.2 mile east along the lakeshore. Brooks Lake Lodge, where rooms and

Meadows below Brooks Mountain.

meals are available, is a recommended resupply point; see the introduction to this Section.)

Just before going through the narrow gate, make a sharp right turn and backtrack at contour on a pack trail. Cross a little creek at 3.6. There are three trails cutting through the willows on the far side; take the one furthest to the left and begin to climb on well-trodden path. (The Trail, proceeding west for the next half mile along the adjoining edges of the topographic maps, is not marked on them.) The turret-like prow of Sublette Peak towers over a small meadow at 4.0. Step across a little creek and bend right. Climb steeply over a ridge and dip to a meadow. A deep notch, through which the route will pass, is visible just before the Trail crosses a creek at 4.3. Hike to the left of a knoll and climb steeply again, with some large whitebark pine mixed in with the firs and spruces.

Cross the rim of a beautiful high plateau at 4.6. Sublette Peak and Brooks Mountain, each topped with band after band of vertical wall, are in the foreground, embracing gardens of wildflowers. Cross a creek at 4.7 and take the trail (which may be indistinct) that forks to the left and follows the north bank of the creek directly toward the notch. Keep straight at 4.9 where a side trail turns left, cuts through willows, and crosses the creek to a scenic campsite. From the junction beneath tall spruces at 5.2, ascend on the left fork. (The right fork curves down to meadows beneath Brooks Mountain.) Climb steeply to 5.5.

The Trail enters meadow again and, after a short level stretch, climbs steeply once more to the east side of the pass between Brooks Mountain and Sublette Peak. The conglomerate rock, of volcanic origin, is breccia. Cliffs are everywhere to the north and east — notably jagged Pinnacle Buttes, beyond the waters of Brooks Lake a thousand feet below. A lone summit, Younts Peak, sticks up on the skyline far to the north northeast.

Proceed through the narrow pass, climbing a bit more to a high point under the layered cliffs of Brooks Mountain at 5.8. There does not appear to be any trail on the west side of the pass. However, the grades are not severe and the forest is full of game tracks that permit passage without much hardship. Any route to the southwest should be all right, as one is bound to intercept either the Brooks Lake dirt road (one-way, westbound) or the highway. The recommended course is to descend to the pond above Wind River Lake and then follow the south shore of the latter, reaching the picnic area (closed to camping) just off U.S. 26 and U.S. 287 at 6.9.

From the picnic area, with a good view of Sublette Peak behind Wind River Lake, walk out to the highway and turn right. Climb slightly to Togwotee Pass, the end of the Section, at 7.5.

Distances and elevations are:

0.0	Cub Creek Pass	9200
0.3	Upper Brooks Lake	9100
0.7		9150
1.2		9100
1.4		9150
1.5	Brooks Lake Creek	9100

63

2.0		9150
2.5	Dunoir Trail junction	9100
3.5	Brooks Lake	9050
3.7	Enter Lava Mountain Quadrangle	9150
4.0	Meadow	9250
4.2		9350
4.3	Creek	9300
4.4	Enter Togwotee Pass Quadrangle	9350
4.6	Plateau	9500
4.7	Creek	9500
5.2	Trail junction	9550
5.5	Meadow	9800
5.7	Pass	10000
5.8		10050
6.2	Enter Lava Mountain Quadrangle	9800
6.4	Pond	9650
6.7	Wind River Lake	9550
6.9	U.S. 26 — U.S. 287	9550
7.2	Enter Togwotee Pass Quadrangle	9550
7.5	Togwotee Pass	9550

GROS VENTRE SEGMENT

Section 1

Togwotee Pass to North Fork, Fish Creek

Distance 11.6 Miles

The Trail samples more subalpine meadows and then descends gradually, through forest interspersed with numerous openings, to a remote valley.

Some of the most scenic terrain comes at the beginning of the Section as the Trail travels on jeepway from Togwotee Pass to Squaw Basin, at 3.2. The route then proceeds cross-country, rising a bit through meadow and crossing a wooded ridge, to another pretty basin at 5.2. Unmaintained footway leads down the valleys of Hereford Creek and Larkspur Creek to Beauty Park at 7.6. Old path is available through forest to the open bottomland of the North Fork of Fish Creek, which is forded at the end of the Section, at 11.6.

For information, check with the Wind River Ranger District of the Shoshone National Forest and the Gros Ventre Ranger District of the Bridger-Teton National Forest. Water is readily obtainable, and there will be no trouble finding good campsites. In early season, caution will be required in fording the North Fork of Fish Creek.

U.S. 26—U.S. 287, which is heavily traveled, provides good access at Togwotee Pass. Although there is no public transportation across the mountains, it is possible to reach Moran Junction in Jackson Hole on the bus connecting Jackson Lake Lodge and the town of Jackson. Togwotee Lodge, about 10 miles west of the pass on the highway, offers good food and lodging.

The Section appears on Maps 10 and 11, as well as two 1:24000 U.S.G.S. topographic maps (*Togwotee Pass* and *Lava Mountain*). Rely on the maps, in particular, between Togwotee Pass and Squaw Basin; when scouted, at the end of June, this high country was covered with snow, which sometimes made it impossible to follow the marked route precisely.

Detailed Trail data are:

Togwotee Pass, at the start of the Section, is named for an

Indian (whose name means "Lance Thrower" in the Shoshone tongue) who guided Capt. W.A. Jones of the Corps of Engineers. Their reconnaisance, in 1873, led to the construction of a wagon road in 1898, followed by an auto route in 1922.

Take the jeep trail starting westward along the log fence from Togwotee Pass. Swing left on the tracks to go through the gap between Two Ocean Mountain and the low knoll. High breccia cliffs and the pyramid of Sublette Peak overlook the meadow.

Climb to the forest boundary on the Continental Divide at 0.9, at a clump of whitebark pine, and cross through a gate in the fence of large logs. After a short additional rise, pass directly beneath the slopes of Two Ocean Mountain and descend gradually. Step over a creek near the bottom of a meadow at 1.6. In another meadow at 2.4, the Trail (which had been headed directly away from the mountain) makes a 90° bend to the left, crossing an intermittent creek. Common birds around the small ponds at 2.6, as elsewhere, include Clark's nutcracker, gray jay, white-crowned sparrow, junco, and robin.

Enter Squaw Basin after the small creek at 2.9 and follow the jeep trail clockwise as it travels beneath the ridge of Two Ocean Mountain. Dip down into the heart of the basin to boulder hop its shrub-lined principal creek at 3.2. In less than 50 yards, and before a second creek, turn left on a jeep trail.

A small land-locked pond is to the right at 3.5. The jeep trail disintegrates here. Proceed cross-country up the open valley (heading about 215°), remaining on the left (west) bank of the creek; the obvious objective is to get across the ridge at the low timbered point on the skyline to the right.

Turn right at 3.8, away from the cliffs, and climb in the gap between stands of timber. Bend left at 4.0 and proceed south southwest, hiking through a brushy draw between the trees at 4.2. Emerge into the upper part of Squaw Basin at 4.3 and continue south southwest to the notch between the sloping ridge on the left and the small timbered knoll on the right. Enter spruce-fir forest at 4.6 and climb very slightly. There is a pack trail through the notch at 5.0, but it may not be easy to locate. Cross the ridge, being careful not to be tripped up by remaining strands of an abandoned barbed wire fence.

Break out into a high and flat basin and cut over to its southeast corner, toward the Wind Rivers in the distance. Step over the headwaters of Hereford Creek at 5.2 and 5.5, just before reaching a line of trees. Descend fairly steeply on an old pack trail. Come to a side creek at 5.9.

Join a better pack trail that comes in from the right, closer to Hereford Creek. Rise a few feet and then continue down the open valley well above the left bank. Cross a minor ridge, passing small side creeks and entering the main valley of Larkspur Creek at 6.3. Step to the left bank at 6.5. From 6.8 to 7.0, descend in forest along footway marked with occasional ancient axe-blazes. Continue in meadow.

Take the right fork at 7.3, crossing Larkspur Creek and coming promptly to a signed trail junction. Turn right, westward, rising a bit as the Trail enters lodgepole pine forest. Proceed at contour, overlooking Hereford Creek, and possibly spotting pine grosbeaks or chipping sparrows. The flowers in early summer include springbeauty, dandelion, lupine, larkspur, long stalk clover, ballhead waterleaf, tongueleaf violet, buttercup, and cinquefoil.

Boulder hop Hereford Creek at 7.6 and enter Beauty Park. Step over a smaller creek at 7.8 and immediately take the pack trail that angles to the left. This is one of many fine campsites. Around 8.0, the route becomes indistinct. Here head to the right, across the puddle-dimpled meadow, to intercept the conspicuous jeep trail at 8.1. Turn left and follow the ruts southeast, returning to forest at 8.3, between a couple of ponds. Avoid the snowmobile trail, marked with red diamond blazes, which angles right. As the route descends, the tracks may be difficult to make out at places, particularly in meadows, but they can readily be relocated.

A lovely long pond is to the right at 8.6. Beyond this point, the occasional diamond blazes can be followed, as they lead down to Fish Creek. A meadow at 9.5 affords a view of a couple of the higher Gros Ventre Peaks to the south southwest. Step over a creek at 9.8.

Reach the grassy bottomland at 10.5. Continue straight here, avoiding the jeep tracks that bear left up the main valley. Walk downstream along Beauty Park Creek, boulder-hopping easily to its right bank at 10.7. Western valerian grows here. Note that the sagebrush (silver sagebrush) has unlobed leaves, distinguishing it from its more ubiquitous cousin, the big sagebrush (which has three rounded teeth at the leaf tips).

Continue through sage down the valley of the North Fork of Fish Creek, with several ups and downs to cross small draws. At 11.4, begin a descent to the creek. The big humped mountain down the valley is Darwin Peak. At 11.6, ford the North Fork at a wide spot, almost 20 yards bank to bank; in high water, it may be knee deep, but ordinarily should present no problem. This is the end of the Section.

Distances and elevations are:

0.0	Togwotee Pass (U.S.26—U.S. 287)	9550
0.7	Enter Lava Mountain Quadrangle	9600
1.0		9700
2.0	Enter Togwotee Pass Quadrangle	9450
2.2	Enter Lava Mountain Quadrangle	9450
2.3	Enter Togwotee Pass Quadrangle	9400
2.6	Enter Lava Mountain Quadrangle	9450
3.2	Squaw Basin	9300
3.5	Pond	9450
4.2	Brushy draw	9550
4.6	Enter forest	9600
5.0	Notch	9650
6.5	Larkspur Creek	9150
7.3	Trail junction	8850
7.6	Hereford Creek	8850
8.3	Ponds	8900
9.5	Meadow	8600
10.7	Beauty Park Creek	8150
11.6	North Fork, Fish Creek	8050

GROS VENTRE SEGMENT

Section 2

North Fork, Fish Creek to South Fork, Fish Creek

Distance 12.1 Miles

The route continues, through rather open terrain, across minor ridges. The highlight is a magnificent viewpoint, from which the Wind River Range, the Tetons, and the Breccia Cliffs are simultaneously in sight. Much of the distance is traveled cross-country or on faint footpath.

From the ford at the start of the Section, the Trail follows the North Fork of Fish Creek downstream to the crossing of Squaw Creek at 1.2. Although the route is obscure, or even cross-country beyond here, it is not difficult to find the way up Squaw Creek to 3.1, up Open Fork to a ridge at 4.5, and then down to Purdy Basin at 5.9. Another gentle climb through mountain meadows leads to the high ridge, at 9.1 and 9.3, which affords the splendid view mentioned above. This is typical summer range for elk.

Route-finding may be difficult as the Trail next passes through forest. The cross-country descent comes to a precipice, at 10.7, high above the South Fork of Fish Creek, and then drops down open slopes. The Section ends with a walk up the South Fork to a ford, at 12.1, which can be a serious obstacle at times of high runoff.

Water supplies are uncertain between Purdy Creek and the South Fork. Some possible campsites can be found along the North and South Forks of Fish Creek and along Purdy Creek; other places with water are likely to be brushy or excessively sloped.

Refer to Map 11 for the route in this Section, which lies entirely within the Gros Ventre Ranger District of the Bridger-Teton National Forest. U.S. Geological Survey 1:24000 topographic maps are *Lava Mountain*, *Tripod Peak*, (a small bit only), and *Sheridan Pass*.

Detailed Trail data are:

From the ford of the North Fork of Fish Creek, follow jeep

tracks down the valley. Walk on a level grade through the sage-brush, well back from the meandering stream. A high red bluff on the other side of the valley is passed at 1.0.

Another set of jeep tracks joins from the right at 1.2, immediately before Squaw Creek. The creek, though shallow, may have to be forded. Climb up the bank to the flat shelf, where there is an indistinct junction. Take the jeep tracks that turn left, and head up Squaw Creek toward the partly timbered hill to the east. A faint jeep track joins from the right at 1.4.

Reach Squaw Creek again at 1.5, just before a ridge descending from the timbered hill. The obvious trail ends here. Hop across Squaw Creek and make a way up the right (east)bank through willows; game tracks can be followed close to the base of the hill. Pack trail can be used from 2.2; it is 50 to 100 yards back from the creek and 50 feet, more or less, above it. Pass abreast the dense stand of timber on the hillside across the creek at 2.5. Note the low steep-sided grassy transverse slope ahead; the Trail will turn right immediately before it. Come to the edge of the ravine at 3.0. (The hillside timber now bears about 240°.) Follow the edge to the right, taking the obvious path down the slope.

Ford ankle-deep Squaw Creek at its broadest spot, at 3.1. There are two pack trails on the far side. Take the one bearing left (south southwest). This treadway is very obscure and probably cannot be followed; it crosses a small side creek (which appears to be the main creek) at a switchback at 3.3. Head due south, staying about 100 yards west of a steep grassy hillside. Remain to the right of a clump of trees at 3.7. The pack trail can be picked up here, but may be lost as it leaves sagebrush. The country is open, however; just keep climbing, in a generally southerly direction, toward the saddle on the ridge ahead.

Attain the ridge at a barbed wire fence (with prominent wooden poles) at 4.5. Tripod Peak is the double-topped moun-tain to the rear. Look ahead to Purdy Basin and descend steeply. Once again the pack trail is too indistinct to be follow-ed. It doesn't make much difference, however, as any path downhill to the south is bound to lead to the valley in Purdy Basin. Stay generally to the left, in the main drainage. The slopes are quite open, with some light aspen near the ridge and lodgepole pine lower down. It is sometimes necessary to use care making a way through low sagebrush. Nineleaf lomatium can be found in early summer. A good landmark is the flat and bare end of the ridge, marked 8508 on the topographic map, on the east side of the valley.

Reach Purdy Creek at 5.9 at its confluence with the side creek which the Trail has been following downstream. The steep forested slopes of the Continental Divide are a couple of miles to the left. Step over the creek and proceed down its left bank. A few yards after intercepting a jeep trail at 6.0, pass remnants of an old corral.

Come to Purdy Creek again at 6.2. Follow the pack trail which, 20 yards before the creek, turns sharply to the left. Using the indistinct tread as much as possible, climb to the low point on the ridge above; reach the crest at 6.5, between the small patch of trees on the left and the large timber stand on the right. From the south side of the ridge, Crystal Peak in the Gros Ventre Range is prominent down the valley.

Take the pack trail that angles left and descends very slightly. The path is good down to the bottom at 6.8. Bend right and pick up the tread again on the right of the first patch of trees. Follow the well-worn pack trail to the right of the grassy mound ahead. Go over the ridge at 7.5. In another hundred yards, at a secondary ridge, take the fork angling left and remaining close to contour. From 7.7, bend right and dip a bit as the Trail crosses small headwaters (probably dry) of Hackamore Creek. An obscure path joins from the left at 7.9.

Reach an unmarked trail junction at 8.0, a couple of hundred yards before running into the densely timbered slope. Turn left, climbing on distinct tread. (To the right is the narrow Hacka-more valley, with Sheep Mountain in the Gros Ventre Range beyond.) Watch for elk, which summer in the high mountains and spend the winter in Jackson Hole; ravens may also be much in evidence.

Turn left at 8.7, at the ridge which divides the basins of Hackamore and Bell Creeks. Continue to ascend on grass and sage with scattered timber. Take the lower, right, fork at 8.9 and go over a spur ridge, just left of the timber, at 9.0.

Follow the left, ascending fork up the bare slope to its crest at 9.1. Here there is a spectacular overlook— toward the Bridger Wilderness to the southeast and toward some of

The ford of the South Fork of Fish Creek.

the Tetons to the west (though only the tip of the Grand Teton can be seen). Drop to the main path and then rise to the crest once more for a repeat of the panorama; this time there is also a view northward to the Breccia Cliffs.

Continue climbing the ridge, largely in forest, to a high point at 9.7. From an opening in aspens here, the outlook to the Tetons is improved, with the Grand and its neighbors to the south in full view. Less imposing, but still worth noting, is Crystal Peak beyond Burnt Ridge.

The following route down to the South Fork of Fish Creek was taken inadvertently by the author; it lies to the west of the Trail marked on the topographic map which, if it can be located, would be an alternate. Descend slightly, running into bothersome aspen deadfall at 9.9. Remain on the apparent ridgeline, dropping steeply to the grassy spot below, where tread can be made out clearly, at 10.2. Stay on the clear path close to the crest, ignoring game trails joining from both sides. Swing left at 10.4, still on very good footway along the forested crest.

Emerge from forest at 10.7 at the top of a cliff which over-looks the South Fork of Fish Creek as well as a narrow un-named side valley. Violet-green swallows swoop by. From this point, switchback sharp left and descend very slightly on sandy path before picking up clear trail once again at 10.8 upon re-entering forest. Descend in the direction of the head of the side valley. Turn right at the grassy draw at 10.9; follow it downhill, soon picking up game trail. At 11.2, follow the tracks a few feet up to cross the open ridge and then descend, quite steeply, angling left toward a jeep trail.

Intercept the jeep trail at 11.4. Turn left and proceed up the valley of the South Fork of Fish Creek. A gooseneck of the creek is just to the right at 11.8.

Reach the ford of the South Fork at the end of the Section, at 12.1. The stream is divided. The first part, about five yards to the gravel island in the center, is the deep section. In high water, it may reach three feet, with a strong current, calling for great caution. The ford of the far channel, at the upstream end of the island, is shallower and should present no problem.

Distances and elevations are:

0.0	North Fork, Fish Creek	8050
0.5	Enter Tripod Peak Quadrangle	8000
1.2	Squaw Creek	8000
1.5	Squaw Creek	8000
1.6	Enter Lava Mountain Quadrangle	8000
3.0		8300
3.1	Squaw Creek	8250
3.4	Enter Sheridan Pass Quadrangle	8350
3.7	Clump of trees	8450
4.5	Ridge (8851)	8850
5.9	Purdy Creek	8100
6.2	Trail junction	8050
6.5	Ridge	8200
6.8		8150
7.5	Ridge	8400
8.0	Trail junction	8350

8.7	Ridge	8750
9.1	Viewpoint	8850
9.2	Pass*	8800
9.3	Viewpoint	8850
9.7		8950
10.2	Grassy spot	8750
10.7	Cliff	8450
10.9	Draw	8350
11.2	Ridge	8100
11.4	Jeep trail	7850
12.1	South Fork, Fish Creek	7900

---

*Dave Clarendon of Banner, Wyoming reports that there is a cowpath from this pass down along the west side of Buck Creek to the ford at the end of the Section; his route would be more direct than the one described in the text.

GROS VENTRE SEGMENT

Section 3

South Fork, Fish Creek to Fish Creek Park

Distance 10.7 Miles

The Trail ascends the valley of the South Fork of Fish Creek, close to the stream's rapids, riffles, and meanders.

The first part of the Section is a hike up a steep-sloped ravine. The valley broadens out near Heifer Creek at 3.5. Jeep trail continues, through forest and sage, to a stretch of improved road (near Park Creek) from 5.3 to 5.8. Jeepway resumes to Leeds Creek at 6.6. Next, follow unmaintained pack trail by small ponds before dropping to Strawberry Creek at 8.0. Some willow thickets complicate the cross-country travel from here until jeep trail appears at 9.2. The South Fork becomes a tumbling stream once again as the Trail climbs into Fish Creek Park, where the Section terminates on the transmountain Union Pass Road at 10.7.

This portion lies entirely within the boundaries of the Gros Ventre Ranger District of the Bridger-Teton National Forest. Water is always readily accessible and there are excellent campsites, especially at Leeds Creek at 6.6 and at 9.8 just before the Trail reaches Fish Creek Park. Traffic on the Union Pass Road (which descends eastward, about 20 miles or so to U.S. 26—U.S. 287) is very light.

Refer to Maps 11 and 12 for an overview of the Section. Three U.S.G.S. 1:24000 topographic maps are required: *Sheridan Pass, Mosquito Lake,* and *Fish Creek Park.*

Detailed Trail data are:

Set out from the ford of the South Fork of Fish Creek. By day, watch for the gray jay, raven, flicker, belted kingfisher, and cliff, tree, and violet-green swallows and, at night, listen for the hooting of the great horned owl. Silky phacelia, chickweed, strawberry, anemone, lupine, clover, locoweed, shrubby cinquefoil, red and yellow species of Indian-paintbrush, and elephantshead grow nearby.

Walking upstream, pass opposite the canyon of Buck Creek. A many-layered bare bluff overhangs the opposite side of the creek at 0.4. A pack trail joins from the right at 0.6. Go through an old fence at 0.8 and bend to the right. (The jeep trail that turns left crosses the creek and enters broad-bottomed Devils Basin.) While passing another set of high outcrops, rise to look over rapids at the bend at 1.2.

The Pass Creek Trail turns right at a signed junction at 1.4. Continue along the South Fork Trail, rising to cross Pass Creek (an easy boulder hop) after 100 yards. A good camp could be made here. Hike through a patch of forest, passing more rapids, and return to meadow at 1.8, opposite steep bald gray slopes. The green Little Devils Basin, partially obscured by trees, opens up across the creek at 2.4. Wilson's warblers breed in the thick growth of willows to the left at 2.6. At 2.7, the jeep trail swings left to ford the tumbling creek; remain right, climbing on the obvious pack trail, to get above the bluff that crowds the bank. Rejoin the jeep trail, which comes in from the left at 2.9.

The character of the stream changes abruptly at 3.3; here enter a green bottomland of placid meandering water, where you may see eared grebes. Step across Heifer Creek at 3.5; a campsite is at the edge of the trees up the slope, back and to the right. From 3.6 to 3.9, follow the upland pack trail in preference to the parallel jeep trail closer to the creek. Then continue on jeepway, climbing well above and back from the water. Reach a spur ridge at 4.5 and dip slightly on the jeep trail, passing a creek and pond at 4.6. Entering grass and sage at 5.1, stay left at the jeep trail junction and cross a culvert at Pelton Creek in about 50 yards.

Intercept a good jeep road, where there may be some misleading signs, at 5.3. Follow the road left. Just after passing a wood pole fence at 5.5, take the good logging road that continues to the left up the main valley. (The jeep trail to the right is the Park Creek Trail up to Buffalo Meadow.) Cross Park Creek right away, at a wide and very shallow ford. Be attentive as the road swings right at 5.8; leave the logging road here and turn left, following the old jeep trail parallel to the fast-rushing South Fork of Fish Creek. Dip to a little side creek at 5.9. Rise, entering forest at 6.2 at another small creek. The trickle at 6.4 is called Currant Creek. Remain on the needle-carpeted jeepway, dipping to a corral on the edge of the South Fork, at its confluence with Leeds Creek, at 6.6. This would be an excellent place to spend the night. A few of the flowers here are upland larkspur, thickleaf groundsel, and woods forget-me-not.

Proceed up the left (south) bank of the South Fork. (Another jeep trail turns left and fords the creek; it climbs to Fish Lake.) The old pack trail seems to disappear almost immediately, at the barbed wire fence. If it is lost, it can be discovered again at the southward bend of the creek at 7.2; the tread there is only a stone's throw from the water, though about 30 feet above it in elevation.

Rise a bit from 7.2. Soon there is a puddle just to the right of the Trail. Keep left, dipping a few feet to a small creek and then climbing the next hill quite steeply. Enter a large meadow at 7.4 and follow faint tracks close to its left edge. Proceeding clockwise, pass the southeast tip of a pond, where lesser scaup are likely to be observed, at 7.6. Head up the narrow valley and, at 7.8, cross the ridge dividing this valley from the South Fork. Descending, look out over another meandering section of the stream. Drop almost to the bank. Just before entering willows, contour right about 50 yards.

Turn left and easily boulder hop Strawberry Creek at 8.0, just below the embankment on the other side. Continue upstream along the South Fork, remaining within about 100 yards of it; there is rarely a distinct trail. A break in the forest cover occurs on the slope to the right at 8.4. Rise a bit to cross the sage-covered ridge at least 50 yards up from its tip, thereby cutting to the southernmost point of a creek bend at 8.5.

Plow through willows (not too bad, as there are game trails) for a couple of hundred yards until it is possible to get above them on the lower part of the dry slope. From here, the route, though remaining in willows, is easier and reasonably well defined. A gently sloping green valley appears on the opposite side of the South Fork at 8.7. Look out over a sharp bend of the creek at 9.0.

The route becomes a jeep trail at 9.2. The South Fork, to the left, is one continuous cascade. Dip from a ridge at 9.7. There's a fine campsite in the narrow band of pines on the water's edge at 9.8. Besides many of the flowers mentioned above, you may find marshmarigold, subalpine buttercup, bistort, thickleaf draba, and shooting star. Chipping sparrows are also present.

The Trail levels out at the next ridge, at 10.1. High mountains appear to the southeast; one of these is Osborn Mountain, visible through Gunsight Pass. Walk about at contour from here, with the creek becoming much more gentle.

Reach the gravel Union Pass Road (passable by car) at 10.6. Turn left to the junction at 10.7, where the Section ends. Fish Creek Park, a huge treeless basin, extends for miles to the southeast.

Distances and elevations are:

0.0	South Fork, Fish Creek	7900
0.8	Devils Basin Trail junction	7950
1.4	Pass Creek Trail junction	8000
2.4	Little Devils Basin	8050
3.5	Heifer Creek	8150
4.8	Enter Mosquito Lake Quadrangle	8350
5.5	Park Creek	8350
6.4	Currant Creek	8450
6.6	Leeds Creek	8400
7.0	Enter Fish Creek Park Quadrangle	8500
7.6	Pond	8550
7.8	Ridge	8600
8.0	Strawberry Creek	8550
9.2	Jeep trail	8650
10.6	Union Pass Road	8850
10.7	Road junction	8850

GROS VENTRE SEGMENT
Section 4
Fish Creek Park to Green River Lakes
Distance 16.8 Miles

This Section provides more hiking through open country, much of it at quite high elevation. The views from Gunsight Pass are superb.

The Trail follows gravel road to 0.8, then continues on jeep tracks around the west and south rims of Fish Creek Park before it begins to climb from about 4.3. The ascent to Gunsight Pass, through open forest, is generally on pack trail; at places, however, the route disappears or is hard to follow. From the scenic crest at 8.8, a good path drops down the mountain for a short distance, but then one must plunge downhill cross-country. It is not difficult, as the slope has light tree cover interspersed with meadows. A jeep trail is intersected in the valley of the Roaring Fork. After a short stretch along the ruts, from 10.4 to 11.2, the Trail crosses Roaring Fork at a ford which can be troublesome in high water. The route again proceeds cross-country, through meadows to the crossing of a minor ridge at 11.8, and then descends quite steeply on sagebrush-covered slopes to the valley of the Green River. The last part of the Section, from 14.3 to 16.8, follows pack trail (sometimes obscure) to the bridge at the foot of Lower Green Lake at 16.8.

Travel is in the Bridger-Teton National Forest—the Gros Ventre District to Gunsight Pass and then the Pinedale District. Although the route was once maintained as part of the "Highline Trail", little evidence remains and one must frequently resort to map and compass. The best campsites are found between Fish Creek Park and Roaring Fork. Water supply is not a problem. Sadly, there may be new clearcuts.

The end of the Section lies just opposite a Forest Service campground at the end of a gravel access road. See the introduction to Section 1 of the Bridger Wilderness Segment for information concerning resupply arrangements.

Maps 12 and 13 show the route. They will need to be supplemented by *Fish Creek Park, Union Peak, Green River Lakes,*

and *Big Sheep Mountain* U.S.G.S. topographic maps, all on
1:24000 scale.

Detailed Trail data are:

The Section begins on the Union Pass Road, at a junction
with a gravel road that turns south toward the Fish Creek
Guard Station. Turn right here and follow the western edge
of Fish Creek Park, quite possibly noting some American
goldfinches. Continue straight on the maintained jeep road
at 0.5, avoiding the drive to the right that leads 0.1 mile to
the guard station.

Historic Union Pass is visible across Fish Creek Park as
the Trail continues. A large party under Wilson Price Hunt
crossed the Continental Divide there in September 1811, en
route from the Dubois region to the mouth of the Columbia
River, exploring a line of communication and locating possible sites for fur trading posts for John Jacob Astor. Union
Peak is the mountain across Fish Creek Park, on the Continental Divide to the south of Union Pass. Still further south,
past the deep saddle, is Triple Divide Peak, where the Columbia and Colorado River Basins meet. Straight ahead is Gunsight Pass, with Osborn Mountain beyond it.

Bear left at 0.8 on the jeep tracks that head toward Triple
Divide Peak. (This is 0.2 mile before the gravel road cuts
through the tip of the timber.) Walk parallel to the improved
surface, remaining below and within 100 yards of it; stay
above the flat bottom of the park, where subalpine blue violets
sprout up in the wet grass. The Trail is at the same elevation as
the road and barely 50 yards from it at 1.7; a venerable lodgepole pine next to the jeep tracks, one of its two trunks already
fallen, is a good landmark.

Swing left to cross the high point of a spur ridge at 2.0.
The Trail then diverges from the road, which curves right
and enters forest. Chipmunks may be seen scampering about
the lichen-covered boulders as the route comes to a small
creek at 2.1; aside from the proximity of the road, this would
be a good campsite.

Follow easily-discerned tracks across the carpet of grass.
Bend gradually to the right, climbing slightly. A distinct jeep
trail joins from the left at a junction at 2.6. Note the sheer

cliffs around Dunoir Butte off in the distance to the north. Turn right for 100 feet, then turn left and head southeast through the grassy draw. Pick up a jeep trail joining from the right at 2.8 and follow it toward the timber, and then left parallel to the edge of the trees.

Dip in wet meadow, walking just to the right of a small pond at 3.3. Remain on the jeep trail, passing next to points of the forest at 3.5 and 3.7. Bend right along the edge of the trees as the Trail approaches the meandering and much reduced South Fork.

Hike by the remains of an old log cabin at 4.0. There is a fine view overlooking Fish Creek Park; the prominent peak to the north northeast is probably part of the Ramshorn, about 25 miles away. A good camp can be made at shaded and grassy Cullys Point at 4.2, with a vista looking up toward Triple Divide Peak.

The jeep tracks soon peter out, though remnants appear from time to time. Make a bend to the right at 4.3, staying along the edge of the trees and above the willows. Keep an eye out for old axe-blazes. Watch for moose in this remote corner of the park (and also, later on in the Section, in the Roaring Fork Basin).

It would probably be best to leave the old blazed route at 4.6, where it bends right and climbs a few feet in forest, as deadfall has become excessive; instead, walk in the meadow, remaining close to the trees. At 4.9, take the path that angles slightly uphill to the right. The treadway is observable, and there are occasional blazes. Stay close to the forest edge, above the willows, crossing some trickling creeks.

The larger creek at 5.5 is a good landmark. Approach it on a grassy slope, pass to the left of a low and small cairn, and then cross it on a prominent jeepway through willows. Another cairn is on the left 50 yards after the creek.

The route from here to 6.4 is the one taken by the author, by mistake; it might be better to stay on the abandoned pack trail, as shown on the topographic map, if it can be located. Continuing on the obvious tread, however, proceed southeast up a long and narrow open valley. Remain on the right (east) bank at 5.8, where the more obvious path crosses the creek. Hike almost to the apparent end of the valley, then climb left where a break in the trees leads up toward a low ridge.

Enter the forest at 6.2, at the top of the opening. Proceed about at contour to the northeast to a large tributary of the South Fork of Fish Creek, at 6.4.

Intercept the poorly-blazed old trail, a faint path through the woods, just before the creek. Head upstream, climbing in meadow for a bit from 6.5. After a belt of forest, the Trail passes to the left of an old corral at 6.7. Enter a large basin, dropping down close to the creek at 6.9 and hopping over a feeder. Climb above the willows and contour left around the ridge, approaching the main creek again at 7.1. The treadway is almost hopelessly obscure, but there are some old blazes. Rise a bit in a meadow and then swing down to the edge of the creek at 7.3.

Good campsites can be found as the Trail enters the next meadow at 7.5; Gunsight Pass lies between the two summits ahead. Hike up the broad avenue of wet meadow between the two ranks of trees. At 7.6, take the blazed trail that cuts through the trees on the left for 50 yards before breaking out into the open again. Cross to the right side of the meadow and follow the edge of the trees to 7.7, where the Trail enters a well-drained park.

Intersect a jeep trail at right angles at 7.8. Continue uphill south of east. Head for the blazed pole and, beyond it through wet meadow, a blazed tree at the extreme southeast end of the park. (This is not the route shown on the topographic map, but it is uncomplicated.) Enter the forest at 8.1 just to the right of a very small creek. From 8.2, climb up the valley, close to the little creek, remaining in meadow. The easiest way through the narrow spot at 8.3 is up the creekbed itself.

Reach a pond, where there is a fine campsite, at 8.4. Don't confuse Clark's nutcracker with the gray jay; both of them may be present along with mountain chickadees. Among the early summer wildflowers, you may expect lanceleaf spring-beauty, marshmarigold, globeflower, and lousewort. Observe that the creek tumbling toward this basin from the east sinks in the limestone at a point several feet below the level of the pond, making an underground channel to an unknown point of reemergence. Turn right at the outlet of the pond and continue on the old pack trail. Climb up the open slope to the right of the talus; Gunsight Pass is directly overhead.

Keep generally to the left, so as to enjoy the view westward toward all the high Teton peaks (which are blocked at the pass itself). The climb is further enriched by the prospect northward beyond Togwotee Pass. Some prominent points are Breccia Peak and Brooks Mountain, distant Smokehouse Mountain, the Pinnacle Buttes, and Crescent Mountain. The expansiveness of Fish Creek Park in the foreground can also be appreciated.

Enter a new world at Gunsight Pass, at 8.8; from here the westward-flowing waters along the Trail empty into the Colorado River. Suddenly there is a picture postcard view toward a jumble of mountains rising steeply out of the Green River Lakes. Big Sheep Mountain stands out in the foreground; Squaretop Mountain is the distinctive monolith at the head of the lakes. Growing along the high ridge are alpine forget-me-not, diamondleaf saxifrage, biscuitroot, early cinquefoil, Indian-paintbrush, shooting star, and bistort.

Descend quite steeply on obvious pack trail along the left bank of the narrow grassy gully. There are more fine views – not only overlooking Green River Lakes, but also up the Roaring Fork and toward Tosi Peak in the southern Gros Ventres. Watch for blue grouse.

Specific route description is impossible beyond 9.2, where the path reaches forest. Some old blazes continue to the top edge of the aspens at 9.3, where a trail down the valley angles right. At 9.4, it seems as if the main path, though unblazed, descends to the right, down the valley through the aspens; it may, but it is clearly not the route shown on the topographic map. Rather than engage in a vain search for the vanished trail, the best thing is to take some bearings and descend the slope cross-country. One good point of reference is the notch at 9200-foot elevation across the Roaring Fork Basin; try to come down opposite it or only slightly downstream from it. A fortuitous choice of route would include open stands of aspen with some meadow, and then light conifers—nothing of any difficulty.

Reach the Roaring Fork Basin, say at 10.4, at the bend of a jeep trail. Turn right and follow the tracks as they approach Roaring Fork; note the fine view upstream. Pass through some timber at 10.6. There is no sign whatever of any tread at 10.8, which is where the "Highline Trail" should come down from the mountain.

Continue westward to 11.2, where Roaring Fork must be forded. (The west edge of a stand of timber is across the creek at this point.) A good campsite is on the left just before the ford. The water may be more than knee deep and the current strong, so considerable caution may be required; the stream has a firm sandy bottom, with few rocks, with the last couple of feet the only difficult spot.

Once past the ford, proceed cross-country through the low scrub, heading generally south southwest along the course of Roaring Fork. Bend west at 11.5, and about 11.7 angle into the thin band of trees, rising only slightly to cross the ridge at a low point.

Pick up a bit of the old trail, with a couple of cairns remaining, at 11.9. Look out toward the Green River Lakes and Squaretop Mountain. The old path vanishes once again, but it is an easy walk down the grassy slope. The route described here, more or less following the one shown on the topographic map, aims for the right side of the narrow pond this side of a bend in the Green River; it would probably save time, however, to make a beeline for the foot of Lower Green River Lake.

Note the path through the sagebrush covering the lower part of the slope. Drop down to that path and follow it into the flat green basin at 12.7; there are a few mucky spots here, but no real obstacles. Around 13.1, come over the lip of the basin, perhaps locating some remnants of the old trail. Once again there are good views up the valley toward Squaretop as the Trail drops down to the narrow pond. Look for waterfowl, such as mallard, Barrow's goldeneye, wigeon, common merganser, and coot.

Turn left at 13.4 and walk along the north shore of the pond. Swing right at 13.7 and cross a strip of wet meadow without difficulty. Climb a few feet over the low ridge and resume the descent toward the river.

Reach the bank of the Green River at 14.3 and head upstream, soon passing below a fence corner. There is a worn path, which sometimes disappears in meadow. It is all right to stay close to the river to 14.5, past the first island. Then turn inland of the low mound to the sagebrush. Follow defined path uphill, passing a second island at 15.0. Cross a side creek at 15.5 and take the left fork up a rise.

Remaining at contour, pass an abandoned pole fence at 16.0. This is a good place to look for Savannah sparrows. Walk high on the flat bench in order to get around the extensive marshes by the river around 16.3. The Trail goes through a corral at old ranch buildings at 16.6. Walk by an old bridge just before reaching a strong new one at the outlet of Lower Green Lake, at the end of the Gros Ventre Segment, at 16.8.

Distances and elevations are:

0.0	Union Pass Road	8850
0.5	Fish Creek Guard Station	8900
2.1	Creek	9000
2.8	Jeep trail	9100
3.3	Pond	9050
4.0	Log cabin	9050
5.5	Creek	9200
6.2	Edge of trees	9350
6.4	Creek	9400
6.7	Enter Union Peak Quadrangle	9450
6.9	Basin	9400
7.8	Jeep trail	9600
8.4	Pond	9800
8.8	Gunsight Pass	10150
9.3	Aspens	9650
9.8	Enter Green River Lakes Quadrangle	9300
10.4	Roaring Fork Basin	8850
11.2	Roaring Fork	8800
11.6	Enter Big Sheep Mountain Quadrangle	8800
11.8	Ridge	8850
12.7	Basin	8250
13.4	Pond (8045)	8050
14.3	Bank of Green River	7950
14.7	Enter Green River Lakes Quadrangle	7950
15.5	Creek	8000
16.8	Bridge	7950

BRIDGER WILDERNESS SEGMENT
Section 1
Green River Lakes to Green River Pass
Distance 16.0 Miles

Squaretop Mountain and neighboring peaks rise abruptly above the Green River Lakes at the start of this Section. The Trail then climbs to the headwaters of the Green River, where it enters a truly alpine landscape.

The route follows the eastern shore of photogenic Lower and Upper Green River Lakes to 4.4. Next, it parallels the Green River along meadows and, beyond, through a forested narrow canyon to a tricky crossing of the stream in Beaver Park at 9.4. The grade is moderate to Three Forks Park, but then the Trail climbs steadily and more steeply to Green River Pass, the end of the Section, at 16.0.

A gravel wilderness access road terminates at a Forest Service campground at the foot of Lower Green River Lake. The nearest community of any sort is Cora, where there are a post office (ZIP 82925) and store; despite the distance (about 40 miles from the roadhead), most vehicles from the campground will go at least as far as Cora. (Along the way is Kendall Warm Spring, home of a dace — a tiny fish — that lives exclusively in this restricted habitat.) It is another 10 miles to Pinedale (ZIP 82941), where complete tourist facilities can be found, but transportation there and back may be more difficult to obtain. Other possibilities for resupply include arranging a food drop with an outfitter, either at the campground or in the Wilderness. (One contact is an outdoor store, Wind River Sporting Goods, Box 727, Pinedale.) The most convenient public accommodations (meals, modern cabins) are at Middle Butte Ranch, 24 miles from the campground. (Address: c/o SeTeton Ranch, Box 224, Pinedale). Adjacent to Middle Butte Ranch is The Place, with bar, grill, and soda fountain.

The Section, following the heavily-traveled Highline Trail, is virtually entirely in the Bridger Wilderness (Pinedale Ranger District, Bridger-Teton National Forest). Water is readily accessible, and campsites can be found without difficulty except in densely forested areas or along steeper portions of the climb. (Campsite recommendations are generally omitted in the Bridger Wilderness, so as to avoid encouraging undue concentration.) Route descriptions at higher elevations may not be precise; when visited in the second week of July, parts of the Trail were still covered by snow. Later in the season, one might consider taking a shortcut (from 14.3) over Shannon Pass, omitting Green River Pass altogether. *Be sure to obtain current regulations, including possible restrictions on camping, before entering the Bridger Wilderness.*

Refer to Maps 13 and 14 for the general lie of the route. U.S.G.S. 1:24000 topographic maps are: *Green River Lakes, Squaretop Mountain,* and *Gannett Peak.*

Detailed Trail data are:

From the bridge at the foot of Lower Green River Lake, cross Mill Creek on a log and start following the east shore of the lake. Ascend the bench and proceed at contour, avoiding the fork to the left at 0.1 that climbs into trees. Enter the Bridger Wilderness at the sign at 0.3. The enormous granite plug of Squaretop Mountain and the dark peaks across the narrow glacial valley to its west contrast with the light cliffs of White Rock, to the east at the end of the lake.

Come to the Clear Creek Trail junction at 2.0. (It is 0.2 mile left to Clear Creek Falls and about four miles to popular Slide Lake.) Remaining on the Highline Trail, dip almost to the level of Lower Green River Lake, near its head; cross a narrow footbridge of logs spanning Clear Creek, an important tributary, for five yards.

Hike, in forest, up the right (east) bank of the Green River. Pass by the junction of the Porcupine Trail (which crosses the river on a wide and strong bridge) at 2.9. Bend east to cross over a low ridge before returning to the foot of Upper Green River Lake, with its head-on prospect of Squaretop Mountain. There's a good closeup view as the Trail passes a burned area and overlooks the lake and mountains from a point well up the steep slope at 3.9. Dip to lakeside and walk beneath the towering layered cliffs of White Rock.

Pass the end of Upper Green River Lake at 4.4 near bridged side creeks. Continue up the right bank of the meandering river

Squaretop Mountain.

along the margin of tree and meadow. Approaching Squaretop Mountain at 6.1, cascading falls are seen (at least in early season) tumbling down from the hanging valley beyond the broad meadow. Openings in the timber cover reveal the next rock mass, Granite Peak, just upstream from much more impressive Squaretop.

Walk through the narrow forested gorge between Squaretop and White Rock and approach the frothing waters of the Green River at 6.6. Continue in timber, well upslope, when passing opposite the sheer walls of Squaretop at 7.7, and then drop down to the riverbank across from Granite Peak at 8.5. Cross both Elbow Creek at 9.0 and Pixley Creek on parallel poles.

Enter beautiful Beaver Park, which is cradled by mountains, at 9.3. (12,198-foot Stroud Peak is the high pinnacle far up the valley.) The "permanent" bridge across the Green River half a mile upstream has washed out; the replacement crossing at 9.4 consists of a cluster of lashed parallel poles about 100 yards after entering Beaver Park. (Inquire, before setting out, whether a new bridge has been erected.) The 15-foot crossing requires considerable caution, especially since the water may be over six feet deep and the current is strong.

Proceed up Beaver Park on the Granite Lake Trail, fording a creek at 9.6 and resuming the traditional route of the Highline Trail at the head of the park (by the bridge washout) at 9.8. Climb through forest, above the left bank, crossing the tumbling waters of Marten Creek by bridge at 10.3. Boulder hop a minor branch of the river at 10.6 and 10.7. Remain in the trees, avoiding side trails that drop left into Three Forks Park.

Begin climbing steadily along Trail Creek, with switchbacks starting at 12.1 and continuing to 12.9. An outcrop at 12.5 looks up at cascades, almost falls. Ford ankle-deep Trail Creek at the foot of Trail Creek Park at 13.3. Stay left on the rising Highline Trail at the junction at 13.5. (The right fork is the Clark Creek Trail.)

There is supposed to be a trail to the left at 14.3, providing an alternate, shorter route to Upper Jean Lake by way of Shannon Pass. (It was not observed by the author, probably because of lingering snow.) Hop across a creek, using logs or boulders, at 14.4. From 14.7, climb along the creek, in open country, between two high and steep rock faces. It is not necessary to cross to the left bank at 15.0 and back again at 15.2 if the water is high.

Reach Green River Pass at 16.0 and enter the high country of the Bridger Wilderness. The pass, at 10,380 feet, is the highest point yet attained on the Continental Divide Trail from Canada.

Distances and elevations are:

0.0	Green River bridge	7950
0.3	Wilderness boundary	8000
0.8		8100
2.0	Clear Creek Trail junction	8000
2.1	Clear Creek	8000
2.9	Trail junction	8000
3.1	Ridge	8050
3.2	Upper Green River Lake	8000
3.9	Burned area	8050
4.4	Head of lake	8000

BRIDGER WILDERNESS SEGMENT

5.7	Enter Squaretop Mountain Quadrangle	8000
7.7	Pass Squaretop Mountain	8150
9.0	Elbow Creek	8050
9.1	Pixley Creek	8050
9.4	Green River	8050
10.3	Marten Creek	8150
10.8	Enter Gannett Peak Quadrangle	8250
11.8	Three Forks Park	8350
12.1	Begin switchbacks	8500
13.3	Trail Creek	9250
13.5	Clark Creek Trail junction	9300
14.3	Trail junction	9600
16.0	Green River Pass	10400

BRIDGER WILDERNESS SEGMENT
Section 2
Green River Pass to Pole Creek
Distance 17.7 Miles

Lofty, jagged peaks overlook the Trail as the route winds through a region of tundra dotted with lakes. The Section, except for a bit at the very end, is entirely above 10,000 feet.

The start of the Section is a walk through the high, flat basin of Summit Lake, followed by a short drop to Pine Creek at 1.5. The Trail climbs gradually in superb alpine country, exceeding 11,000 feet at 5.9 on the ridge that connects Bow Mountain (13,020') and Elbow Peak (11,948').

The Trail descends past pretty Upper and Lower Jean Lakes. There is a strong bridge over Fremont Creek, a large stream carrying runoff from a cluster of peaks along the Continental Divide, at Fremont Crossing at 9.8. Island Lake at 11.4 is one of the most popular points in the Bridger Wilderness, deservedly so; a side trip into nearby Titcomb Basin would be worthwhile. Several peaks over 13.000' (though probably not Gannett Peak, highest point in Wyoming) are visible as the Trail reaches its maximum elevation in the Section at Lester Pass (11,100'). The descent is steep at first, with caution required while snowbanks remain. The final part of the Section, from Cook Lakes at 16.6 to the ford of broad Pole Creek at 17.7, is in subalpine forest and meadow.

Travel may be difficult until mid-July — not only because of snow, but also because of high water. Pole Creek, though wide and fairly deep, does not have a strong current; Pine Creek at 1.5, while narrow, can be a more substantial problem. Water is plentiful and campsites are easy to find. (But check the current Forest Service regulations.) Much of the route was snow-covered during the author's trip in early July. Some of the description is therefore imprecise, particularly between Fremont Crossing and Island Lake.

Despite the high elevation, the tall peaks along the Continental Divide are largely obscured by the ridge on the west side of the Titcomb Basin. Still, this is magnificent country and certain to be enjoyed.

BRIDGER WILDERNESS SEGMENT

The Section, which is in the Pinedale Ranger District of the Bridger-Teton National Forest, appears on Map 14 and on the U.S.G.S. *Gannett Peak, Bridger Lakes,* and *Fremont Peak South* (1:24000) quadrangles.

Detailed Trail data are:

Green River Pass, the start of this Section, is a tundra basin with several lakes. From the actual crest, at 0.0, walk to the left of the first pond and jump over a creek at 0.2. Continue on the Highline Trail, fording another creek at 0.5. (Because of high water here, the author remained to the left, rejoining the Highline Trail at 1.5 after a difficult descent of a steep rock face; ordinarily it would be best to remain west of Summit Lake.)

Hike along the west side of Summit Lake. Disregard the side trails which turn right at 0.8 and 0.9 and lead to several wilderness access points in the valley far below. From the south end of the lake, descend to cross Pine Creek at 1.5; though narrow, the stream may be difficult to cross when the runoff is great.

After climbing in a small belt of forest, cross turbulent Elbow Creek beneath cascades, by bridge, at 1.9. Still rising, pass to the right of a small pond. Reach a junction with the Bridger Lakes Trail, which angles right, at 2.3. Stay on the Highline Trail and continue up to the low rocky ridge.

As the Trail leaves Pass Lake at 2.5, it enters the world of the high peaks of the Wind River Range. The tallest mountain in sight is Fremont Peak (13,745'), just north of east. Flanking it in the foreground are Bow, American Legion, and Henderson Peaks on the left and Elbow Peak to the right. Dip to cross Elbow Creek at the wide and shallow ford at the inlet to Upper Twin Lake at 2.8. Climb fairly steeply for nearly a mile, arriving at a high basin, with the pyramids of Henderson Peak prominent north of east. The Trail dips down at 4.0 to boulder hop a narrow point in a small lake at the foot of Sky Pilot Peak (named for a pretty alpine flower).

Reach the shore of Elbow Lake at 4.7. Towering above the lake, to the northeast, is Bow Mountain. Rosy finches inhabit the tundra. Ford the ankle-deep inlet creek and climb to a saddle between Bow Mountain and Elbow Peak, at 5.9. (Just to the

Island Lake.

north is Shannon Pass, the route of the shortcut from 14.3 in
Section 1.)

Descend a narrow valley. High cliffs rise to the east, above
Upper Jean and Lower Jean Lakes. Fremont Creek is forded
twice between the lakes. The Trail angles away from Lower Jean
Lake at 8.7. Note the creek plunging from the wall on the
opposite side of the valley; a good view of Island Lake can be
obtained from a point closer to the creek.

The Trail descends to Fremont Creek, which is much enlarged
with the drainage of the Titcomb Basin, and crosses the sturdy
bridge at Fremont Crossing at 9.8. Climb to a junction, at about
10.4, and take the left fork. This is a good side trail, marked
with cairns, that passes several small ponds and then reaches
Island Lake at 11.4, just about opposite the island. One finally
gets a close view of some of the high mountains on the Continental Divide, including Fremont and Jackson Peaks. The steep-
walled canyon to the north is the Titcomb Basin, a mecca for
climbers and other wilderness visitors.

Pick up the Indian Pass Trail at the southeast corner of Island Lake. Swing right and climb to the pass at 12.2. (Old-man-of-the-mountain is the large yellow flower that is so conspicuous here.) After dipping to a bottom at 12.6, climb again and come to a junction with the Highline Trail at 12.8. Rise a bit more and then drop down to a junction with the Seneca Lake Trail at 13.2.

Keep to the left, remaining on the Highline Trail. Boulder hop a creek and climb to a lake at 13.6. Directly ahead are the gently sloping, though rocky, slopes of Lester Pass. After following a ridge between lakes, the Trail begins to climb, with switchbacks at higher elevations; cairns of small stones mark the way.

From the higher slopes, there are views of the fluted peaks to the north, along the Continental Divide. The prospect changes as the Trail reaches Lester Pass, at 14.6. There are still tall steep-sided mountains southward along the Divide, but not the incredible jumble of spires and domes that dominate the scene to the north. New Fork Peak is the mountain that stands out all by itself straight ahead from the pass. The Wyoming kittentails, noteworthy for its colorful stamens and lack of petals, is one of the many alpine flowers that grow here.

The difficult part of the crossing of Lester Pass is the descent on the south side, at least so long as the snowbanks remain. The slope may be convex, with cornices, and should be treated with respect. It may be possible to find a safer route by walking south 500 yards along the ridge and then following the spur down to the valley, heading about 160°.

Once the initial drop is over, the descent is very gradual. Tommy Lake, with Mount Lester as an imposing backdrop, is on the left at 15.7. The Trail drops down to Cook Lakes, with a boulder hop across the connection between two of the lakes. After a small rise, the Trail dips through forest to a junction, at 17.2, in a meadow.

The route continues by taking the fork to the right, using the Highline Trail. (To the left is the Fremont Trail; it remains at higher elevations and would be a good alternate.) Using the Highline Trail, follow the trees on the right side of the meadow to 17.5. Hop a small creek and proceed along the water's edge to Pole Creek at 17.7.

The ford of Pole Creek, the end of the Section, may require caution. It appears that the best place to cross is just below the low cascades; the water is about 100 feet wide and two feet deep, but the current is not strong.

Distances and elevations are:

0.0	Green River Pass	10400
0.9	Summit Lake	10350
1.5	Pine Creek	10150
1.8	Enter Bridger Lakes Quadrangle	10250
1.9	Elbow Creek	10300
2.3	Bridger Lakes Trail junction	10400
2.5	Pass Lake	10500
2.8	Upper Twin Lake	10400
3.7		10850
4.6	Enter Gannett Peak Quadrangle	10800
4.9		10850
5.0	Elbow Creek	10800
5.6	Shannon Pass Trail junction	10950
5.9	Saddle	11050
6.8	Enter Bridger Lakes Quadrangle	10800
7.9	Fremont Creek	10650
8.3		10700
9.8	Fremont Crossing	10250
10.4	(Trail junction)	10400
10.8		10500
11.4	Island Lake	10350
11.8	Indian Pass Trail junction	10400
12.2	Pass	10650
12.6	Creek	10500
12.8	Highline Trail junction	10550
12.9		10600
13.2	Seneca Lake Trail junction	10350
13.6	Lake	10550
14.6	Lester Pass	11100
15.4	Enter Fremont Peak South Quadrangle	10700
15.7	Tommy Lake	10650
16.6	Cook Lakes	10200
17.2	Fremont Trail junction	10250
17.7	Pole Creek	9950

BRIDGER WILDERNESS SEGMENT

Section 3

Pole Creek to North Fork Lake

Distance 14.8 Miles

This is an easy Section, a hike in upland forest broken by frequent meadows and lakes.

There are fords of Pole Creek at the start of the Section and again at Pole Creek Lakes at 1.4 and 1.7. Much of this travel is in meadow, as is the next stretch — about level past the Chain Lakes and Barnes Lake and then dropping modestly to Horseshoe Lake. From the south end of Horseshoe, at 8.6, the Trail swings left, generally climbing, toward the mountains. This is dense forest, with some more small lakes, until the Trail emerges into more open country again as it approaches beautiful North Fork Lake, where the Section ends at 14.8.

The only difficulty in hiking this Section will be the fords of Pole Creek, during high water. Travel through the forest in the second half of the Section would also be a problem, because of the numerous ponds and absence of landmarks, were it not for the well-worn pack trail. Water is readily available; camping is not recommended between Horseshoe Lake and the end of the Section, however.

The Section, still in the Pinedale Ranger District of the Bridger-Teton National Forest, is shown on Map 15. The 1:24000 U.S.G.S. topographic maps are: *Fremont Peak South*, *Bridger Lakes*, and *Horseshoe Lake*.

Detailed Trail data are:

Continue on the Highline Trail from the ford of Pole Creek at the start of the Section. Cross a boot-deep creek at 0.1 and then drop, first through spruces and then in meadow, to another ford of Pole Creek at 1.4. The Pole Creek Trail comes in from the right at 1.5. A third and final ford of Pole Creek is at 1.7. (Do not try to bypass the stream crossings except, perhaps, when the water is extremely high; travel along the left bank requires a scramble over a ridge, to get by a rock face that drops precipitously into the water, and then a steep descent.)

Head south, rising slightly in meadow and crossing small creeks. Pass a divide at 2.6 and come to Chain Lakes, situated in a basin of rocky knolls and low forested ridges. The Trail here, and for several miles, has small grades, so that travel is easy. Continue on the Highline Trail at the junction at 3.8. (The Bell Lakes Trail angles left and provides a connection to the Fremont Trail.) The meadow here boasts the typical diversity of wild-flowers — shooting star, marshmarigold, cinquefoil, spring-beauty, bistort, microseris, draba, dandelion, bracted lousewort, and violet among them.

After passing the turnoff of a side trail to Spruce Lake, at 4.3, stay well to the right of the meadow as it drops to Barnes Lake. Contour along the lake from 4.9 to a junction at 5.6. Take the left fork, hiking along the combined route of the Highline and Timico Lake Trails. Baldy Creek, about 10 feet wide and a foot deep, is forded at 5.7. Cross a ridge, in forest with a ground cover of grouse whortleberry.

Dip to meadow, remaining straight at the junction at 6.2. (Continue on the Highline Trail; the path forking left is the Timico Lake Trail.) At 6.3, ford Fall Creek, which is about the same size as was Baldy. Walk through a ravine to a junction at 6.5 and ford again. (The trail remaining on the left bank should be all right, too; it would rejoin the described route at 7.2, just after a shallow ford at the far end of the meadow.)

Descend from 7.2. Reach a junction 100 yards or so before Horseshoe Lake. Take the trail (not indicated on the topographic map) that once again fords Fall Creek and follow the east shore of the lake, with some small ups and downs, Reach the meadow at the southeast corner, at 8.6. Turn left on the Highline Trail, heading southeast. (Avoid the Horseshoe Lake Trail, which con-tinues straight up the valley to the south.)

Climb in spruce forest, then level out in meadow. Follow the shoreline along Lake George. Midway down the lake, at 9.7, take the fork heading to the right. Stay left at the junction at 9.9, hiking from here on the combined routes of the Highline and North Fork Trails.

Twist about, generally rising, through buggy, viewless spruce forest broken by occasional meadow. Edmond Lake, at 11.7, is a welcome oasis. The character of the Trail remains much the same down to Macs Lake where, at 12.8, the Ethel Trail joins from the right. Ascend gradually past several ponds, with the forest finally breaking up and the mountains coming into view close ahead.

Swing far to the left of a meadow at 14.1. Leave the High-line Trail, which turns sharp right at 14.2. Following the obvious main track, marked by cairns, walk to the left of a pond and come to a four-way intersection at 14.6. Keep going straight, dropping down to the shore of North Fork Lake. Follow the edge around to the north and east. The Section ends at a junction at 14.8, by the lake, as the Fremont Trail joins from the left.

Distances and elevations are:

0.0	Pole Creek	9950
0.6		10050
1.4	Pole Creek (enter Bridger Lakes Quadrangle)	9700
1.5	Pole Creek Trail junction	9750
1.7	Pole Creek	9700
2.1	Enter Fremont Peak South Quadrangle	9750
2.3	Enter Horseshoe Lake Quadrangle	9750
2.6	Divide	9850
2.8		9800
3.0		9850
3.3	Chain Lakes	9800
3.8	Bell Lakes Trail junction	9850
4.3	Trail junction	9850
4.9	Barnes Lake	9750
5.6	Timico Lake Trail junction	9750
5.9	Ridge	9850
6.2	Timico Lake Trail junction	9800
6.3	Fall Creek	9700
6.5	Fall Creek	9700
7.0	Meadow	9650
7.8	Trail junction	9450
8.2		9500
8.6	Horseshoe Lake Trail junction	9450
9.7	Lake George	9700
9.9	North Fork Trail junction	9750
10.2		9800
10.4		9750

11.4		10000
11.5		9950
11.6		10000
11.7	Edmond Lake	9950
12.8	Ethel Trail junction	9650
14.2	Highline Trail junction	9850
14.6	Trail junction	9800
14.8	North Fork Lake	9750

BRIDGER WILDERNESS SEGMENT
Section 4
North Fork Lake to East Fork River
Distance 16.3 Miles

For mile after mile, the Trail travels along a high plateau at the edge of the mountains forming the spine of the Wind River Range. The landscape is dotted with lakes separated by low divides. The first half is lightly forested, the second half wild and nearly treeless — but it is all very grand.

The route follows the Fremont Trail throughout the Section. (Trail designations are confusing. The name "Highline Trail" appears on some signs along the way as well as on the outdated Mt. Bonneville topographic map. The terminology here conforms to the 1975 wilderness plan.) From North Fork at the start of the Section, the Trail climbs easily, passing Pipestone Lakes at 2.4 at the base of Medina Mountain. It rises to a ridge at 3.9, where the prominent turrets of Mount Bonneville, a distinctive landmark, appear for the first time.

The route drops to ford the Middle Fork of Boulder Creek at 6.4 and continues in delightfully open country past several lakes to the easy crossing of the South Fork, with good views of the mountains, at 9.3. Several miles of rolling tundra mark the way to a high point at 14.7, followed by a dropoff to the end of the Section, at the ford of the broad East Fork River, at 16.3.

Sheep grazing, an activity dating back to the turn of the century, continues in the Bridger Wilderness. The Fremont Trail is a major driveway, and large flocks may be encountered. Sheep may not tarry, however, in the especially lovely area by the North Fork and around North Fork Lake. While on the subject of sheep, it is worth mentioning that some 1200 of them were slaughtered in a scrap between cattlemen and sheepherders, in 1903; the skirmish is commemorated by the name of Raid Lake, along the Trail at 9.3.

Aside from this animal intrusion, there should be no problems in finding good campsites. Water supplies are plentiful. There are opportunities for many outstanding side trips, if time permits.

The Trail, in the Pinedale Ranger District of the Bridger-Teton National Forest, appears on Maps 15 and 16. The topographic maps are the 1:24000 *Horseshoe Lake* quadrangle and the 1:62500 *Mt. Bonneville* quadrangle. (The latter is to be superseded by new 1:24000 maps, which are to be available about 1981.)

Detailed Trail data are:

From the junction at the northwest corner of North Fork Lake, follow the worn tread eastward toward Mt. Victor, the prominent peak in the foreground. In addition to such ubiquitous flowers as lupine, cinquefoil, and bistort, there are many more of special interest, such as Colorado columbine and pygmy bitterroot. Look for pipits and spotted sandpipers, too.

The North Fork of Boulder Creek can soon be heard and seen to the right. The Trail cuts across scenic meadow to reach a ford at a wide spot, 100 feet across and knee-deep near the west shore, at 0.5. (It may still be possible to avoid the ford by taking the old bridge — reduced to a single solid beam in 1976 — to the right at 0.3, just downstream from the scattered timber on the far side; from that crossing, at a point where the creek is channeled into a chute of deep and fast water, it is easy to return to the Trail by following the bank.)

Climb in forest to 1.6. As the scene opens up, there are good views northwest up North Fork Canyon toward Round Top Mountain and northeast up Europe Canyon toward the Continental Divide. Note the enormous whitebark pines at a high point at 1.9. Straight ahead is Mt. Geikie; Medina Mountain is the grassy-sloped summit close by to the left.

A trail from Europe Canyon joins from the left at 2.2 as the route drops down to the creek, easily boulder-hopped, between the Pipestone Lakes at 2.4. The Trail follows the shore of the second lake, then climbs over a couple of ridges, mostly in light forest. At the second one, at 3.9, after circling to the right of a lake, the view southward includes Mt. Bonneville for the first time. Its unique profile — several rock towers like the stacks of a ship — contrast with the conventional pyramids, including Raid Peak and Mt. Geikie to its right.

Descend a winding route to Halls Creek at 4.8; cross at a very wide ford, barely ankle-deep, at a gravel bar. (For a good side trip, follow the creek up to Halls Lake and then climb to the Continental Divide; many other opportunities for exploration are available in this area as well.) Walk through pleasant meadows, over a low ridge, and on to the Middle Fork of Boulder Creek at 6.3. There is little current at the ford, which is knee-deep and 25 yards wide.

Pass the sandy point of Sandpoint Lake at 6.7. After the next divide, Mt. Bonneville stands out on the dip to Bobs Lake. The high country now becomes a vast open park, with very enjoyable travel. Dream Creek at 8.1 is an easy ford. After passing a back cove of Dream Lake at 8.5, the Trail climbs over a hill. As it descends by a pond, there is a superb unobstructed view of Mt. Bonneville and its neighbors straight ahead to the east. Go around the pond and drop to the easy ford of the shin-deep South Fork of Boulder Creek, where it enters Raid Lake, at 9.3. The Trail winds through several rock fields on its way to Raid Creek, which can be boulder-hopped, at 10.5.

Some of the nicest high grassland, looking up at the Bonneville Basin and the summits from Raid Peak to Mt. Geikie, is found as the Trail climbs to Sheep Creek at 12.0; mountains fill the skyline from northwest to southeast. Among the birds are white-crowned and chipping sparrows, pipits, Clark's nutcrackers, and mountain bluebirds.

Use the old bridge to cross Sheep Creek. Climb along the edge of a stand of trees. After passing a pond, come to a ridge at 12.8, where the Scab Creek Trail joins from the right. Here one has the first view of the complex of spires along the west side of the Cirque of the Towers, as well as the last unblocked sighting of the mountains to the north. Another valley, with a small creek at 13.5, is followed by a climb to an extensive plateau. From the high point at 14.7, the Cirque is especially impressive.

The Trail then drops along a creek, mostly through light forest, to a park where several streams converge. The largest, the East Fork River, requires a ford of 10 yards; the water is nearly three feet deep, but the current is quite modest. Cross opposite some boulders, below the confluence with one branch of Washakie Creek, where the Section ends at 16.3.

Distances and elevations are:

0.0	North Fork Lake	9750
0.4	North Fork, Boulder Creek	9750
0.5	Enter Mt. Bonneville Quadrangle	9750
1.9		10200
2.2	Trail junction	10150
2.4	Pipestone Lakes	10100
2.9		10200
3.2		10100
3.9	(10290)	10300
4.8	Halls Creek	9800
5.4	(9916)	9900
5.8		9750
6.3	Middle Fork, Boulder Creek	9800
7.4	Bobs Lake	9900
8.1	Dream Creek	9900
8.9	(9979)	10000
9.3	South Fork, Boulder Creek	9950
10.5	Raid Creek	10050
12.0	Sheep Creek	10250
12.8	Scab Creek Trail junction	10350
13.5	Creek	10150
14.7		10550
16.3	East Fork River	9750

BRIDGER WILDERNESS SEGMENT
Section 5
East Fork River to Big Sandy Entrance
8.2 Miles

The Trail diverges a bit from the high mountains, passing several popular fishing lakes before leaving the Bridger Wilderness and dropping close to a roadhead.

The route is the Fremont Trail (though once again there are confusing "Highline Trail" signs along the way). The only significant climb is at the start of the Section, from the East Fork River to meadows at 0.8. The Trail remains quite open as it passes Marms, Dads, and Mirror Lakes and dips to heavily-grazed Fish Creek Park at 5.0. Beyond a divide at 6.0, the hike is downhill, largely in forest. The Section ends at 8.2, just outside the Bridger Wilderness boundary, at a trail junction in a meadow near Meeks Lake.

The end of the Section provides good access to resupply points. It is about 1.6 miles to the Forest Service's Big Sandy Campground; by the graded road, it is then 48 miles to U.S. 187 at Boulder (ZIP 82923). Hikers are also welcome at the rustic and friendly Big Sandy Lodge, on the south side of Mud Lake, a recommended place to have some good meals and enjoy a rest. Allow several weeks to get a reply to inquiries, as they pick up mail infrequently at Boulder; there is no phone. Big Sandy Lodge is about 2.4 miles off the Trail from the meadow at the end of the Section.

Camping opportunities are good betweeen the East Fork River and Dads Lake, and there is plenty of water throughout the Section, which lies in the Pinedale Ranger District of the Bridger-Teton National Forest. The U.S.G.S. topographic maps are *Mt. Bonneville* (1:62500) and *Big Sandy Opening* (1:24000). The former will soon be replaced by new 1:24000 quadrangles. Refer also to Map 17.

Detailed Trail data are:

From the confluence of Washakie Creek and the East Fork River, climb in forest and then meadow, to 0.8. To the north, note Pyramid Peak — not the highest of the summits, but with proportions fit for Cheops. After some rises and dips, swing right and come to an old sign at 1.3 marking a junction with a side trail (no longer evident) down to the sheep bridge across the East Fork.

Cassin's finches and pine grosbeaks might be observed along the forest edge as the Trail drops to the junction with the Washakie Trail (joining from the left) at 2.1. Walk along Marms Lake, with good views north toward Mt. Geikie and Mt. Hooker. Hike in meadow down to Dads Lake. Parallel the east shore with several ups and downs, including a dip to boulder hop Donald Creek, near the lake, at 3.6. As the Trail rises to Mirror Lake, look back up Desolation Canyon, the alpine basin of the East Fork along the back side of Mt. Bonneville. This view becomes even more rewarding as the Trail, after dipping for a ford of shallow Fish Creek at 5.0, climbs a broad avenue of grass between the forest on both sides.

The rest of the Section is downhill from the crest at 6.0. As the Trail comes past the south end of Laturio Mountain, the sheer north face of Temple Peak stands out boldly. Descend in forest, mostly spruce, leaving the Bridger Wilderness at 7.4. Come to the junction of the Fremont Trail and the Meeks Lake Trail in a flat meadow adjacent to Meeks Lake, at 8.0. Turn left, staying on the north edge of the opening, following the tall poles. (The Fremont Trail, to the right, provides an alternate route to Big Sandy Lodge.) A camp could be made near the small creek at 8.1. Intersect the Diamond Lake Trail at the forest edge at 8.2, where the Section ends.

(To get to Big Sandy Campground or Big Sandy Lodge from the end of the Section: Take the Meeks Lake Trail, continuing across the meadow to the east edge of Meeks Lake, where an osprey might be soaring, at 0.3. Drop down to the edge of the Big Sandy River at 0.9 and follow it downstream. At the junction at 1.2, elevation 9100, it is 0.4 mile downstream on the river trail to the campground. To go to the lodge, take the right fork at 1.2 and again at 1.8; dip to cross Iron Creek at 2.0 and follow the west shore of Mud Lake to reach the lodge at 2.4.)

Distances and elevations are:

0.0 East Fork River   9750

0.8		10050
1.0		10000
1.1		10050
2.1	Washakie Trail junction	9900
3.2	(9746)	9750
3.5		9800
3.6	Donald Creek	9750
4.4	Enter Big Sandy Opening Quadrangle	9850
5.0	Fish Creek	9800
6.0	Crest	9950
7.4	Wilderness boundary	9550
8.0	Meeks Lake Trail junction	9300
8.2	Diamond Lake Trail junction	9300

BRIDGER WILDERNESS SEGMENT

Section 6

Big Sandy Entrance to Temple Peaks

9.9 Miles

Reaching its highest point in Wyoming, the Trail climbs through alpine basins of exceptional grandeur. There are several lakes along the way, as well as the opportunity for a short side trip into the famous Cirque of the Towers.

From the start of the Section, the Trail immediately returns to the Bridger Wilderness and climbs in forest broken by meadow past V Lake and Diamond Lake to Big Sandy Lake. Here, at 4.8, it picks up the Little Sandy Trail and ascends in gradually thinning tree cover, past Clear Lake at 6.1, into alpine terrain. The climb continues past Deep Lake at 7.6 and Temple Lake at 8.7, at the bottom of cirques at the foot of East Temple and Temple Peaks, respectively. The Section ends at the pass between these two summits, at 9.9, after the steep ascent of a rocky couloir.

Big Sandy Lake, because of its beauty and accessibility to the roadhead, is an especially popular campsite. There are many more good places, however. (As elsewhere in the Bridger Wilderness, inquire about camping restrictions.) Water is plentiful throughout. The only obstacle to be considered is the snow that lingers on the final part of the hike, above Temple Lake, to mid-July.

See the introductory text for Section 5 regarding opportunities for resupply at the Big Sandy Entrance.

The Section, in the Pinedale Ranger District of the Bridger-Teton National Forest, appears on Map 17. 1:24000 U.S.G.S. topographic maps are: *Big Sandy Opening* and *Temple Peak*. The side trip to the Cirque of the Towers is shown, inaccurately, on the 1:62500 *Moccasin Lake* quadrangle, which is to be replaced by new 1:24000 maps.

Detailed Trail data are:

Follow the Diamond Lake Trail from its junction with the Meeks Lake Trail in the meadow above Meeks Lake. Enter forest and the Bridger Wilderness right away. Climbing, pass V Lake at 0.7 and Diamond Lake at 2.0; both offer excellent views of Temple Peak. Clark's nutcrackers and gray jays may be seen in the more open places, western wood pewees and hermit thrushes in the forest. The meadows are filled with cinquefoil, bistort, larkspur, alpine dock, lupine, shooting star, microseris, and other flowers.

Join the Big Sandy Trail, which comes in from the right at 2.5. Climb gradually in forest, crossing minor creeks, until the southern tip of Big Sandy Lake is reached at 4.0. The view from the meadows on the north side is especially fine; the arc of mountains swings leftward from dominating Schiestler Peak to flat-topped Haystack Mountain.

Following the lakeshore, come to a junction at 4.8 and take the Little Sandy Lake Trail, which bends to the right at contour. (The route rising to the left crosses Big Sandy Pass and drops down to Lonesome Lake in the Cirque of the Towers, a glacial basin enclosed by 2000-foot towers of rock. From the junction, it is about 2.4 miles to the Continental Divide and a total of 3.2 miles to Lonesome Lake. At 1.0, while first approaching Shaft Lake, the trail forks. The elevation here is 10,250 feet. The right fork is the pack trail, which climbs another 100 feet before dropping to the head of Shaft Lake at 1.5, elevation 10,150 feet; the left fork may be easier and more direct. Continuing up to Arrowhead Lake at 10,350 feet, you may then climb the very steep path, past the talus on the west side of the lake, to the low col at 2.4, at 10,650 feet, descending cross-country to Lonesome Lake at 10,150 feet; or follow the pack trail to the pass slightly farther east, at 10,750 feet, and then head down on marked path. Looking up from the cirque, Warbonnet and the Warriors are the towers closest to the pass. The most prominent landmark, the rounded obelisk rising directly from Lonesome Lake, is Pingora Peak; its name, in the Shoshone tongue, refers to a high, inaccessible tower. It is a rewarding side trip, enjoy the scenery and the flowers at high altitudes, such as old-man-of-the-mountain, alpine and cutleaf daisies, phlox, biscuitroot, alpine avens, thistle milkvetch, Parry's lousewort, and Parry's primrose. Watch for marmots, pikas, chipmunks and yellow-rumped warblers too.)

From the trail junction, proceed along the shore. The much-divided creeks in the meadows around 5.1 may be boot-wetters,

Big Sandy Lake.

but are easy to cross. Some more flowers on the upland include woolly groundsel, varileaf cinquefoil, and small-flowered penstemon; mountain gooseberry is a common shrub. Spotted sandpipers feed along the edge of the lake, and a California gull may be observed soaring over the waters.

Pass by the side trail that goes off to the left at 5.3 toward Black Joe Lake. Leave the basin at 5.5 by turning left at the sign and climbing, in forest, on the Little Sandy Lake Trail. Reach the grassy shore of Clear Lake at 6.1. The commanding feature is Haystack Mountain, with the sharp-pointed pyramids of Steeple Peak and East Temple Peak close by to its right. Be alert for black rosy finches here and at higher elevations.

Follow the lake shore and then, from 6.9, climb the right (east) bank of the creek, beyond treeline. At about 7.3, cross the creek, which is a film of water flowing down a slide of slab rock. Continue up the slope, with views back to Pingora and

Deep Lake, with East Temple Peak.

other peaks in the Cirque of the Towers. Cross the lip of a basin at the foot of Deep Lake at 7.6; Steeple Peak and East Temple Peak rise majestically above.

Hike on south, climbing steadily up from the lake toward Temple Peak; there are some cairns, but they are not always easy to spot. Cross a pass at 8.3. Briefly, you will be able to see the deep cleft separating a high spire of East Temple from the main mass of the mountain. Swing left toward Temple Lake and Temple Peak, marked by steep snowbanks rising out of the water. Reach the shore of the lake at 8.7.

Proceed over a rise to the south end of the lake. Then begin a very steep climb up a gully, where residual snowfields are likely to be encountered. (It may be possible to avoid most of the snow by climbing almost immediately from 8.7, then contouring at about 10,850 feet; some fairly steep scree slopes have to be crossed this way, however.) Much of the Cirque of the Towers can be seen beyond the hanging valley of Temple and Miller Lakes, and Mt. Geikie is visible to the northwest. The last bit of the climb is relatively flat.

The unnamed pass at 9.9, at the end of the Section, is the highest point on the Continental Divide Trail in the northern Rockies (Montana, Idaho, and Wyoming).

Distances and elevations are:

0.0	Trail junction	9300
0.1	Enter Bridger Wilderness	9350
0.4		9500
0.7	V Lake	9450
1.3	Enter Temple Peak Quadrangle	9450
2.0	Diamond Lake	9500
2.5	Big Sandy Trail junction	9500
4.0	Big Sandy Lake	9700
4.8	Little Sandy Trail junction	9700
5.3	Trail junction	9700
6.1	Clear Lake	10000
7.6	Deep Lake	10500
8.3	Pass	10750
8.7	Temple Lake	10650
8.9		10750
9.1		10650
9.9	Pass	11500

BRIDGER WILDERNESS SEGMENT
Section 7
Temple Peaks to Sweetwater Guard Station
13.6 Miles

Alpine tundra, montane forest, and grassland with sagebrush are all found in this varied Section as the Trail leaves the Bridger Wilderness.

The Trail quickly drops down the steep face of a cirque to 0.5, then descends another several hundred feet in the narrow canyon of Little Sandy Creek to a good campsite at 2.6. The route, continuing in forest, swings away from the creek and passes to the west of Little Sandy Lake, reaching a junction at 7.0. Next, there is a climb to the Continental Divide; the crossing of the Divide at 8.7 is the first in about 140 miles. Leaving the Bridger Wilderness at 10.9, the Trail follows jeep road from 11.7 to a junction, close to the former Sweetwater Guard Station, at the end of the Section at 13.6.

Expect to find steep snowbanks on the high slopes at the start of the Section well into July; an unarrested fall here could result in serious injury. Another complication is the inaccuracy of maps in the vicinity of Little Sandy Lake. (See the detailed text for miles 3.9 through 8.7.) There are adequate sources of water, though a canteen might be welcome on the stretch from Little Sandy Creek at 7.0 to Larsen Creek at 10.2.

The Trail is in the Pinedale Ranger District of the Bridger-Teton National Forest, all but the last 2.7 miles in the Bridger Wilderness. The Section receives relatively little use; perhaps for this reason, there is a good chance to observe bighorn sheep in the upper portions. Although there is light traffic on the road at the end of the Section, it would not be particularly convenient to attempt to resupply from this point.

Refer to Maps 18 and 19. Four 1:24000 U.S.G.S. topographic maps are required. They are: *Temple Peak*, *Sweetwater Gap*, *Jensen Meadows*, and *Sweetwater Needles*.

Detailed Trail data are:

The Section begins at the 11,500-foot pass on the ridge

connecting Temple and East Temple Peaks, the highest point on the Continental Divide Trail in the northern Rockies. The vista southward is a gray, barren landscape of cliff and talus, gouged by the deep glacial cut of Little Sandy Creek. The final high peaks of the range are visible — Wind River Peak being the round dome to the left, Mt. Nystrom far down the valley, and a bit of Atlantic Peak to Nystrom's left.

The Trail swings left a bit, beginning its steep descent eastward above the lake (northernmost of the Frozen Lakes) at the head of Little Sandy Creek. Short, but fairly steep, snowbanks may remain late in the summer. Once down off the mountain, the cairns may be hard to find, but cross-country travel would not be difficult. Cross Little Sandy Creek about 1.0 and proceed down the right bank. Enter forest at 2.2. The meadow at 2.6 is especially scenic, with a massive unnamed monolith overlooking it and a creek fed by a large cascade tumbling down the mountainside. The Continental Divide, just across Little Sandy, is capped with impressive towers and pinnacles.

Boulder hop the rushing side creek and continue down the west side of the valley. For a short way around 3.1, follow the path on an island formed by a small branch of the creek. The stream's rushing descent is interrupted by a large marshy area, with meanders, that starts at 3.4.

The stream broadens into ponds, as indicated on the Sweetwater Gap quadrangle. Unfortunately, that map doesn't show the Trail. So keep an especially careful lookout for a stone marker, signaling the turnoff from the valley floor, at 4.7; this is roughly 200 yards before the south tip of the narrow pond. (The author missed the turn and ended up bushwhacking. Details for the next 1.9 miles were kindly furnished by Dave James of Englewood, Colorado; he reports that the route may be hard to follow at places.) Head straight up into the trees and then gradually curve south. Hike just east of a lake, crossing its outlet at 5.1. Continue south, well above the valley of Little Sandy Creek, passing to the west of one small pond at 5.5 and east of another one at 5.8. After a bit of a rise, the route descends to a junction at 6.6. Turn right at this junction. (The trail to the left leads, after 0.3 mile, to Little Sandy Lake.)

Be alert for an obscure junction on the pack trail, at 7.0. It will be found where Little Sandy Creek is first seen and heard. Make a sharp left here, almost immediately crossing the creek. A large log will probably be available for an easy crossing. Once again, the maps prove to be unreliable; the crossing of the creek is considerably further downstream and the direction of the pack trail far more southerly than indicated on the Jensen Meadows quadrangle. From Little Sandy Creek, head generally south, then east. At 8.0, go through or just north of the pass at 9761 feet on the Continental Divide. At 8.2, there is a good view over Little Sandy Lake toward Temple and Wind River Peaks. From here, except for the omission of some switchbacks, the maps appear to be accurate.

Cross the Continental Divide at 8.7. Drop rather steadily in forest, boulder hopping to the right bank of small Larsen Creek at 10.2 and then climbing over a low ridge at 10.4. The transition from high mountains to plains brings different birds, such as mourning doves, brown creepers, and woodpeckers. Leaving the Bridger Wilderness for the last time at 10.9, drop to a large meadow at 11.4 and, after a small rise, come to a roadhead at 11.7 where the Sweetwater Gap Trail joins from the left.

Keep descending, on jeep road, alternating between patches of forest and openings of sagebrush. Off to the left are the rocky slopes of Sweetwater Needles and Atlantic Peak. At 12.0, get a first glimpse of the high plains ahead. Scarlet gilia, umbrella plant, lupine, and larkspur are among the flowers adding a touch of color. According to a sign, the poor jeep tracks joining from the right at 12.7 connect with the Lowline Trail.

The Section ends at the road junction at 13.6. The site of the Sweetwater Guard Station, built in 1913, is 0.4 mile to the left. (To get there, take the right fork where the side road divides a couple of hundred yards from the junction at 13.6.) The old log cabin (destroyed in 1978 by a 1000-acre fire) and a public campground nearby were attractively situated on the banks of the Sweetwater River, with a clear view out to Atlantic Peak. There is a good spring about 100 yards behind the cabin site, accessible by footpath; it emerges from the right bank of Station Creek. There are also a number of birds to enjoy, including belted kingfishers, common nighthawks, song sparrows, and Wilson's warblers. Red squirrels and mantled ground squirrels add to the scene, too.

Distances and elevations are:

0.0	Pass	11500
0.1	Snowbank	11450
0.3	Snowbank	11200
0.4	Snowbank	11050
1.0	Little Sandy Creek	10600
2.6	Creek	10050
3.9	Enter Sweetwater Gap Quadrangle	9750
4.7	Leave valley	9750
4.9		9850
5.1	Lake	9750
5.3		9800
5.5	Pond	9700
5.8	Enter Temple Peak Quadrangle	9650
6.0		9800
6.6	Trail junction	9500
6.7	Enter Jensen Meadows Quadrangle	9500
7.0	Trail junction (Little Sandy Creek)	9400
7.5	Enter Sweetwater Needles Quadrangle	9600
8.0	Pass (9761)	9750
8.2	Viewpoint	9900
8.7	Continental Divide	10150
10.2	Larsen Creek	9200
10.4	Ridge	9250
10.9	Wilderness boundary	9050
11.4	Meadow	8850
11.7	Roadhead	8900
12.7	Lowline Trail junction (8599)	8600
13.6	Road junction	8300

SWEETWATER RIVER SEGMENT

Section 1

Sweetwater Guard Station to East Sweetwater River

Distance 10.4 Miles

The Trail, using secondary roads and jeep trails, crosses several minor grassland ridges.

The first 2.2 miles are on graded road. The Trail then turns southeast, dipping to the Sweetwater River at 4.4. The route continues on jeep roads, with easy grades up and down to the grassy bank of the Little Sweetwater River at 8.7. After climbing over another low ridge, on less-traveled jeep trail, one reaches the East Sweetwater River, where the Section ends, at 10.4.

A number of prominent landmarks can be made out to the south, along the rim of the Great Divide Basin. These include Steamboat Mountain, about 50 miles, and — to its left — the nearer heights of the Oregon Buttes and then Continental Peak. The best campsites are at the Sweetwater Guard Station site and at the Little Sweetwater River, at 8.7. Water sources are few, but they are conveniently spaced.

From 6.8 on, the Trail is in the Pinedale Ranger District of the Bridger-Teton National Forest. The first several miles are on public land (Rock Springs District, Bureau of Land Management).

In addition to Map 19, use the two U.S.G.S. topographic maps (1:24000), namely *Sweetwater Needles* and *Christina Lake*.

Detailed Trail data are:

The Section begins at the junction where the wilderness access jeep road meets the turnoff to the left (east) to the Sweetwater Guard Station. A camp can be made here, with water from Station Creek, but more attractive sites can be found along the Sweetwater River near the guard station. (See the preceding Section for details.)

The Trail follows the road heading south; from here, it is passable by car. Cross the culvert of Station Creek and leave the national forest. There are small rises and dips; Mt. Nystrom is still visible to the north. Pass a small creek at 0.7 and rise to 1.0,

116

where a side road turns right to the Sweetwater Gap Ranch. Bend right on the road, at 1.7, after the next dip. Ahead is broad South Pass, where the historic Oregon Trail crossed the Continental Divide; several distant buttes rise up from the horizon to the south.

Descend to 2.2. Turn left here, on the jeep trail on the south side of the draw. Keep straight where a jeep trail turns right at 2.9 and again when others join from the left at 3.2. There may be good opportunities for viewing wildlife — possibly a badger as well as antelope and sage grouse. Swing to the right of a small rock outcrop and intersect a well-worn jeep road at 3.3. Turn left and follow the jeep road. Walk between two clumps of aspen, bypassing the jeep trail that turns right at 3.5.

Soon descend to the Sweetwater River, which is crossed by a vehicle bridge at 4.4. (It is just a large creek, barely ankle-deep, and could easily be forded here.) Pass through the Bureau of Land Management's Sweetwater Campground, where an overnight stop could be made. Trash cans are available. Yellow warblers nest in the willows along the bank, and spotted sandpipers can be observed along the edge of the stream.

Follow the jeep road eastward, climbing along the right (north) bank of Clear Creek. A beaver pond is to the right at 5.7. Avoid the poor trail forking to the left, and cross the culvert with small Clear Creek at 5.8. Climb to a hilltop at 6.1, with views southward once again toward Continental Peak and the Oregon Buttes; off to the east are the minor outlying summits of the Wind River Range, notably Granite Peak to the right of low Sioux Pass. Stay on the good jeep road, ignoring trails on both sides.

Reenter the Bridger-Teton National Forest at a cattle guard at 6.8. Come to a four-way intersection, with good views back toward Mt. Nystrom and beyond, at the top of a rise at 7.1. Here turn left and follow the ridge. Vesper sparrows are fairly common in the sagebrush and short grass. Avoid jeep trails heading toward the right at 7.6 and 7.8. Pass just to the right of the corner of an aspen stand at 7.9. After a short and rather steep dip, take the right fork at 8.6. (The jeep trail ascending to the left is the Little Sweetwater Trail.)

Swing right and cross the bridge over the Little Sweetwater River, which is just a typical creek, at 8.7. White-crowned sparrows and MacGillivray's warblers in the willows may provide company at the excellent grassy campsite here. From this point on, the tread gradually deteriorates. The Trail climbs at first, then nearly levels out in meadows filled with chives, wild onion, elk thistle, pussytoes, mariposa, umbrella plant, arnica, and other wildflowers. Pass through a belt of aspen at 9.9 and soon reach a crest, with a view up to Sioux Pass. A poor trail comes in from the left at 10.2.

Reach the valley of the East Sweetwater River, which is immediately ahead, at 10.4. The Section ends here, as the main jeep trail curves to the right.

Distances and elevations are:

0.0	Road junction (Station Creek)	8300
0.1	Forest boundary	8350
0.2		8400
0.7	Creek	8300
1.0	Road junction	8350
1.5		8250
1.7	Bend	8350
2.2	Draw	8200
2.9	Jeep trail junction	8150
3.3	Jeep road junction	8150
3.5	Jeep trail junction	8100
3.8		8150
4.4	Sweetwater River	7850
5.8	Clear Creek	8100
6.1		8250
6.8	Forest boundary	8050
7.0		8000
7.1	Intersection	8050
7.9	Enter Christina Lake Quadrangle	8150
8.3		8200
8.7	Little Sweetwater River	8100
10.1	Crest	8350
10.4	East Sweetwater valley	8300

SWEETWATER RIVER SEGMENT

Section 2

East Sweetwater River to Wyoming Highway 28

Distance 10.9 Miles

The route crosses the forested southernmost ridge of the Wind River Range, then descends through grassland to the vicinity of historic South Pass. Special care will be required, as so much of the way uses unmaintained trail.

The Section begins by following jeep tracks to 0.6, then continues on the often-obscure Sweetwater Trail. The route climbs gradually in forest, with small meadows, well above the East Sweetwater River. It turns south after crossing one of the forks of the river, at 3.4, and ascends the Pine Creek Trail to a viewless crest at 5.1. Route-finding can be difficult on the dip to 6.5, where jeep tracks are intersected. The remainder of the Section, to Wyoming Highway 28 at 10.9, includes views over the Great Divide Basin, interesting rock formations, and attractive rolling country — all on fair to good jeep travelway.

The Trail is in the Pinedale Ranger District of the Bridger-Teton National Forest to 5.1, then in the Lander District of the Shoshone National Forest to 8.1. The remainder of the Section is public land (Rock Springs District, Bureau of Land Management) except for the final half-mile, which may be privately owned. There are good campsites in the East Sweetwater valley, at 0.2, and at the stream at 3.4. South of the crest, the best bet is a spot where the jeep road crosses Little Pine Creek, at 9.1. There are several water sources, but Little Pine Creek is the only reliable one between 6.4 and South Pass City.

The sole public transportation on Wyoming 28 is once-a-week service by Zanetti Bus Lines between Lander to the east and Farson and Rock Springs to the west; resupply would be easier using the post office at South Pass City. The nearest communities on the highway are Lander (where complete backpacking equipment and supplies are available) and Farson; each is about 40 miles from the end of the Section.

The route is shown on Maps 19 and 20. U.S.G.S. 1:24000 topographic maps are *Christina Lake*, *Anderson Ridge*, and *South Pass City*.

119

Detailed Trail data are:

The Section commences where the jeep trail reaches the valley of the East Sweetwater River. Turn left, heading upstream to the faint tracks about 50 yards up the low sagebrush slope. To get there, it is necessary to cross a bit of wet marsh and a small creek with a soft bottom. (Jeeps must cross somewhere up this side creek.)

There is an excellent campsite to the right, beneath the trees by the river, at 0.2. The jeep tracks give out entirely at 0.6, at another small side creek, where the first blazes of the Sweetwater Trail can be picked up. The route conforms very well to that shown on the Christina Lake map, and the first mile has a well-defined tread.

Ford the very shallow East Sweetwater River at 0.8. From 1.4, there is considerable deadfall, but bypasses have been worn around the worst spots. After a high point at 1.6, the Trail drops fairly steeply to a creek at 1.8, where the old path has been completely obliterated by fire. Instead of trying to pick a way through the maze of downed pole timber, cross the creek and head uphill perhaps 100 yards to a meadow. Pass close by the abandoned beaver dam in the meadow and then aim northeast for the top of the open knoll that can be seen through the trees. Before reaching that hilltop, the old path should be rediscovered.

Follow the blazes to the right, northeast, and still climbing, as shown on the topographic map. Stay on the right of the ridge, then drop to a wet meadow and cross it at contour. (Blazes may be missing from here to 3.2.) Pass just to the right of a rocky knob overlooking the valley at 2.2. There is excellent footway as the Trail dips to the upper end of a meadow at 2.4. Angle slightly to the right, pick up good path again, and walk to the right of a prominent outcrop. Stay low (heading about 055°) in the very wet meadow at 2.5. A few feet beyond the line of trees on the far side, pick up the tread and follow it to the right. Keep a heading of close to east, following a discernible path. Climb gradually in forest. Talus-topped summit 9656, to the south, can be used as a landmark. Pass a short section with deadfall at 3.0.

At 3.2, reach a fine open vantage point overlooking a broad grassy valley, with Granite Peak rising behind it. Blazes reappear.

Take the footway that swings left from the east edge of this viewpoint. Drop into the valley, where there are good campsites. Avoid the blazed trail descending the small creek, one of the forks of the East Sweetwater River; instead, take the path rising on the opposite bank at 3.4 and follow it upstream.

There is quite acceptable blazed trail, in the trees but as close as 20 yards or so from the edge of the meadow. Swing away from the valley gradually. The junction shown on the topographic map at 3.8 is undiscoverable, or at least was not observed by the author. (The good blazed trail keeps rising to the east, crossing a spur ridge and entering the hollow to the west of Pabst Peak, which was so named after the beer that the first climbers drank on its summit.)

The best thing to do is to contour to the right from 3.8 until you find the Pine Creek Trail or until you intercept the valley once again at 4.1. This is another camping opportunity. There is blazed trail, though with occasional deadfall, that should be located readily along the right (east) bank. It crosses the two branches of the creek at 4.7. The downed wood may be particularly bad for the next couple of hundred yards, but then the Trail climbs through well-drained lodgepole pine forest, reaching the crest of the Wind River Range at 5.1. Unfortunately, the tree canopy blocks the view.

Enter the Shoshone National Forest and descend on the clearly-defined Pine Creek Trail. Cairns are helpful in getting through the aspens at 5.4; drop down on the left of the ridge to cross the headwaters of Pine Creek at 5.5. At the meadow at 5.6, diverge from the creek to cross a ridge with sculptured rock formations at 5.7.

Another rise leads to the top of an opening at 6.2. South Pass and the westward route of the pioneers stretch out below; some landmarks include Oregon Buttes (due south) and, to its right, Steamboat Mountain (186°), South Table Mountain (190°), and Essex Mountain (205°). Once again look for the cairn straight down the hill along the Trail's heading, then bend left and pass through a belt of forest.

Be alert at the small creek at 6.4; bend left, climbing, instead of following a false lead down the bank. After rising about 100 yards, intercept jeep tracks and turn right. Stay on the descending jeepway, which gradually improves. Fine vistas over the Great

Divide Basin are punctuated by the Oregon Buttes, the elongated feature to the south, and by Continental Peak, the conical hill further east. Umbrella plant, stonecrop, bitterroot, hawksbeard, and penstemon dot the slopes of sagebrush.

A jeep trail joins from the left at 7.1. Stay left where the route apparently divides and rejoins at 7.3. Continue on the obvious jeep trail where secondary paths turn to either side. The landscape is mixed — mostly sagebrush, but with patches of forest as well. Large outcrops of fractured rock, such as the high one just to the right at 8.4, may be the haunt of rock wrens.

Drop to Little Pine Creek, with a grassy bank suitable for a campsite, at 9.1. Fifty yards or so beyond the small creek, keep straight where a jeep road joins from the right. Rise to the sagebrush flats at 9.2 and there take the right fork where the jeep road splits. In another 100 yards, at a four-way intersection, turn right on the descending jeep trail, heading 130°.

Walk along a low ridge crest, keeping straight at 10.0 where another jeep trail crosses. Crawl under the barbed wire gate at 10.5 and curve left to cross the dry gully of Dead Ox Creek. This is sage thrasher habitat. Reach Wyoming Highway 28 at another fence, where the Section ends at 10.9.

Distances and elevations are:

0.0	East Sweetwater valley	8300
0.8	East Sweetwater River	8300
1.6		8700
1.8	Creek	8600
2.0		8700
2.1		8650
2.2	Rocky knob	8700
2.4	Meadow	8650
3.2	Overlook	8900
3.4	Creek	8800
3.8	(Junction)	8950
4.1	Valley	8850
4.7	Creek	9050
5.1	Forest boundary	9300
5.5	Pine Creek	9100
5.6		9000

5.7	Ridge	9050
6.1		8900
6.2	Opening	8950
6.4	Creek	8900
6.5	Jeep tracks	8950
7.4	Enter Anderson Ridge Quadrangle	8650
8.1	Forest boundary	8550
8.8		8350
8.9		8400
9.1	Enter South Pass City Quadrangle (Little Pine Creek)	8350
9.3	Jeep trail junction	8400
10.0	Jeep trail junction	8250
10.5	Dead Ox Creek	8150
10.7		8200
10.9	Wyoming Highway 28	8150

SWEETWATER RIVER SEGMENT
Section 3
Wyoming Highway 28 to Lewiston
Distance 17.9 Miles

This Section is rich in pioneer and mining history. For several miles the route follows the old Oregon Trail. And South Pass City, now partially restored, was once a thriving gold-mining community. The hike for the most part uses dirt roads and jeep trails through open country dominated by sagebrush.

The Trail proceeds east to South Pass City (0.3 mile from the intersection at 2.7). It follows the course of Willow Creek, first along the top of its overlooking bluffs and then in the valley, close to the stream, from 6.5 to 11.1, where the Oregon Trail is intersected. After crossing a minor ridge, you will come to Rock Creek at 13.4; nearby is the Mormon Cemetery, where a number of westbound emigrants froze to death in the blizzards of late October 1856. The route descends slightly, using graded road, to the mining camp of Lewiston, a ghost town on Strawberry Creek. The Section ends here, at 17.9.

South Pass City is a state park area, not a community with motels, cafes, and stores. (Some supplies might be purchased, however, five miles east at Atlantic City.) There is a branch post office (ZIP 82520); don't rely upon it to hold packages unless you have checked in advance. A public telephone is available.

The water in Strawberry Creek is sluggish and not recommended for drinking. Willow Creek's upper reaches (6.6) and Rock Creek (13.4) look better, though purification is advisable. Other water sources are South Pass City (2.7), Spring Gulch (8.0), and Giblin Gulch (0.2 mile north at 17.0).

The route lies within the Bureau of Land Management's Rawlins District. A few stretches are on private land: the longest of these, in the bottomland along Willow Creek, could readily be bypassed if necessary. There are campsites at South Pass City. With permission of the landowners, Rock Creek and Spring Gulch could also be used for camping. Please be careful to keep a clean camp. A stove will be needed for cooking, as is often the case over the remainder of the Trail in Wyoming. (The Section may be relocated; from South Pass City, it would lead to Burnt Ranch and would then follow the course of the Sweetwater River eastward.)

Use Maps 20 and 21 for this Section. The 1:24000 U.S.G.S. topographic maps are *South Pass City*, *Atlantic City*, and *Radium Springs*.

Detailed Trail data are:

Hike straight across Wyoming Highway 28 and follow jeep trail to the south of the low hill, descending slightly. Follow jeep trail east to 2.7; here, just after crossing the spur rail line serving the U.S. Steel Columbia-Geneva taconite (iron ore) mine, intersect a graded dirt road. Inspect the old cemetery, where only a few graves are still marked. (Make a detour downhill, 0.3 mile to the left, to South Pass City.)*

Take the jeep road that goes around the right of the fenced cemetery. Two landmarks on the Oregon Trail — the round knob of Continental Peak and the Oregon Buttes — are prominent to the south. Also, observe the Carissa Mine on the hill beyond South Pass City. It was the first and the largest of the gold mines here, with shafts sunk as much as 400 feet in the ground. Continue on the good jeep road, often overlooking the deep ravine of Willow Creek.

Note the fence corner to the right at 5.4. Just beyond, stay right where the road forks. At about 5.8, take the good left fork (which does not appear on the topographic map) and follow it, at first quite level and then descending, to Willow Creek at 6.5 just below its juncture with Deep Gulch. The road ends a short way above the creek. Head downstream through the sagebrush, dropping down to jump the creek to visit the two well-preserved log cabins on the far side at 6.6.

Follow the worn trail down the left bank, remaining above the willows. Stay outside the fence, after approaching it at 7.7,

---

* My route went north of the hill, then dropped down to Willow Creek, and followed the creek to South Pass City. That was a bad choice for several reasons, notably the difficulty in getting by the unanticipated high railroad embankment. Use the South Pass City quadrangle as a guide for travel between Wyoming 28 and the road at 2.7. *J.W.*

to 7.9. Then duck under the fence at a convenient spot and cross the meadow, where rocky mountain flag (wild iris) will be found into July. The water from Spring Gulch at 8.0 should be pure. Some of the larger birds in the vicinity are magpies, sage grouse, harriers, and kestrels.

Run into a jeep road at 8.1, below an abandoned house and corrals. Follow it down the left bank to a gate and decrepit bridge, where Willow Creek is crossed at 8.2. Rise on the jeep trail, passing a barbed wire gate at 8.5 and immediately turning left. Hike on jeep road along the fence line and parallel to Willow Creek. Another good road joins from the right at 8.7. The snowcapped peaks of the Wind River Range are still visible to the northwest, but southeast there is a flat horizon.

Come to a jeep road at 9.1; at one time this was a stage route to supply South Pass City from the railroad at Point of Rocks (about 50 miles to the south, beyond the Great Divide Basin). Jog to the left to pass through another fence, and continue southeast; a shrubby lupine vies with sagebrush to take over the old pathway.

Walk just to the left of an abandoned log cabin, a rare sanctuary of shade, at 9.5. Another decrepit structure appears on the slope on the opposite side of Willow Creek at 9.9. Keep an eye out for antelope and horned larks, both of which are common in the Wyoming grasslands. Pass a barbed wire gate at 10.5 and, after dipping close to the lush meadows along the creek, still another one at 11.1.

Turn left here, walking a corridor (a stock driveway) between two fence lines. This is the approximate location of the Oregon Trail. Ford the two principal branches of Willow Creek, both narrow and shallow; the first, however, may be a bit mucky. Go through a barbed wire fence at 11.3 and continue on jeep road. Note the concrete Oregon Trail-Pony Express monument to the left. Avoid the jeep trail that forks left here and the one that forks right after 100 yards.

Come to a graded dirt road, passable by car, at 11.6. Cross it at right angles and continue on jeep road. Bear right in 50 yards, where poor tracks bear left. As the Trail rises a bit, look backward at the Oregon Buttes from an attractive perspective. The Wind River Range becomes more intereesting as distance permits a line of sight above its closest ridge. A jeep trail joins from the left at the low crest at 13.0, and another set of tracks bears right just on the other side. Remaining on the good path, bend left and very gradually descend. Keep straight at 13.1, with jeep roads coming in from both sides.

The Trail turns right, on graded road passable by car, at a junction at 13.4. Immediately cross the bridge over Rock Creek; note the dredge spoils (left from gold-recovery operations) along both banks. A good camp, with water warm enough for a comfortable dip, might be made by the bridge. Barn swallows and cliff swallows grace the site, along with pussytoes, daisies, clover, and other flowers.

Proceed eastward along the gravel road. To the right at 13.5, 100 yards back through the grass, is the Mormon Cemetery, where a monument tells the story of Captain James Willie's handcart company of Mormon emigrants. The band, "greatly exhausted by the deep snows of an early winter and suffering from lack of food and clothing, had assembled here for reorganization by relief parties from Utah, about the end of October, 1856. Thirteen persons were frozen to death during a single night and were buried here in one grave. Two others died the next day and were buried nearby. Of the company of 404 persons, 77 perished before help arrived. The survivors reached Salt Lake City November 9, 1856."

Walk on through rolling grassland, avoiding side roads to the north. Cross a cattle guard at a monument at 15.4. Keep straight on the road, following the Oregon Trail markers at the intersection at 17.0. (The side road forking left leads to two maintained cabins on Strawberry Creek; the creek in Giblin Gulch, next to the cabins, provides good water. The side road ascending to the right leads to some abandoned mines.)

The old gold mining camp of Lewiston is now reduced to partial shells of two buildings. At 17.6, take the jeep trail that forks left around the fence. Step across the very small Strawberry Creek and visit the ghost town. The Section ends at Lewiston at 17.9.

Distances and elevations are:

0.0	Wyoming Highway 28	8150
0.9	Junction	8100

1.6	Junction	8050
2.3	Junction	8000
2.7	Road (South Pass City 0.3 north)	7950
3.1	Junction	7950
5.4	Forks	7800
5.7	Enter Atlantic City Quadrangle	7800
5.8	Forks	7800
6.6	Log cabins	7550
8.0	Spring Gulch	7450
8.2	Willow Creek	7450
8.5	Gate	7500
9.1	Stage road	7450
10.5	Gate	7400
11.2	Willow Creek	7350
11.6	Intersection	7400
13.0	Crest	7450
13.3	Enter Radium Springs Quadrangle	7350
13.4	Junction (Rock Creek)	7350
15.4	Cattle guard	7500
17.0	Intersection (7369)	7350
17.6	Jeep trail junction	7300
17.9	Lewiston	7300

SWEETWATER RIVER SEGMENT
Section 4
Lewiston to St. Mary Station
Distance 13.0 Miles

The narrow canyon of the Sweetwater River is a scenic oasis. Beyond the canyon, the route once again follows the Oregon Trail on jeep road.

Travel from Lewiston down Strawberry Creek is cross-country, but uncomplicated. At 4.1, the Trail reaches the edge of the Sweetwater River and continues downstream on footway through the Sweetwater Canyon. The heart of the gorge extends to 9.3, where jeep routes resume. The Oregon Trail, intercepted at 11.1 as the valley widens out, is followed for the remainder of the Section to the site of the old St. Mary Stage Station.

The Section is in the Bureau of Land Management's Rawlins District. Sweetwater Canyon is public land, and it should be protected from motorized intrusion; its interesting geology, and the varied plant and animal life which flourishes in its isolated riverside environment, offer the hiker a rewarding change of scene. The Strawberry Creek valley is private property from about 0.9 to 3.2; be careful not to disturb the grazing cattle unduly. The last stretch, from 9.3 on, is also privately held, but use of the jeep road by the public appears to be permitted. (As previously noted, the Trail may be relocated to include more of Sweetwater Canyon and eliminate the walk down Strawberry Creek.)

The beauty of Sweetwater Canyon was a source of inspiration to the early explorers. Thus Lt. John Fremont, passing through in 1842, remarked that "wildness and disorder were the character of the scenery...On both sides the granite rocks rose precipitously to the height of three and five hundred feet, terminating in jagged and broken pointed peaks." The 1849 journal of Capt. Howard Stansbury, traveling westward, records:

". . . The stream, as I had anticipated, was shut up between lofty, rocky eminences, coming down directly to the water at an angle of from 45° to 60°, along the sides of which we scrambled, sometimes walking and leading our mules over crags where it was impossible to ride, crossing and recrossing the stream ever and anon, to enable our animals to get along at all. A short distance after entering the canon, the red sandstone was found cropping out at an angle of 45°, with a dip to the north; and a little farther on the crystalline rocks appeared, forming the sides of the canon. The prevailing rock was gneiss; but sienite and granite were found in some places constituting the bulk of the formation. A narrow bottom occasionally gave room for some fine groves of large aspens, the sight of which, after our long and dreary ride without a particle of shade, was truly refreshing. The bed of the river was filled with large boulders and fragments of rock which had fallen from the cliffs above, among which the waters foamed and fretted with a gurgling murmur, which, when contrasted with the flat, silent waters of the Platte, was very pleasant to the ear. It reminded one of the clear, purling streams we had left at home.

The river here is truly a mountain-stream, with great fall, rapid current, and water as clear as crystal, of the temperature of 55°. On emerging from the district of primary rocks, we came upon the stratified, which were formed of micaceous, slaty shales, and red sandstone, all evidently metamorphic. . . The aspen, beech, willow, and cotton-wood were found growing on the bottoms, and on the hills cotton-wood, pine, and cedar. Sage hens, a species of grouse, were seen in great numbers, and the men shot as many as we could conveniently carry. They are very good eating, and some of the older ones were larger than a full-grown barn-door fowl."

The most convenient water source is the Sweetwater River, readily accessible from 4.1 to 9.7. Other possibilities include Deep Creek (1.8), an unnamed side creek at 9.0, and the spring at 12.9 as the Trail approaches St. Mary Station. The choice campsites, of which there are several, are in the Sweetwater Canyon area.

The Section is shown on Map 22. The 1:24000 U.S. Geological Survey topographic maps are: *Radium Springs*, *Lewiston Lakes*, and *Barras Springs*.

Detailed Trail data are:

The Trail leaves jeep tread at Lewiston and proceeds cross-country down the left bank of Strawberry Creek; at times, stock trails or vehicle tracks mark the way. Some beaver ponds are just to the right after the route passes a jeep trail at a ford at

Sweetwater Canyon.

0.2. Cross Deep Creek, a small run, at 1.8. Continue down, without difficulty, remaining on the left bank at all times (except for 100 yards at a narrow spot at 3.7). The valley is rich in game — sage grouse, especially, and with deer and moose in the lower portions.

Reach the valley of the Sweetwater River, just below its confluence with Strawberry Creek, at 4.1. The river here is about 15 yards wide and one foot deep. Among the birds of the upper part of the canyon are green-winged teal, spotted sandpipers, flickers, crows, Brewer's blackbirds, yellow warblers, and violet-green swallows. The banks are lined by birch (or alder), Rocky Mountain juniper, and limber pine.

The relatively wide bottomland, good for camping, extends only to 4.5. The Trail then enters the canyon proper, winding about on the slopes above the left bank. The narrowest part occurs just after Mormon Creek empties into the river from the deep S-shaped valley on the opposite bank, at 5.7. Parts are rocky, but usually a game trail helps to point the way. A satisfactory campsite is available at 6.5 a little bit before the side canyon to the left, and others that are rock-free can be found along the river, beneath the 400-foot bluffs, at frequent intervals.

Only the valley floor itself is verdant; plants a few feet farther from the stream must survive on much less water. So look for prickly pear cactus as well as wild roses, common juniper, and currants (with tart but tasty fruit), goldenrod, shrubby cinquefoil, blanketflower, and sunflowers. There are also cottonwoods at some places.

Cross a broad bottomland before passing the confluence of Willow Creek, which flows through the deep canyon on the opposite bank at 7.5. There are some narrow spots remaining between slope and stream, but it is an easy walk along the stock trail. Stay high to cross a small creek, a good place to fill a canteen, near the upper edge of the willows at 9.0. Some water-buttercups grow submerged in the water, and yellow monkeyflowers are found on the bank of the creek.

Pick up a jeep trail, just after beaver ponds, at 9.3. There are a number of good campsites along the Sweetwater at 9.7, near the cottonwoods where a side jeep trail comes down from the upland. Keep going along the river, immediately stepping over Chimney Creek. (Note the old chimney standing to the left.) Among the birds are harriers, red-tailed hawks, perhaps even a golden eagle, rock wrens, sage thrashers, and western kingbirds. There is a final narrow gap at 10.6, at the end of Sweetwater Canyon. Pass the barbed wire fence and continue on jeep trail; the pocked cliffs across the way are nesting sites for violet-green swallows.

Rejoin the Oregon Trail (the jeep road up the hill to the left) at 11.1 and continue down the left side of the Sweetwater valley. Remain on well-worn jeepway, well back from the stream, avoiding minor side trails. Pass a barbed wire fence at 12.4 as the Trail approaches twin buttes that crowd the river.

Make a swing to the right at a junction at 12.9. (The road to the left continues up the gulch of dry Silver Creek.) In a few yards, note the eroded gully in the grass to the right. There is a spring of fine water at its head. Stock up, as this is the last clean drinking supply before Sweetwater Station at the end of the next Section. (The spring has a very small flow and may dry up altogether in times of drought.)

The old St. Mary Station is marked by a simple pillar to the left at 13.0. The original building was erected in 1859, then burned by raiding Indians in 1865. (The men keeping the Station escaped by hiding in an abandoned well.) A new structure was put up, but no traces of it remain.

Distances and elevations are:

0.0	Lewiston	7300
1.8	Deep Creek	7250
2.7	Enter Lewiston Lakes Quadrangle	7200
4.1	Sweetwater Canyon	7050
5.7	Mormon Creek (opposite)	6950
7.5	Willow Creek (opposite)	6800
9.0	Creek	6800
9.7	Chimney Creek	6750
10.6	Fence	6700
11.1	Oregon Trail	6700
12.2	Enter Barras Springs Quadrangle	6700
12.9	Spring	6700
13.0	St. Mary Station	6700

SWEETWATER RIVER SEGMENT
Section 5
St. Mary Station to Sweetwater Station
Distance 12.2 Miles

The hike in this Section follows the meandering Sweetwater River through rolling grazing land.

From St. Mary Station, the Trail uses jeep routes along the left bank of the Sweetwater River to 6.2, then veers north to intersect U.S. 287 at 9.9. The remainder of the Section, to the bridge at Sweetwater Station, is a walk along the highway.

The detour to the highway might be avoided by taking alternates up Alkali Creek and crossing to Happy Spring. But Sweetwater Station provides very convenient access to public transportation, for the first time on the route of the Trail since Yellowstone Park. The gas station there carries some canned goods and serves sandwiches; it is a flag stop on the Zanetti bus route, which runs daily from Lander to Rawlins and back. The nearest large town is Jeffrey City, ZIP 82310, about 20 miles to the east; for full services, including any desired backpacking supplies, take the bus 40 miles northwest to Lander, ZIP 82520.

While there are campsites along the Sweetwater River in the middle of the Section, the water has become cloudy and somewhat sluggish; purify it, or carry a supply from St. Mary Station. Another possibility is to hike through the Section and camp, for a small fee, at the private River Camp Ground at the end of the Section. (Showers and some groceries are available; address is Rawlins Route, Box 67, Lander.)

Although the Section is in the Rawlins District of the Bureau of Land Management, the first several miles (as far as 7.0) are largely privately owned, except for Section 16 (2.3 to 3.4). Hopefully, there will be no objection to well-mannered hikers traveling through. But please do not camp or tarry near the Ellis Ranch, at 2.1.

See Map 23 for the route of the Section. The U.S.G.S. 1:24000 topographic maps are: *Barras Springs, Red Canyon* (a small bit), and *Sweetwater Station*.

Detailed Trail data are:

Follow the route of the old Oregon Trail eastward from St. Mary Station; there are several gates in the first mile. A side road joins from the right at 0.7. Bear left on the main jeep road at the junction at 1.1 and pass another barbed wire gate at 1.7. Short-horned lizards might be seen underfoot.

Take the left fork at 2.0, just after another gate. (The right fork goes to the bridge over the Sweetwater River to the Ellis Ranch, an active operation; an alternate route up Alkali Creek would cross the river here.) In 100 yards, cross the graded road and continue parallel to the willows on the valley floor. There are more fences (at 2.3, 3.4, 4.2 and 6.2).

The Oregon Trail veers left from the jeep road at 3.5; it shows up as a scar on the hillside. Look for loggerhead shrikes, a rarity on the Trail, as the route approaches the river at 3.9. Here, and on several other occasions when the jeep road is next to the stream, it would be possible to make a satisfactory camp. The river is now meandering and its bottom is silty; it would be best to purify the water before drinking. The last easy access to the river is at the gauging station at 6.5; here the bottom is rockier, and there are camping opportunities nearby.

Beyond the corrals and cattle guard at 7.0, traffic can be seen as glitters on the highway in the distance. Oregon Trail landmarks include Atlantic Peak to the west northwest and Dishpan Butte, the small round protuberance to the north. Remain at all times on the good jeep road, avoiding several grassy jeep trails to both sides. One of these is the Oregon Trail, marked by monuments and crossed at an acute angle in a draw at 7.8. A good jeep road joins from the grassy flat on the left at 9.0. Continue north, passing under utility wires at 9.1.

Reach U.S. 287 and turn right, walking along the highway. Dip to cross the bridge over the dry gulch of Crooked Creek at 10.2. To the southeast are Crooks and Green Mountains, which are along the route of the Trail. Pass a highway rest area, with shaded picnic tables, at 11.6.

Sweetwater Station, a gas station with a few groceries, is on the right at 12.0. See the introductory text with respect to bus service and information about the River Camp Ground, which is on the right at 12.1. The Section ends at 12.2, at the bridge where U.S. 287 crosses the Sweetwater River.

SWEETWATER RIVER SEGMENT

Distances and elevations are:

0.0	St. Mary Station	6700
2.1	Ellis Ranch	6650
3.5	Oregon Trail	6650
6.0	Enter Red Canyon Quadrangle	6600
6.5	Enter Sweetwater Station Quadrangle	6600
7.0	Corrals	6650
7.8	Oregon Trail	6600
9.0	Jeep road junction	6600
9.9	U.S. 287	6600
12.0	Sweetwater Station	6550
12.2	Sweetwater River	6550

GREEN MOUNTAINS SEGMENT

Section 1

Sweetwater Station to Happy Spring

Distance 8.6 Miles

The Trail, generally on jeep road, crosses low sagebrush-covered ridges to reach the base of Crooks Mountain.

Starting at the Sweetwater River, the route remains on U.S. 287 only to 0.3, where it turns south on the graded Bison Basin Road. It cuts off on jeep trail at 1.5, dropping slightly to intercept the Oregon Trail (for the final time) at 2.7 and crossing Warm Springs Creek at 3.2. After going over another low ridge, the Trail passes the dry gully of Bull Canyon at 5.5 and continues with modest changes in elevation to the end of the Section at Happy Spring at 8.6.

The Section is entirely on public land (Rawlins District, BLM) except for the immediate vicinity of Happy Spring, where there is an excellent protected water source. The immediate area is uninhabited and, if permission of the owners can be obtained, the lush grass would be fine for camping. The only other place to obtain drinking water is along Warm Springs Creek; this, too, would be a good campsite but, because of heavy grazing, water purification is recommended.

See the introduction to Section 5 of the Sweetwater River Segment with respect to transportation and other services at Sweetwater Station on U.S. 287.

The U.S. Geological Survey's topographic maps for the Section are the *Sweetwater Station* and *Happy Spring* quadrangles, both 1:24000. Refer also to Map 24.

Detailed Trail data are:

The Section begins at Sweetwater Crossing, the highway bridge just east of the store at Sweetwater Station. Follow U.S. 287 across the river, passing a dirt road that leads to the right at 0.1 and an Oregon Trail historical monument on the left at 0.2. Take the next dirt road (the graded Bison Basin Road) to the right at 0.3. Soon bend left and climb gradually, reaching a flat ridge at 1.0. Horned larks are abundant.

At the far side of the ridge, at 1.5, leave the Bison Basin Road as it swings to the right. The route of the Trail is the conspicuous jeep track stretching out far ahead toward Crooks Mountain to the south. This vantage point affords 50-mile views eastward as far as Ferris Mountain and west northwest to the Wind River Range (with Wind River Peak's snowy summit especially prominent).

Descend gradually, taking the left fork as the Trail levels out at 2.2. Keep straight at 2.7 at the oblique crossing of another jeep track (the approximate location of the Oregon Trail). More jeep tracks come in from the left at 2.9, from the right at 3.0, and then again from the left. Stay on the main route until just after it swings right around the base of a low ridge at 3.1. Here turn left, remaining on the track closest to the fence on the left.

At 3.2, come upon Warm Springs Creek, which will not be visible until you are right on top of it. Although the creek is only a couple of feet wide and about three inches deep, it should be a reliable source of water; because of grazing activity along the creek, water purification is advisable.

About 50 yards past Warm Springs Creek, take the jeep trail up the rise — not the one that heads left along the fence line. Cross a jeep road at 3.4 and proceed south on better-defined route. Go over a minor ridge at 3.6. Here cross a jeep road that appears to follow a pipeline along a corridor lined with tall poles. Disregard the jeep track that leads off to the right at 4.0. Climb gradually, passing a pair of jeep tracks from the left and to the right at 4.4, and another from the left at 4.8. Go over a high point at 5.1. Descend gradually, passing tracks from both sides, and then more steeply.

The road divides at 5.4 into two good divisions; take the left fork, crossing the dry gully of Bull Canyon Creek at 5.5. A faint track turns to the right, at 5.6, heading up Bull Canyon; remain on the good jeep road. Climb to the right of the hill ahead, passing jeep tracks bearing left at 6.0 and joining from the right as the Trail goes around the hill at 6.2.

Take the right fork at 6.4, as the road divides just before a high point. Descend, passing a track coming from the left at 6.6. This a likely place to flush sage grouse; perhaps there will be a short-horned lizard, too. Rise to go around a bend at 6.9; the peaks to the east are in the Granite Mountains (also called the

Sweetwater Rocks). Cross a poor jeep track at 7.0. Keep straight at 7.2 where a jeep road turns left toward the prominent low rock outcrop.

Approaching a fence corner at 7.5, note the sheep watering impoundment below and to the left. Follow the road as it swings around the west end of this pond. Avoid several side trails around 8.0 by keeping close to the fence on the left of the road, but not passing through it. Mountain bluebirds make this fence a favorite perch.

Climb gradually to Happy Spring, which is in a hollow between the road and the derelict building to the left at 8.6. Turn left at the fence corner and drop down from the gate to the grassy area close to the protected spring. This is the end of the Section and the last source of water for several miles.

Distances and elevations are:

0.0	Sweetwater River	6550
0.3	Bison Basin Road	6600
1.5	Jeep track	6700
2.7	Oregon Trail	6550
3.2	Warm Springs Creek	6550
3.7	Enter Happy Spring Quadrangle	6600
5.1		6750
5.5	Bull Canyon	6700
6.4	Road junction	6800
6.7		6750
8.6	Happy Spring	6900

GREEN MOUNTAINS SEGMENT
Section 2
Happy Spring to Cottonwood Creek
Distance 11.5 Miles

This Section is an easy walk, on jeep road, at contour along the north flank of Crooks Mountain. The treeless expanse of sagebrush is antelope country.

The Trail turns east at Happy Spring. As it proceeds on a level course close to Crooks Mountain, it overlooks the broad basin that was once the route of the Oregon Trail. Just after circling a spur ridge of the mountain, it comes to the colorful quicksand-like Soap Holes at 6.6. There are some minor ups and downs as the Trail continues its way eastward, several hundred feet below the crest, passing Haypress Creek at 9.2 and dipping to a graded dirt road at Cottonwood Creek, at the end of the Section, at 11.5.

Virtually all of the Section is on public land, BLM or state. The exceptions to this include the few drinking water sources along the Trail — Happy Spring, Soap Holes (a questionable spring), Haypress Creek, and Cottonwood Creek. When scouted, access and transit were not restricted at any of these; keep them clean so as to avoid possible problems in the future. Happy Spring and Cottonwood Creek are both very good, grassy, campsites which, in particular, must not be abused.

The U.S. Geological Survey 1:24000 topographic maps are *Happy Spring*, *Soap Holes*, and *Crooks Mountain*. Also use Maps 24 and 25.

Detailed Trail data are:

Obtain an ample supply of water before setting out from Happy Spring — preferably, enough to reach Cottonwood Creek. (Haypress Creek, the only other dependable running water along the Trail in this Section, may be contaminated by stock.)

Follow the jeep trail that backtracks to the north, circling the hill overlooking the spring. Bend right at 0.2 where a horse trail goes straight toward the impoundment. Soon pass a gate through a barbed wire fence and begin a long walk east, with very little elevation change, along the obvious jeep marks. A jeep trail (probably a waterless shortcut from mile 7.2 in Section 1) joins from the left at 0.9 a little way before a gully. Cross a jeep track at 1.6.

Some prickly pear cactus may appear along with the sagebrush and rabbitbrush as the Trail passes beneath summit 7369, one of several low hills with rock outcrops and scattered trees to the south. Richardson's ground squirrels may be observed scampering off to the safety of their burrows. Flocks of horned larks continue to be common. Dip to cross another dry creekbed at 2.5. Cross a jeep track at 2.9 and continue eastward, passing between the mountain ridge on the right and a conical cairn-topped mound to the left at 3.4.

A secondary jeep track bears left at a crest at 3.7; another one angles down the hillside to join the Trail from the right at 4.5. Take the much poorer right fork, remaining more nearly at contour, as the road divides at 5.1 until it rejoins at 5.4. A set of jeep tracks joins sharply from the left as the Trail swings right, around a ridge, at 6.0. Some tracks at 6.3 drop to the green bottom where running water might be found in a little creek.

Remain on the jeep road, climbing a bit and passing to the left of a stagnant impoundment at 6.6. To the left of the road is a shallow red-walled canyon that should be explored with care, for its name of "Soap Holes" refers to the quicksand consistency of its muddy floor. The creek has its source in this multihued draw — reds, whites, browns set off against the green of the algae and grass — but the water is too shallow to collect easily.

Come to the intersection of well-traveled jeep roads at the far end of the pond at 6.7. Take the road in the middle, which bears left. Follow the left fork at 6.8 and bend left, climbing over a ridge. Dip to the right to cross a gully, possibly with a trickle, at 7.1. Continue ahead, then slightly right, where the Trail crosses a good jeep road at 7.4. The main ridge of Crooks Mountain is just ahead as the Trail goes over a rise at 7.5. Follow the main track down to a dry gully at 8.0 and then over a spur ridge, avoiding side trails to the right. Descending, swing north toward a distant clump of cottonwoods. Take the poorer right fork at the junction at 8.7. Make a sweep to the right; with a jeep trail joining from the left at 8.8, stay right and head uphill.

Cross willow-lined Haypress Creek, where the onetime impoundment has washed away, at 9.2. This is a possible campsite, though not attractive. The flow is very small and may be contaminated by livestock. Keep going straight, uphill to the east, at the crossroads about 60 yards past the creek. There is a good view back toward Wind River Peak (recognizable by the precipitous drop on the north side of its summit).

Stay left at contour at 9.8. (The track to the right leads up the right bank of a dry creek.) Keep level again at 10.2 and 10.7 where jeep trails head left toward the enormous flat valley. Jeffrey City is visible, to the northeast, from the crest of a spur ridge at 11.1. Descend toward Cottonwood Creek, disregarding the tracks that bear left at the crest. (The latter probably rejoin the route at 11.4.)

The Section ends at 11.5 as the Trail reaches a maintained and graded dirt road that is passable by car. Just across this road is a good flat grassy campsite, beneath some aspens, on the left bank of Cottonwood Creek. Although there is a fairly generous flow in this stream, grazing in the area may make it desirable to purify the water. There is little traffic on the road, which leads to an intersection with U.S. 287 about seven miles north of this point.

Distances and elevations are:

0.0	Happy Spring	6900
0.9	Jeep track	6850
1.5	Enter Soap Holes Quadrangle	6800
1.9		6850
2.1		6800
2.3		6850
2.5	Creekbed	6750
3.7	Crest	6800
4.1		6850
4.3		6800
4.9		6850
5.1	Road forks	6800
5.4	Road reunites	6800
6.0	Road junction	6850
6.3		6800
6.6	Soap Holes	6850

6.7	Intersection	6850
7.1	Gully	6950
7.5	Rise	7050
8.0	Gully	7000
8.4	Spur ridge	7050
8.8	Junction	6950
9.2	Haypress Creek	7000
9.6	Enter Crooks Mountain Quadrangle	7100
9.8	Junction	7050
10.7	Junction	7000
11.1	Ridge	7150
11.5	Cottonwood Creek	6950

GREEN MOUNTAINS SEGMENT
Section 3
Cottonwood Creek to Crooks Creek
Distance 8.8 Miles

The Trail in this Section, still following the north side of Crooks Mountain, passes through a couple of oil fields, largely on improved road.

The first part of the Section, to Nancy Creek at 2.6, is on good road, but it may be unnecessarily circuitous and uneven in elevation. The Trail then follows secondary routes through the Jade Oil Field, over small ridges, until improved road is rejoined shortly before reaching Woods Gulch at 4.2 and O'Brian Creek at 4.5. The Trail, for the most part descending gradually, proceeds through the Crooks Gap Oil Field to Crooks Creek at 8.4 and the intersection with a high-standard, well-traveled, gravel road (which connects with Jeffrey City, about seven miles to the north, on U.S. 287) at the end of the Section at 8.8.

The one good water source and campsite in this Section is at its start, on Cottonwood Creek. Crooks Creek, besides having a clouded appearance, is in a developed and noisy area. The other creeks are very small and likely to be contaminated by grazing or oil field operations. Unless you detour to Jeffrey City on the gravel road, it would be best to continue straight through to Sheep Creek at the end of Section 4.

Except for the campsite on Cottonwood Creek, and perhaps some of the route in the Jade Oil Field, the Trail is on public right-of-way. (The "jade" refers to the semiprecious mineral, the official stone of Wyoming, that is found in the area; stay off any land that is posted against trespassing rock hounds.)

The Jade Oil Field has been developed since publication of the 1:24000 1951 Crooks Mountain quadrangle. As a result, that map is incomplete and misleading. The Trail description that follows is also unreliable from the crest at 0.5 to Nancy Creek at 2.6, but the distances, elevations, and locations given for the remainder of the Section should be quite accurate. In addition to the *Crooks Mountain* quadrangle, part of the Section is on the *Jeffrey City* quadrangle, also 1:24000. Map 25 in this volume shows the route.

Detailed Trail data are:

The Section begins as the Trail descends a jeep route to an intersection with graded road just east of Cottonwood Creek. There is a fine campsite here, which is sometimes used by residents of the area. Cottonwoods grow upstream, aspens and limber pine downstream. There are a number of flowers, including lupine, yarrow, gumweed, and thistle. Wild roses are plentiful, along with gooseberries and currants.

From the junction at the start of the Section, turn right and cross Cottonwood Creek in 50 yards. Carry a good supply of water from here. Follow the main graded road to the east, climbing and bending left to reach the crest of a spur ridge at 0.5. The Trail continues over the crest and down toward a house, avoiding the several roads that turn off to the right at the ridgetop.

Beyond the house, bend right and descend on the good road. The deep notch in Split Rock, a famous landmark on the Oregon Trail, stands out on the skyline to the east. Swing uphill at 1.6, immediately past a culvert where a jeep road forks left. A jeep road joins from the left at 2.1. Continue climbing parallel to utility lines above the left (west) bank of Nancy Creek.

Leave the road at 2.5, following a gas line marked by warning signs. Cross trickling Nancy Creek just above a shed and rise a few feet to the road, at a gas well, at 2.6. A poor camp could be made a few yards upstream on the right bank. Turn left for 100 yards, then take the right fork on jeep road, passing to the right of a little knoll at 2.7. Where several roads join at 2.8, head east and climb just to the right of cylindrical towers and another knoll. Take the left fork at the crest at 3.1 and proceed east along a gas line. A couple of huge boulders sit atop the rise to the left of the Trail at a crest at 3.5. Drop by an oil well at 3.7; then keep to the right, at contour.

Continue east on the graded and maintained road that joins from the left at 3.9. A very small creek flows through a culvert in Woods Gulch at 4.2. Follow the main road just beyond, where a jeep road turns sharp right. Climb over a minor ridge and drop to another little stream, O'Brian Creek, at 4.5. Descend gradually, passing a cattle guard at 4.7. Good views of flat-topped Green Mountain are obtained for the first time.

Campsite by Cottonwood Creek.

Boggy Springs Pond, an impoundment, is seen about 300 yards to the left from a gully at 5.4. Curve right and climb to a high point at 5.9 before dropping along the south side of summit 6953. Walk under utility lines and curve left. Cross a couple of gullies at 6.4. Continue on the main road, where a side road turns right toward an oil well, at 7.0.

Just past the gully at 7.2, angle left following jeep tracks along utility lines, taking a shortcut back to the road at 7.4. Note the mining operation, with criss-crossing roads, ahead on Sheep Mountain; the Trail will take the access road up the hollow to its left. The prominent pointed summit just to the south is Crooks Peak. Pass storage tanks and a house at 7.8. At 8.4, cross a wooden bridge over murky Crooks Creek, a stream several feet wide and with a strong current. Despite all the human activity nearby, mule deer and antelope may be observed close to the water.

The Section ends at 8.8, as the Trail comes to a T-intersection with a heavily traveled gravel road. Jeffrey City, on U.S. 287, is about seven miles to the left. The Trail continues by turning to the right.

Distances and elevations are:

0.0	Cottonwood Creek	6950
0.5	Crest	7100
0.7		7050
0.9		7100
1.6	Culvert	6850
2.1	Jeep road junction	7000
2.5	Gas line	7150
2.6	Nancy Creek	7100
3.1	Crest	7200
3.4		7100
3.5	Crest	7150
3.9	Road junction	7000
4.2	Woods Gulch	7000
4.5	O'Brian Creek	6900
5.4	Boggy Springs Pond	6750
5.9		6850
6.4	Gullies	6750
6.5		6800
6.7		6700
6.8		6750
7.2	Gully	6700
7.4	Enter Jeffrey City Quadrangle	6700
8.4	Crooks Creek	6550
8.8	Intersection	6600

GREEN MOUNTAINS SEGMENT

Section 4

Crooks Creek to Sheep Creek

Distance 3.0 Miles

The Trail in this Section passes through the heart of a major uranium mining operation. Because of access restrictions, it may be necessary to detour a bit to the north.

The route turns east at 0.3 and, climbing several hundred feet, goes through the Western Nuclear, Inc. mining area from 1.2 to 2.2. The ore is deep-mined, so the principal signs of the operation are ore and tailing piles, hoists, ventilators, settling ponds, and support buildings — no deep pits. The Trail then goes over a saddle on Sheep Mountain and drops into the undeveloped valley of Sheep Creek, where the Section ends at 3.0.

A camp can be made at an attractive spot on Sheep Creek. The water is turbid, probably as the result of earth-moving upstream, though it is presumably all right to drink. Another possibility is to fill canteens and bottles at the mine.

The nearest community is Jeffrey City, on U.S. 287, about seven miles north on the gravel road at the start of the Section. Full services are available, including post office (ZIP 82310), meals, lodging, and laundry. There is daily bus service on Zanetti Bus Lines westward to Lander (via Sweetwater Station) and eastward to Muddy Gap and Rawlins.

Although the Trail could be relocated to a more northerly route, there would be little scenic advantage to doing so. The mines are a point of interest in an undramatic portion of the Trail and, with the permission of the company, they should remain on the route notwithstanding their industrial character. The entire Section is on fair to good road. (However, under current mining regulations, random entry is not allowed. You can inquire by writing Western Nuclear, Inc., Box 630, Jeffrey City.)

The route appears on the U.S. Geological Survey 1:24000 *Jeffrey City* quadrangle as well as Map 25. (See the same U.S.G.S. map for the detour — north to intersection 6512, then east to Sheep Creek, which is followed upstream; the detour would add 1.5 mile to the journey.)

Detailed Trail data are

The Section starts at the intersection of the roads from the Crooks Gap Oil Field and Jeffrey City. Proceed south to a major intersection at 0.3. Here turn left and climb gradually on the right (north) bank of a gully, on high-standard gravel road. A settling pond is on the right at 1.2 as the route enters a ravine. Mine shafts are on the left at 1.5; beyond them, stay on the main road as it bends right.

Turn left at a four-way intersection at 1.8. (Straight ahead it is 0.2 mile to the Golden Goose 2 Mine.) Continue climbing, still on high-standard surface. Just before crossing a saddle on Sheep Mountain at 2.2, pass the road leading 100 yards to the right to the hoist at the entrance to the Reserve Mine. (Water may be obtainable at the nearby service building.)

At the crest of the ridge, take the good (though secondary) road that bears left and descends. Walk beneath utility lines at 2.5. The Section ends at 3.0, where a jeep road joins from the left. There is a good campsite 100 yards east of this junction, in a grassy spot surrounded by a meander of Sheep Creek, beneath tall narrowleaf cottonwoods. Once again there are wild roses, gooseberries, and currants — along with common and Rocky Mountain junipers, serviceberry, and snowberry. The water is sluggish and cloudy, but is permanently flowing. The constant roar of the ventilation equipment of the mines may be bothersome, however.

Distances and elevations are:

0.0	Intersection	6600
0.3	Intersection	6650
1.2	Settling pond	6800
1.8	Intersection	7000
2.2	Reserve Mine	7150
2.5	Utility lines	7050
3.0	Jeep road junction	7000

GREEN MOUNTAINS SEGMENT

Section 5

Sheep Creek to Willow Creek

Distance 13.3 Miles

The Trail climbs to the tableland atop Green Mountain. The Section is a rewarding montane interlude, the only one in the 200-mile circuit of the Great Divide Basin.

The route begins by climbing along Sheep Creek, largely on jeep trail at the beginning, but with some bushwhacking at higher elevations. At 2.7, it suddenly reaches a large open plateau, Sheep Creek Park, on the summit ridge of Green Mountain. The Trail swings counter-clockwise along the wooded rim of the mountain, climbing gradually on jeep route. There are good views toward the distant horizon beyond the Great Divide Basin.

Beyond 4.9, the Trail is quite level for several miles, with only small dips and rises. It travels on graded road, part of a scenic loop drive connecting with U.S. 287, from 6.3 to 7.7, along the way passing by Sagebrush Park (another large open flat) and then the Green Mountain Guard Station at 7.5. The next part is on good jeep road, to East Cottonwood Park at 9.7 and from there along a razorback to the picnic area at panoramic Wild Horse Point at 10.8. Old and abandoned jeep trail is used to descend the mountain to the end of the Section on Willow Creek at 13.3.

Water is scarce in this Section. Sheep Creek, particularly around 2.0, should supply some of good quality. Also, an excellent reliable spring is located close to the guard station at 7.5. As there is little level ground along Sheep Creek, its best campsite is probably the one at the start of the Section. Or, you can carry water and spend the night on the mountain at Sheep Creek Park. However, the choice spot, particularly because of its scenery, is at the edge of Sagebrush Park near the guard station and spring.

A short stretch along Sheep Creek (from about 0.1 to 1.3) is on private land. There appear to be no travel restrictions, however.

U.S. Geological Survey topographic maps are *Jeffrey City*, *Crooks Peak*, and *Sagebrush Park* — all 1:24000 scale. The final few feet of the Section are on the *Whiskey Peak* quadrangle. See also Maps 25 and 26.

Detailed Trail data are:

From the jeep road junction (and campsite) at 0.0, the Trail heads up the valley parallel to the left (west) bank of Sheep Creek. At 0.5, as the road approaches a hill to its right, turn left and leave it. Cross a tributary creek and follow a stock trail along the left bank of Sheep Creek, at first about 50 yards or so from the stream. Continue on this as it becomes a jeep track and angles to the right, away from the creek. Remaining above the aspens, walk by a stake (a onetime fence corner) on a section line at 0.8. Beaver ponds are to the left at 0.9. Just beyond, take the right fork. (Both forks are very faint here.) Follow a left-forking jeep track at 1.1 as the more obvious track bends right to climb a ridge; head southeast, toward the mouth of Sheep Creek's forested hollow.

At 1.3, intercept a better jeep trail just before a line of trees. Turn left, crossing the gully of Sheep Creek (likely to be dry) at 1.4. Continue cross-country, climbing through low and fairly scattered sagebrush up the right bank of the gulch, possibly observing rock wrens and mule deer. The Sheep Mountain Mine is at a slightly higher elevation to the west, and there is an endless view of high plains to the northwest.

Return to the left bank at 1.6. Pick up an old bulldozer road which ends at 1.8. Angle uphill on jeep trail. Stay close to the creek (more likely to have water here) where another track cuts sharply right at 1.9, and cross over to the right bank at 2.0. The track is badly eroded at 2.1 and it is best to continue on game trail along the right bank, climbing in aspens and pine. The gully above here is once again likely to be dry. The game trail, which may be difficult to follow, remains within about five to ten yards of the creekbed to 2.4, after which it becomes too obscure to use. Climb along the right bank, despite the nuisance of some deadfall.

Emerge abruptly into open and flat Sheep Creek Park at 2.7. Look for antelope or other game. Pleated gentians are among the most colorful of the many flowers. In a very few yards, turn right on a jeep track, which is joined almost immediately from the left by another one. Follow these trails as they swing back to the right, descending slightly and entering lodgepole-aspen forest at 2.8. Stay to the left at 3.3, where another jeep road comes up from the valley and joins from the right. Climb steadily, avoiding the jeep trail that bears left at 3.5 and the several that converge from both sides at 3.6.

Enter meadow and an excellent opportunity to look out to the west over Sheep Mountain and beyond Crooks Peak — the last view of Jeffrey City and the first sighting of the vast Great Divide Basin. Swing left at 3.8, still climbing and now following the main ridge of Green Mountain southeastward. Keep going straight, passing several side roads. There are fine views of the Basin from the open ridge at 4.1. The Trail, rising hardly at all, is again open and very windy at 4.9 where another jeep trail joins it from the left.

A couple of jeep trails head left at a high point at 5.3. The prominent bare butte to the southeast is the southern portion of Stratton Rim. Keep on the main ridge where a good road turns to the right at 5.5 and, also, where several jeep trails join from the left.

Dipping to a pass at 6.3, pick up the graded Green Mountain Loop Road, negotiable by car, and follow it east. Climb to flat Sagebrush Park, bending right and leveling out at 6.7; at its far end, at 7.4, a partially sheltered camp can be made in the edge of the trees to the left of the road. There are excellent views from the edge of the plateau. Starting with Wind River Peak and its neighbors in the Bridger Wilderness, the vista picks up a number of landmarks on the west and southwest rim of the Great Divide Basin, and some even farther away — including Oregon Buttes to the west, Black Buttes to the southwest, with several in between them (reaching out almost 100 miles, beyond Rock Springs, to Pilot Butte).

Leaving Sagebrush Park, bend left and cross a culvert at 7.5. The BLM Green Mountain Guard Station is just to the left. (Drop to the right below the culvert, in about 100 yards coming to an excellent piped spring, which is a reliable water source.) The road to the right at 7.6 doubles back to the spring.

Take the jeep road to the right, toward Wild Horse Point, at the major road junction at 7.7. (The loop road descends to the left, to the Cottonwood Campground and U.S. 287.) Keep close to the edge of the mountain, with little elevation change, avoiding the jeep road that bears left at 7.8. The road divides in a park at 8.3 and rejoins at 8.5; use the more scenic route on the right. Bend sharply left at 9.3 where poorer jeep trail continues ahead to an antenna in the sagebrush. (The latter swings around and rejoins at 9.4.)

Pass through East Cottonwood Park, which affords views both north and south, to a road junction at 9.7. Keep straight, immediately crossing a cattle guard. Hike east on a narrow forested ridge, bypassing the side trails at a dip at 9.8 and one to the left at 10.6.

Come to the traffic loop at the Wild Horse Point Overlook at 10.8, with vistas on both sides of the crest. (The mountain was covered with fog during the author's visit, but presumably Split Rock and the Sweetwater Rocks are prominent.) Here there is a large picnic area, set among lodgepole pine and boulders, with tables, grills, trash barrels, and outhouse, but no water supply. Among the birds of the higher elevations are nutcrackers, juncos, and red-breasted nuthatches.

Two jeep tracks lead away from the road — one blocked off and going up to the high point on the ridge and the other bearing right at the end of the loop. Take the latter, descending steeply, with flat Stratton Rim ahead. Go through a severed barbed wire fence at 11.2 and through a fence gate at a saddle on the ridge at 11.4. Keep dropping eastward. Swing to the right of the main ridge at 12.4, with Whiskey Peak ahead and Ferris Mountain further off and slightly to the left.

As the jeep trail curves right at 12.9, take the poorer tracks to the left, heading northeast to the valley of Willow Creek beneath a hill scarred with old uranium test drilling roads. This reaches the valley at the intersection of two good jeep roads, at 13.3, where the Section ends. The Trail continues on the road that parallels Willow Creek going downstream. A camp can be made in a flat grassy area opposite this point and along the creek — unless a uranium mine takes it over. There is no obvious spring, as shown on the topographic map (Whiskey Peak Quadrangle), though seeps make the soil close to the road very wet.

Distances and elevations are:

0.0 Jeep road junction   7000

0.5	Creek	7050
0.9	Beaver ponds	7250
1.4	Sheep Creek (gully)	7550
1.6	Enter Crooks Peak Quadrnngle	7650
2.0	Sheep Creek	7800
2.7	Sheep Creek Park	8400
3.3	Jeep road junction (8464)	8450
3.7	Meadow	8700
4.9	Jeep trail junction	9000
5.3	High point	9000
5.6	Enter Sagebrush Park Quadrangle	9000
6.3	Loop road	8850
6.7	Sagebrush Park	9050
7.5	Green Mountain Guard Station	9050
7.7	Road junction	9050
8.3	Park	9000
9.5		9050
9.7	East Cottonwood Park	9000
9.8		8950
10.8	Wild Horse Point Overlook	9050
11.2	Fence	8700
11.4	Saddle	8550
12.4	Ridge	8000
12.9	Junction	7650
13.3	Road junction (enter Whiskey Peak Quadrangle)	7400

GREEN MOUNTAINS SEGMENT
Section 6
Willow Creek to Muddy Gap
Distance 12.1 Miles

In this Section, the Trail descends gradually through a rolling landscape of sagebrush-covered hills. Antelope are abundant.

The Trail follows the general course of Willow Creek downstream from 0.0 to the Diamond Hook Ranch, where it crosses the creek at 5.0 and heads east over arid plains. At 8.9, it drops into a colorful red canyon and aims for the parallel ridges of Ferris Mountain directly ahead. From 10.3 to 11.4, it detours north to a crossing of Muddy Creek, then returns south along U.S. 287 to the small settlement of Muddy Gap (about a mile south of the U.S. 287-Wyo. 220 road junction), where the Section ends at 12.1. There is a bit of easy cross-country travel, but nearly all of the hiking is on fair to good jeep road.

The Diamond Hook Ranch straddles Willow Creek for about three miles, virtually requiring that the Trail traverse private land. It is to be hoped that hikers will be permitted to walk through the property, which was unoccupied when the route was scouted. The part of the Trail that crosses the ranch is 4.4 to 5.2; remain there no longer than necessary.

There is a service station, with telephone and a limited grocery stock, at Muddy Gap. Hot sandwiches and pizza are available. Camping is permitted nearby, on rocky ground, for a nominal fee; there are no other lodgings, however. Zanetti Bus Lines provide daily service south to Rawlins and west to Lander (by way of Jeffrey City and Sweetwater Station). There is also bus service between Casper and Rawlins by way of Muddy Gap. (Additional supplies, as well as meals and lodging, may be available at Lamont, 10 miles south of Muddy Gap; the nearest post office is at Bairoil, ZIP 82322, five miles west of Lamont.)

Willow Creek and its tributaries furnish the only drinking water in the Section. Most of it is cloudy, but potable. (Uranium prospecting was observed by the author; development of the area could affect this water.) The best campsite is at 2.2, on Willow Creek; other possibilities are near the creek at the beginning of the Section and at 5.2, just beyond Diamond Hook Ranch.

In addition to Maps 26 and 27, use the 1:24000 *Whiskey Peak* and *Muddy Gap* quadrangles.

Detailed Trail data are:

The Section starts at the intersection labeled 7390 on the Whiskey Peak quadrangle. A camp can be made opposite this point, in the grass along Willow Creek. Proceed north on the good jeep road, passing to the left of an aspen stand and crossing trickling Rabbit Creek, which has discolored its bed, at 0.5. Climb the next hill, avoiding the road to the right. (It was not scouted, but it may provide a good alternate route down Willow Creek.) Approaching the first crest, at 0.6, keep straight and bypass the good road that bears left and climbs.

Go over a rise at 0.8 and begin a long descent. A series of beaver ponds is just to the right of the road from 1.6 to 1.9. Return to the main valley of Willow Creek as a jeep road joins from the right at 2.0. A fine grassy campsite is set among the water birches on the left bank of the creek at 2.2, directly beneath the timber-topped summit on the opposite side. Common crows and vesper sparrows are likely to be observed nearby.

A large granite dome is seen to the north, beyond the Sweetwater River, as the Trail at 2.7 veers away from Willow Creek. With the Trail bending to the right around a hill, pass an unattractive and unprotected spring, which is about 50 yards to the left, at the head of a two-foot-deep gully. Keep straight on jeep trail, toward the basin on the right, at 3.3. (The main road bears left toward U.S. 287, whose traffic is faintly visible.) Cross another jeep trail, at an angle, at 3.9 and keep descending.

Go through a barbed wire gate at 4.4, entering Diamond Hook Ranch. Swing right to pass the ranch buildings at 4.9, taking the road here to cross Willow Creek at 5.0. This is the last drinking water in the Section. Do not camp along the creek, which is private; a poor camp can be made as the Trail leaves the ranch at a gate at 5.2.

The Trail, after going through the fence, continues straight on jeep trail. (Avoid the jeep trails that head up the hill to the left and follow the fence to the right.) Walk beneath utility lines

at 5.7 and then bend right, parallel to the poles, toward Ferris Mountain. After turning to the right side of the wires, cross Rawlins Draw (a dry gully) at 6.4. Rise slightly to a junction at 6.8 where the Trail takes the left fork, continuing parallel to the fence just ahead.

Pass a barbed wire gate in another fence at 7.1. A jeep trail joins from the right before the route crosses a low ridge at 7.4. Descending, pass under the wires at 7.5. Mountain bluebirds, along with the more common vesper sparrows, may be seen at the next rise, at 7.9. A jeep road joins from the right, from the direction of Whiskey Peak, at 8.3.

At 8.8, intersect the good jeep road, lined with poles, that serves the radio tower on the hill to the right. Leave the road here and continue straight ahead. Walk over the brow of the hill at 8.9 and drop down into the gully, heading east toward Ferris Mountain. Go through a barbed wire fence at 9.4 and proceed down the left side of the valley on jeep tracks. Note the thin vertical flake of rock that runs along the red hillside across the gully. Be alert for both coyotes and their rabbit prey, probably the desert cottontail.

Angle left, hiking to the left of a knoll ("6412" on the map) at 10.3. Swing northward. Pass through a barbed wire gate at 11.1. Leave the jeep tracks here and bear right toward the concrete highway underpass, a stock driveway. Walk through sagebrush, reaching Muddy Creek at 11.4 at a break in the willow thickets lining its banks. Boulder hop the creek without difficulty, go through the underpass, and climb over the fence where it abuts the concrete retaining wall.

Reaching U.S. 287 at 11.5, turn south and continue to the settlement of Muddy Gap. Pass a picnic table, brick highway maintenance building, and then a gas station, where the Section ends at 12.1. See the introduction for a description of services, including transportation, available here.

Distances and elevations are:

0.0	Road junction (7390)	7400
0.5	Rabbit Creek	7300
0.8	Rise	7400
2.2	Campsite	7050

GREEN MOUNTAINS SEGMENT

2.5	Rise	7100
3.0	Spring	7000
3.3	Junction	6950
4.4	Gate (6795)	6800
4.9	Diamond Hook Ranch	6750
5.0	Willow Creek	6750
5.2	Gate	6750
6.4	Rawlins Draw	6650
6.8	Junction (6687)	6700
7.4	Ridge	6750
7.8		6650
7.9	Rise	6700
8.3	Junction (enter Muddy Gap Quadrangle)	6600
8.8	Road junction (6650)	6650
9.4	Fence	6500
10.3	Ridge	6350
11.1	Fence	6300
11.4	Muddy Creek	6250
11.5	U.S. 287	6300
12.1	Muddy Gap	6300

EAST RIM SEGMENT
Section 1
Muddy Gap to Ferris Mountain Ranch
Distance 10.8 Miles

This inviting stretch, for the most part climbing gradually on jeep trail, threads through open canyons formed by the parallel ridges of Ferris Mountain. Whiskey Gap, site of the nation's first prohibition raid, is easily accessible.

From Muddy Gap, the Trail rises to cross a saddle at 1.7. It drops to a jeep road junction close to Whiskey Gap at 2.8. It cuts off on to poor track at 3.5, climbing gradually through a notch to enter secluded Black Canyon at 4.9. The Trail leaves the canyon at 7.2, continuing cross-country over a ridge at 7.6. After picking up jeep trail again, it descends Indian Creek and then the dry gully of Currant Creek before reaching the fertile oasis of the Ferris Mountain Ranch at the end of the Section at 10.8. Antelope are plentiful in the second half of the Section; some mule deer may be observed as well.

There are bits of private property at both ends of the Section — 0.0 to 0.2 and 10.2 to 10.8 but, as of this writing, travel is not restricted. The author was welcomed cordially by the proprietor of Ferris Mountain Ranch, Mr. R.B. Raymond; please respect his privacy and avoid any disturbance of his land. Whiskey Gap and its good springs, slightly off the Trail, are also privately-owned. Suggested campsites on public land are at 0.5 and beneath the aspens along Indian Creek (likely to be heavily grazed) at 8.5. There is excellent spring water at Whiskey Gap near 2.8, and several creeks furnish something to drink at reasonable intervals elsewhere.

The main emigration route was being shifted from the Oregon Trail to the Overland Trail in 1862. Some of the soldiers assigned to the move were tipsy, prompting a search of their party's wagons and the discovery of a barrel of whiskey. The commanding officer ordered the keg to be destroyed, and it was smashed near the springs at their campsite, now Whiskey Gap. The troops quickly scooped up what they could. One soldier recorded that it was the best spring water he had ever tasted; their commander more soberly observed that it was a good thing the night passed without Indian attack.

See the introduction to Section 6 of the Green Mountains Segment with respect to transportation and other facilities at Muddy Gap.

Nearly all of the Section appears on the U.S. Geological Survey 1:24000 *Muddy Gap* quadrangle. The *Youngs Pass* and *Lamont* quadrangles (both 1:24000) also depict small portions of the route. Refer to Map 27 in this volume.

Detailed Trail data are:

Begin at the service station in Muddy Gap next to the highway maintenance station. Head east on the good dirt road to the north of the service station. Pass a cattle guard at 0.2. The road to the left at 0.3 is another connection to the highway. A camp can be made on public land near the culvert at 0.5, with good water available from the spring up the hill to the left. Take the better right fork at 1.5.

Cross a saddle at 1.7, with Ferris Mountain and the open valley of Whiskey Creek straight ahead. Drop slightly, reaching a junction at 2.8. Stay to the right. (There are several springs in Whiskey Gap, the deep notch 0.3 mile to the left. The best, perhaps, is beyond the Gap, where water flows from the base of the rocks through a green carpet of watercress. You are likely to encounter a flock of pinyon jays, as well as the less robust mountain bluebird and the small rock wren.)

The road, passable by car to this point, levels out at 3.5. Several jeep trails converge upon the barbed wire gate here; go through the gate and take the route on the far right, closest to the fence. After crossing the Hays Ditch, carrying water from Whiskey Creek, turn left on the jeep tracks at 3.6 and climb very gradually. Take the right fork at 4.1. A mining prospect is on the right as the Trail reaches a dry gully at 4.6. Just after crossing one fork of the gully, bear right at the jeep trail junction at 4.9.

Head up Black Canyon, away from colorful outcrops, passing to the right of the hill with the prominent microwave reflector. The gully will probably have a fairly good flow of water at first, though it will disappear farther up Black Canyon. Pass between the microwave reflector on one side and a tributary canyon on

Whiskey Gap.

the other at 5.8. Take the right fork at 6.1, close to the gully which once again has water. The walk is scenic — with red bluffs to the right, the limestone flatirons along the crest of Ferris Mountain to the left, and the domes of the Granite Mountains in the distance to the rear.

The Trail comes to a small impoundment at 6.4. Feeding this is a creek flowing from a clean (though unprotected) spring, 0.2 mile uphill to the left, beneath a juniper. A camp could be set up near the pond, which is marked on the topographic map. Continue up the main valley, following jeep tracks. (Avoid the side valley off to the right at 6.5.) A spur ridge from the left crowds the Trail, starting at 6.9.

Take faint tracks bearing right at 7.1 toward the knolls with free-standing boulders on top. Cross two dry gullies, less than 100 yards above their junction; from here, on the southwest edge of Black Canyon at 7.2, climb fairly steeply up the tributary gully to the left. Enjoy the vista to the northwest, past the rounded contours of Black Canyon and on to the far horizon.

Proceed, from 7.4 to 7.6, through a straight and level walkway between two low parallel ridges. (The one to the right looks out over the Ferris Mountain Ranch and much of the eastern portion of the Great Divide Basin. Prominent features in the middle distance are Table Mountain and the Haystack Mountains; farther off, to the southeast, are Elk Mountain and the Snowy Range and, to the south southeast, mountains along the Continental Divide extending to Colorado.)

Use care crawling under the tightly-strung barbed wire fence at 7.7. Pick up jeep tracks in a few yards and descend to the southeast. After dipping to a gully, rise to cross a ridge at 8.0, with views of the great vertical flakes of Ferris Mountain. Take the jeep tracks descending ahead toward the aspens. Bend right at 8.2 and descend the right bank of Indian Creek, which is a good water source. Walk beneath an avenue of aspens at 8.5; the grassy ground in the shade of the trees across the creek is a fine campsite.

Turn right, following the creek downstream, where another jeep trail joins from the left bank at 8.6. Go through a barbed wire gate at 8.8 and swing to the left, crossing Indian Creek (a culvert) in a few yards. The Trail steadily descends, moving away from Ferris Mountain. After passing to the east of a gray butte, it follows the course of Currant Creek (which is likely to be dry). Pass through a barbed wire gate at 10.2 and enter the Ferris Mountain Ranch. Walk between hayfields to the road junction at 10.5. Turn left, reaching the ranch buildings beneath large cottonwoods at 10.8, the end of the Section.

Distances and elevations are:

0.0	Muddy Gap	6300
1.7	Saddle	6700
2.8	Junction (Whiskey Gap 0.3)	6600
3.5	Fence	6650
4.1	Fork	6700
4.9	Jeep trail junction	6900
6.4	Impoundment	7250
7.2	Gullies	7500
7.6	Ridge	7700

7.9	Gully	7550
8.0	Enter Youngs Pass Quadrangle	7600
8.4	Enter Muddy Gap Quadrangle	7300
8.8	Fence	7150
9.5	Enter Youngs Pass Quadrangle	6900
9.7	Enter Muddy Gap Quadrangle	6900
10.4	Enter Lamont Quadrangle	6800
10.5	Road junction	6800
10.8	Ferris Mountain Ranch	6850

EAST RIM SEGMENT
Section 2
Ferris Mountain Ranch to Sand Creek
Distance 15.2 Miles

Lofty Ferris Mountain, its flank punctuated with impressive free-standing outcrops, dominates the scene. The route, which involves little climbing, follows jeep trail in a straight line on the south side of the long ridge. The Trail enters the Great Divide Basin, for the first time, for several miles in the middle of the Section.

The route starts out by following Muddy Creek upstream to a crossing at 2.5; it then climbs slightly and contours along the lower slopes of Ferris Mountain, entering the Great Divide Basin around 4.9. There is a pond, set incongruously in a circle of sand dunes, just before the Trail reaches the Larsen Place (still maintained, but not regularly occupied) at 8.8. The ruins of an abandoned homestead, the Marvin Place, are at 10.8. The Trail leaves the Great Divide Basin around 12.2. It drops several hundred feet and, after crossing Sand Creek at 13.8, follows that stream to the intersection with a good road at 15.2 at the end of the Section. In addition to antelope — which continue to be abundant — deer, elk, and golden eagles may be spotted.

Much of the land in the Section is privately-owned, but there appears to be no restriction to hiking on the rarely-used jeep travelway. The best campsites are at Muddy Creek (2.5) and at the Larsen Place (8.8), where there is a spring. Water is available from several small creeks; if heavy grazing is apparent, purification is recommended.

New foot trail could be constructed along the crest of Ferris Mountain, if necessary to avoid conflict with other land uses; the described route is scenic, varied, and entirely satisfactory, however.

In addition to Map 28, refer to the following U.S. Geological Survey 1:24000 quadrangles: *Lamont* (a small bit), *Lamont NE*, *Ferris*, and *Bradley Peak*.

Detailed Trail data are:

This Section starts at the Ferris Mountain Ranch. Brewer's blackbirds and meadowlarks can be expected; and a rufous-sided towhee may lurk in the brush. Cross Birch Creek, which flows through a culvert. Stay to the left at 0.1, avoiding the main ranch road that doubles back to the west. There may be some ducks on the Marsh Reservoir, to the right at 0.3. Dip to cross Cottonweed Creek's culvert at 0.8. Take the right fork immediately beyond and continue on good jeep road, paralleling Muddy Creek and Ferris Mountain. Cross cattle guards at 1.1, 1.8, and 2.4.

Continue east after the Muddy Creek culvert at 2.5. A camp could be made by this permanent creek. The road swings left and faces Youngs Pass (a deep notch on the crest of Ferris Mountain) as it comes to a cattle guard at 3.5. Take a shortcut by leaving the road temporarily and following the right side of the fence eastward. Elk, counted in the hundreds on Ferris Mountain, are likely to be found below Youngs Pass and near the creek at 3.7. Look for golden eagles as well.

Shortly after passing through a barbed wire gate, pick up the good (though somewhat sandy) jeep road again, at 4.0. Take the left fork at 4.5, at 4.7 passing on the uphill side of the large corral ahead. Sand dunes appear to the right; then, 50 yards after going through a four-way intersection with a jeep trail at 5.0, pass over a very small creek flowing through a culvert. This creek apparently sinks in the sand dunes and thus lies in the Great Divide Basin, across the indistinct Continental Divide from the Muddy Creek drainage. A line of iron poles marks a section boundary at 5.2.

From the ridge at 5.7, Bradley Peak is directly ahead and Whiskey Peak directly to the rear. Take the left fork as the road splits at 5.8 and rejoins at 5.9. Go through another barbed wire fence at the next section line, at 6.3. The stock pond just past the fence will probably have a trickling inflow. After crossing the dam, climb to a ridge at 6.6. Walk by a fence angle at 7.0 and then dip, remaining left of the fence. Step over a good-sized permanent creek at 7.2. Rise slightly to the next section boundary, going through the barbed wire fence at 7.3. Step over another creek at 7.7. A stock pond is above the Trail, to the left, at 7.9.

Keep straight where poor tracks bear right at 8.1. (The latter leads to a pretty pond, at the base of dunes, a Sahara-like setting and well worth the detour of 500 yards or so each way; watch for prickly pear cactus in the sandy soil.) Just after the small creek at 8.5, take the jeep tracks bearing right. The route becomes confusing around 8.7, with several interwoven jeep tracks; head generally to the east, remaining north of some small ponds. The jeep track is well-defined again at 8.8, where it splits once more.

Take the fork continuing straight. (The sandy right fork leads a quarter mile to the Larsen Place, where there is a cabin that is no longer occupied on a permanent basis; a good spring is a few yards southeast of the house. This is private property; with the consent of the landowners, it would be a good campsite.)

The tracks are sandy and overgrown with sagebrush as they proceed on the left of some old fence poles. A plank bridge over a creek at 9.0 is decrepit and unusable. A hundred yards beyond, keep straight where good jeep tracks cross, running up and down the hill. (The Larsen Place is visible from here, 0.2 mile to the right.) Climb gradually, passing jeep tracks joining from the right at 9.6 and from the left at 9.8. After the grassy gully at 10.1, look out over the foreground sand dunes and northeast corner of the Great Divide Basin toward Bradley Peak and the Haystack Mountains. Ferris, the site of some oil storage tanks a couple of miles to the southeast from here, is uninhabited.

The Trail bends left at 10.6, crosses small but permanent Garden Creek and comes to the shells of log cabins at the abandoned Marvin Place at 10.8. The spring is likely to be dry, but creek water is available for a camp. After passing between the two main buildings, take the uphill jeep tracks and climb to the left. Cross two sets of tracks at 11.0 and continue almost at contour, rising slightly. Just beyond the second set, pick up a jeep trail joining from the right and follow it eastward.

Reach a high point at a cattle guard at 11.4. Sage grouse may be flushed nearby. Head east toward Bear Mountain and the serrated, more distant peaks to its left. The log cabin ruins next to the Trail at 12.2 mark the approximate location of the Continental Divide. Take the left fork at 12.7 and drop gradually to the valley on the left. (This route, shown on the topographic map, is no longer used by jeeps.) Tracks join from the right at

13.3. Cross a culvert with a small creek at 13.4. Descend its left bank past beaver ponds.

Jeep tracks coming downhill join from the left just before the Trail crosses Sand Creek, a relatively large stream (with culvert and bridge ruins) at 13.8. A camp might be set up, but it is not an attractive site. Proceed on jeep road above the left bank of Sand Creek. Poor tracks join from the right at 14.2. After crossing a small side creek, by bridge at 14.5, climb to a ridge at 14.7 facing a colorful hillside of red rock. Reach an intersection, the end of the Section at 15.2, where the Trail continues by making a sharp right turn onto graded road.

Distances and elevations are:

0.0	Ferris Mountain Ranch	6850
0.2	Enter Lamont NE Quadrangle	6800
0.8	Cottonwood Creek	6900
2.5	Muddy Creek	7000
3.5	Cattle guard	7250
4.0	Jeep road	7300
4.5	Fork (7354)	7350
4.9	Enter Great Divide Basin	7400
5.7	Ridge	7450
6.3	Stock pond	7350
6.6	Ridge	7450
7.2	Creek	7350
7.3	Enter Ferris Quadrangle	7400
7.7	Creek	7300
8.5	Creek	7200
8.8	Larsen Place	7200
10.1	Gully	7300
10.7	Garden Creek	7200
10.8	Marvin Place	7250
11.4	Cattle guard	7400
12.2	Leave Great Divide Basin	7200
13.4	Creek	6750
13.8	Sand Creek	6700
14.5	Creek	6600
14.7	Ridge	6700
14.8	Enter Bradley Peak Quadrangle	6650
15.2	Intersection	6550

EAST RIM SEGMENT

Section 3

Sand Creek to Deweese Creek

Distance 9.2 Miles

The Trail crosses the northeast tip of the Great Divide Basin. Uninhabited by man, this land boasts an abundance of wildlife, notably the waterfowl around its numerous potholes. Some of the route is confusing; but the open terrain and prominent landmarks make it easy to keep one's bearings.

The first part of the Section, entering the Great Divide Basin around 1.0, is on good jeep road. The Trail cuts off the maintained surface at 2.7 and follows jeep tracks, which may be hard to follow, past the McCargar Place at 3.3 to the Boot Ranch at 6.4; both of these have been abandoned. Cross-country travel can be difficult, as there are several parallel low ridges separated by long ponds that can only be bypassed by long detours. From Boot Ranch, the Trail turns east on more obvious routes and, after crossing creeks at 7.3 and 8.0, climbs over a saddle between Junk Hill and Bradley Peak. Leaving the Great Divide Basin here, at 8.7, it drops to Deweese Creek, the end of the Section, at 9.2.

There are several small creeks, with possible campsites, as described in the text. Running water is absent from the creek at 1.4 to Boot Ranch at 6.4; carry something to drink on this stretch, particularly since there may be route-finding difficulties. The portion of the Section in the Great Divide Basin is mostly in private ownership, though not in economic use except for a little grazing; foot travel is unlikely to be restricted.

The text below is in part hypothetical, as the author's actual route snaked through the maze of ponds east of the McCargar Place. That way was unnecessarily circuitous, but it was especially rich in bird life — mallard, redhead, green-winged and blue-winged (or cinnamon) teal, snipe, and coot, among others.

See the U.S. Geological Survey 1:24000 *Ferris* and *Bradley Peak* quadrangles, along with Map 29.

Detailed Trail data are:

The Section begins at a road junction at the eastern tip of the

Ferris Mountains. Here the Trail makes an abrupt turn to the right and starts its southward leg around the Great Divide Basin. The Trail, on good jeep road, drops steeply for 50 yards, crossing a culvert at Sand Creek. (Just downstream is a confluence where Sand Creek's volume is doubled; take a walk up the side stream a short distance to view a rocky cascade of muddy water tumbling through a barren gorge bounded by sand dunes. There is likely to be a large flock of pinyon jays near the confluence.)

As the road climbs under utility lines, at 0.1, it passes fairly good grassy campsites at bends along Sand Creek. The water may be somewhat silty, however. Walk beneath more lines at 0.3, with the sandy ravine to the left. As the road bends right at 0.4, it would be possible to take a cross-country shortcut between Bear Mountain and Junk Hill. Remaining on the road, pass under wires again at 0.5.

Curve left, rising, at 0.7. (A cleared pipeline route continues straight just before the curve.) Go over a low ridge at 0.9. Pass under utility lines in a few yards and again at 1.2 where poor tracks bear off to the right. Dip slightly to cross a fair-sized creek at a culvert at 1.4; the sandy gully downstream is eroded into interesting stepped bluffs. The water is clearer than Sand Creek and a camp could be set up alongside. Carry water from here.

A large pond is immediately to the left at 1.6. Keep straight at 1.7, climbing where a good side road turns to the right past a small pothole. There are good views from the ridge at 1.8, the approximate location of the Continental Divide. Dip, passing to the left of another pond and then crossing a cattle guard at 2.1. More potholes appear on both sides of the road after it levels out.

New road construction may result in some confusion; follow the main road straight to the southwest where, at approximately 2.7, you should pick up a jeep trail that veers south to the McCargar Place. (If you miss the junction, as the author did, you will come to a cattle guard just before another pond on the left of the road. From there, cut cross-country to the south southeast to resume the correct route. Another thing to note is that the McCargar Place lies about 100 yards east of the easternmost set of utility lines.)

Pass a demolished shed at 3.1 and at 3.2 reach the abandoned McCargar Place. The several structures here include a long ranch house, open to the elements but with the roof fairly intact, and a large corral. Take the jeep tracks that cross a marshy spot opposite the corral; the small green amphibians that may be seen here are chorus frogs. Head eastward toward Junk Hill. This path is easy to discern as it winds through sagebrush, but much of it is soft sand and rather difficult going. There are more ponds to the left. From the rise at 3.9, a good log cabin can be spotted less than a mile to the east.

The Trail crosses another set of jeep tracks at 4.0 and then makes a sweeping bend to the right. This does not seem consistent with the route appearing on the Bradley Peak quadrangle, and the author elected to head cross-country for the cabin. This was a mistake, as the building sits in a country of long ponds separated by low ridges, with the ponds blocking travel across their path. So at 4.1 remain on the jeep tracks. Hypothetically, they head generally southeast and climb gradually, with some small dips.

Come to the top of a ridge at about 5.5 (where the author relocated the tracks). The metal-roofed barn of the abandoned Boot Ranch can be seen almost directly in line with the sand dunes on the lower slopes of Bradley Peak. Dip to 5.7, then climb gradually again to 6.2. Make a sharp left turn on the tracks here and pass immediately through a gate of woven wire.

Intersect another set of tracks, turn left, and come to the Boot Ranch at 6.4. A good camp could be made on flat grass in the shadow of Bradley Peak. Just before the barn, cross the gully on the right and pick up jeep tracks heading eastward. Keep straight at 6.6, paralleling the fence, where a set of tracks turns right toward Bradley Peak. Take the right fork, dipping, at 6.7. Cross another set of tracks, at an angle, at 6.9; keep straight, using the descending path nearest to the fence.

Good water and campsites are available as the Trail crosses small School Creek at 7.3. Climb on jeep trail, passing a fence corner at 7.5. Jeep tracks join from the right at a high point at 7.7.

Step across West Junk Creek at 8.0. In 50 yards or so, turn right on an intersecting jeep trail and continue climbing up the right (north) bank. Jeep tracks soon join from the left. Keep climbing at 8.1 where tracks bear right toward the creek. (These may also lead to the pass ahead, but would require a steeper climb.)

Reach the pass between Junk Hill and Bradley Peak at 8.8; a spring is off to the right shortly before the top. Leave the Great Divide Basin for the last time and pass through a woven-wire gate. Descend gradually, with glimpses of Pathfinder Reservoir to the northeast. (Jeep tracks to the right at 8.9 appear to offer a shortcut to the Trail at 0.4 in the next Section.)

Come to a junction with a jeep road and turn right. The Section ends here, at 9.2, as the Trail immediately crosses a small unnamed creek that flows into Deweese Creek. A usable campsite may be found on the far side of the latter, but most of the ground is wet, sloping, or covered by sagebrush or cowpies. Water birches, along with some smaller trees and shrubs, grow along the creek. Flickers and meadowlarks are among the birds of the area.

Distances and elevations are:

0.0	Intersection	6550
0.0	Sand Creek	6500
0.7	Pipeline	6600
0.9	Ridge	6650
1.0	Enter Ferris Quadrangle	6600
1.4	Creek	6650
1.8	Enter Great Divide Basin	6700
2.0	Enter Bradley Peak Quadrangle	6700
2.5	Enter Ferris Quadrangle	6700
2.7	Jeep trail junction (?)	6700
3.3	McCargar Place	6700
3.6	Enter Bradley Peak Quadrangle	6700
3.9	Rise	6750
5.5	Ridge	6900
5.7	Dip	6850
6.4	Boot Ranch	6900
7.3	School Creek	6850
7.7	Jeep tracks	7000
8.0	West Junk Creek	6950
8.7	Leave Great Divide Basin	7250
9.2	Jeep road junction	7050

EAST RIM SEGMENT
Section 4
Deweese Creek to Saltiel Creek
Distance 9.1 Miles

Bradley Peak, a reddish summit patched with clumps of aspen, is the focus of the Section. The Trail uses jeep trails to make a circuit of the mountain, reaching the highest elevation on the Segment at a saddle on Bradley Peak's east side.

The Trail climbs up the valley of Deweese Creek, reaching the pass between Bradley Peak and other summits of the Seminoe Mountains at 2.8. The rest of the way is a nearly uninterrupted descent. The ruins of the old Elkhorn Stage Station are at 6.8, beyond which the Trail drops along small Saltiel Creek to the end of the Section at 9.1.

There is considerable grazing, especially along Saltiel Creek, and water purification may be prudent. Coal Creek, at 6.2, is a good uncontaminated source; several other creek are available, however. Scenic campsites looking back toward Bradley Peak can be found along Saltiel Creek near the end of the Section. Although most of the land is privately owned, there appear to be no travel restrictions. Relocating the Trail over the summit of Bradley Peak is an interesting possibility.

The U.S. Geological Survey 1:24000 topographic maps are *Bradley Peak* and *Wild Horse Mountain.* The route also appears on Map 29.

Detailed Trail data are:

The Section begins as the Trail turns right at a road junction and begins its ascent up the west bank of Deweese Creek. A jeep trail joins from the left at 0.2. Climb gradually, passing a clump of aspens at 0.4. Jeep tracks coming up from the right beyond the trees appear to be a shortcut from 8.9 in the preceding Section.

Cross a small creek at 0.9 and a larger one at 1.5. There are good views back toward Ferris Mountain, with Junk Hill to its right; Whiskey Peak is still visible far to the west. Take the steep trail uphill at 1.6, cutting across a couple of long switchbacks.

Ferris Mountain, from the head of Deweese Creek.

Turn right on the main road at 1.7. Follow the middle, climbing, trail at 2.0. (The one to the left goes through a fence to a private cabin set among aspens; the right one is an alternate, rejoining the route at 2.1.)

Twin Creek flows through a culvert at 2.2. The woods contain some limber pine as well as aspen. Look for the hermit thrush, as well as crows, nuthatches, and Cassin's finches; several raptors, including kestrels, golden eagles, and Cooper's hawk, may also be present. Avoid the side roads at 2.3, one turning sharply right and climbing toward the true summit of Bradley Peak and the other heading downhill through the fence on the left.

At 2.6, cross Deweese Creek, here no more than a trickle from a stock-trampled seep a short way above. Bend right, close to the aspens. There are good views northward, to the right of Ferris Mountain, the last glimpse of the Oregon Trail country.

173

The Trail at 2.8 crosses the saddle between Bradley Peak and its neighboring summits in the Seminoe Mountains. Seminoe Reservoir is seen in the plains below, with the massive hump of Elk Mountain beyond. Descend on good jeep road, toward the reservoir. Continue downhill at 3.2 where less-traveled trails join from both sides and at 3.4 where one joins from the aspens on the right.

Leave the main road at the junction at 3.7; turn right and drop off into the valley. Step over a very small creek at 3.9; this is typical habitat for the green-tailed towhee, which finds shelter in patches of chokecherry and other shrubs on open slopes. Bend left, continuing to descend, and pass another little creek at 4.1.

Coming around a bend at 4.4, take the better fork, to the right. (The author descended on the left fork, which becomes very poor beyond a fence half a mile downhill.) From the topographic map, it appears that this road crosses a small creek at 4.6, remains at contour to 4.9, then drops to a junction at 5.1. It then turns left and goes directly down the slope to a junction near the head of Indian Creek at 5.8.

Curve right and climb, along a fence, to the right of a rocky knob. Boulder hop cascading Coal Creek at 6.2, near its source. This is a good place to get drinking water; the sloping terrain is poor for camping, however. Continue along the right side of the fence.

Pass the stonework ruins of the old Elkhorn Stage Station at 6.8 as the jeep road descends steeply toward Saltiel Creek. Go through a barbed wire gate here, crossing under power lines, and take the jeep trail descending along the left bank of Saltiel Creek. Although the creek is only a few inches wide, it has a good flow that is probably permanent. There are occasional places to camp by the stream as the Trail gradually and steadily drops through treeless grassland. One good spot is the sagebrush-free bluff across the creek at 8.5.

Log cabin ruins are to the right at 8.6, at the confluence with an intermittent creek. A tall chimney-like cairn stands on a butte to the left of the Trail at 9.0. The Section ends at a junction of jeep trails at 9.1, where the route continues by turning right and crossing Saltiel Creek.

Distances and elevations are:

0.0	Jeep road junction	7050
0.9	Creek	7300
1.5	Creek	7400
1.7		7600
2.0	Junction	7700
2.2	Twin Creek	7750
2.6	Deweese Creek	7800
2.8	Saddle	7900
3.2	Junction	7800
3.7	Junction (7649)	7650
3.9	Creek	7550
4.1	Creek	7500
4.4	Junction	7500
5.1	Junction	7400
5.8	Junction	7200
6.2	Coal Creek	7250
6.8	Elkhorn Stage Station	7150
7.7	Enter Wild Horse Mountain Quadrangle	6950
8.5	Campsite	6850
9.1	Saltiel Creek (6764)	6750

EAST RIM SEGMENT
Section 5
Saltiel Creek to Seminoe Road
Distance 15.1 Miles

Water would be difficult to obtain along the crest of the Haystack Mountains, which form the rim of the Great Divide Basin. The Trail therefore detours several miles to the east to pass by a permanent spring.

The Trail starts by crossing Saltiel Creek at 0.0 and Rankin Creek at 0.7, then follows sandy jeep tracks over Cheyenne Ridge at 2.1 and down its other side to Tapers Ranch at 4.9. Here it leaves the Continental Divide and proceeds east in a wide sagebrush valley between Cheyenne Ridge and Coal Creek Rim, descending very gradually. The Trail passes O'Brien Spring at 9.7, emerges into the plains along the North Platte River, and turns south on poor tracks. The most interesting feature on the Section is an archaeological site at 14.0, where Indians once stampeded buffalo into a rock-rimmed cul-de-sac. The Trail reaches the paved Seminoe Road at the end of the Section at 15.1.

It might be desirable to relocate the Trail beyond Tapers Ranch so as to avoid the road walking in the next two Sections. This would require careful scouting in the Haystack Mountains, particularly with respect to water supply. It would also be possible to take a shortcut from Rankin Creek to O'Brien Spring, crossing Cheyenne Ridge much further east, and this too would be worth investigating.

There are three creeks — Saltiel at 0.0, Rankin (probably, though not definitely, permanent) at 0.7, and O'Brien at ID Camp at 10.2. All of these may be contaminated by grazing, but can be used with purification. Good drinking water is best obtained, however, from Coal Creek (6.2 in Section 4) and O'Brien Spring (9.7 in this Section). Although about half of the Section is on private land, the author found no restrictions to foot travel; please help to preserve the same opportunity for other hikers.

The end of the Section is on the lightly-traveled paved road connecting Seminoe Dam and Reservoir to the oil-refining community of Sinclair on Interstate 80.

The U.S. Geological Survey's 1:24000 *Wild Horse Mountain*, *Seminoe Dam SW*, and *Lone Haystack Mountain* quadrangles, as well as Maps 29 and 30, show the route of the Trail.

Detailed Trail data are:

Bradley Peak, to the north, is the dominating summit at the jeep trail junction at the start of the Section. Cross Saltiel Creek, which flows through a culvert. Obtain water. Disregard tracks joining from the right at 0.1 and 0.4. Note the route of the Trail as a clearly visible scar angling up Cheyenne Ridge ahead.

Walk on a dike at 0.6, with an impoundment of Rankin Creek to the right. Just before reaching the four-way fence intersection, bend sharply to the left and follow the tracks past a barbed wire gate at 0.7, using the stile to cross. Jump over Rankin Creek in less than 100 yards and follow the jeep trail south, straight up the bank. Going over a rise to a junction at 1.0, take the poorer tracks that bear right and can be seen climbing Cheyenne Ridge. The ground is sandy, with cactus and Russian thistle, but between the ruts it is for the most part stabilized by grass. Walk through a barbed wire gate at 1.3. Detour to the right around a small sandpit at 1.7.

Enjoy the panorama from the crest of Cheyenne Ridge at 2.1. Stretching off to the south, beyond the Haystack Mountains, are the distant Snowy Range and the mountains of the Continental Divide reaching into Colorado. The Great Divide Basin shows up as a flat plain to the featureless horizon in the west. The Ferris and Seminoe Mountains stand out in the north, while off to the east lie the waters of the Seminoe Reservoir.

Descend gradually and steadily on sandy jeep trail. Keep an eye out for a small toad, the plains spadefoot, that will burrow into the ground to escape your view. Continue straight, toward the dunes, crossing another jeep trail at an angle at 3.2. After passing a fence at 4.3, walk beneath and to the left of high bare sand dunes.

Angle away from the dunes to a junction at a fence corner at 4.9. Here make a sharp left turn. (A hundred yards to the right is Tapers Ranch, apparently still occupied on an occasional basis. Aside from a broken windmill, there is no apparent source of drinking water. Mallards or teal might be seen on a stagnant pond near the ranch. Other birds in the area might include snipe, magpies, Brewer's blackbirds, and horned larks.)

Follow well-used, though still somewhat sandy, jeep road. Go through a pole gate at 5.3. Keep heading east, between converging Cheyenne Ridge on the left and Coal Creek Rim on the right. Curve left as a jeep trail joins from the right at 5.9.

Cross a cattle guard, with old wagonwheels on both sides, at 6.4. Poor tracks turn off to the left at 6.7. A large area of sand dunes is to the left of the Trail around 7.5. Keep straight on the road at 8.2 as one jeep trail joins from the right and another bears to the right of a little rise. Proceed through a swinging metal gate at 8.9; to the left are grassy meadows where there may be some standing water. Pass a fence corner and stagnant pond at 9.1.

Go through a pass on Coal Creek Rim at 9.7. The road that joins from the left here can be taken 0.2 mile to O'Brien Spring. (Following the side road, take the right fork 100 yards after leaving the Trail. The spring consists of many seeps from the side of a gully. Many animals have breathed their last at this waterhole. So fill your canteens at a clean seep as the drops emerge, and try to avoid one too close to a carcass.) Pass another swinging metal gate at 9.8. The buildings of the abandoned ID Camp are on the left at 10.2, across O'Brien Creek.

Make a sharp right on the jeep trail opposite ID Camp and head south. After 100 yards, cross another jeep trail at an angle, and continue straight. (The one to the right parallels Coal Creek Rim.) Go through a barbed wire gate at 10.4. A good landmark is the low small butte ahead called the Pool Table. At 10.8, walk over a dry gully at the confluence of intermittent Coal and Corral Creeks. Russian thistle is abundant near the bridge ruins.

Avoid the tracks that bear right 50 yards beyond the gully. Continue straight, south, crossing another jeep trail at right angles at 10.9. The Trail can be discerned as a wide path through the shadscale bushes and sagebrush, though wheel ruts may be indistinct. Chipmunks are common, and there may be a few antelope as well. Faint tracks intersect the Trail, as it climbs very gradually, at 11.4 and 11.6. Pass a low ridge at 11.9. Just after walking to the right of an outcrop at 12.2, bear slightly to the right where some very faint tracks continue ahead. The route is again indistinct except as a grassy path through the brush. Cross another set of tracks at 12.7.

Use caution at the junction just beyond, at the crest of a low rise. Bear right, heading only slightly left of the Pool Table; the better tracks to the left descend eastward along the waterless draw. Cross that draw at 12.9. Keep a lookout for a junction at 13.3; here bear left to cross another dry draw (now impassable by jeep) whereas the track straight ahead continues toward the Pool Table. Just after the draw, leave the main tracks and follow faint ones close to the east bank of the gully.

From 13.5, low sandstone outcrops crowd the left side of the Trail. At 13.8, a rock promontory sticks out from the main band of cliffs, forming a cul-de-sac. Enter this cove, away from the draw. This steep-walled amphitheatre was an Indian buffalo trap. The bison would be stampeded into it. As they rushed for safety at the far end, some would fall into a 15-foot-deep pit, with overhanging walls, from which there was no escape. This is at 14.0, almost up to the sculptured formations along the back rim. (A ladder down to the bottom looks untrustworthy.) There are said to be some remnants of Indian habitation along the top of the surrounding rock. Rainwater may be found in some of the potholes, but it is hardly a reliable source for something to drink.

Climb through a notch at the very head of the canyon and continue between outcrops to 14.2, where jeep tracks are intersected. Turn left, uphill. Turn right, on good jeep trail, at the T-intersection at 14.3. Walk beneath power transmission lines at 14.9. A patch of Seminoe Reservoir is visible to the left just before the Trail reaches the paved Seminoe Road, the end of the Section, at 15.1. Turn right and continue south.

Distances and elevations are:

0.0	Saltiel Creek	6750
0.7	Rankin Creek	6750
1.0	Junction	6850
2.1	Cheyenne Ridge	7300
3.2	Jeep trail	7100
4.9	Tapers Ranch	6900
5.9	Junction	6800
8.2	Junction	6750
8.9	Meadows	6600

EAST RIM SEGMENT

9.6	Enter Seminoe Dam SW Quadrangle	6600
9.7	O'Brien Spring	6600
10.2	ID Camp	6550
10.8	Gully	6450
11.4	Enter Wild Horse Mountain Quadrangle	6500
11.9	Ridge	6550
12.9	Draw	6500
13.3	Draw	6500
14.0	Buffalo pit	6600
14.3	Intersection	6650
14.6	Enter Lone Haystack Mountain Quadrangle	6650
15.1	Seminoe Road	6650

EAST RIM SEGMENT
Section 6
Seminoe Road to Sinclair
Distance 20.6 Miles

This Section, mostly on paved surface, is hardly a backpacker's delight. Its redeeming feature is the middle third, a scenic stretch along the North Platte River; the riparian birds there, several of them uncharacteristic of the Trail, are worthy of note.

From 0.0 to 8.0, the Trail travels southward on the Seminoe Road, across dry expanses of sagebrush. Reaching the North Platte River, it follows the road along the bank as the stream cuts a winding channel through a series of parallel ridges crossing its path; this canyon, with steep slopes rising on both sides, is known as the Lower Dugway. As the river passes this barrier, at 10.8, the Trail leaves the highway and continues upstream close to the water, following jeep routes to 14.9, where a secondary paved road is intersected. It then turns southwest and heads directly for the oil refining town of Sinclair, where the Section ends at 20.6.

Aside from taxi service out of Rawlins, there is no public transportation at Sinclair; Greyhound buses on Interstate 80 will drop passengers there on request, however. Meals are served at a coffee shop in the old, and once fashionable, hotel in Sinclair (where rooms can be rented). The post office is ZIP 82334.

Cloudy water can be obtained from the river, if necessary. (Treat it before before drinking.) Passing vehicles are another possible source of liquids. Creekbeds are seasonal channels and likely to be dry; the best chance to find good creek water is at a small run at 8.2. A short detour to the pumping station or public park near the Trail at 14.9 will also provide access to water.

A camp can be made at a bend in the Lower Dugway at 8.9 or, away from the road, close to the river between 10.8 and 13.5. Some of the land by the river is privately-owned, though unoccupied; as always, respect the landowner and his property. (Portions on public land are the bend in the Lower Dugway from 8.5 to 9.3 and the riverbank from 10.8 to 11.2.)

Wilson's warblers (probably migrants) may be found in the willow thickets along the river (at the end of September). Other species that might be seen in late season include mallard, common merganser, blue-winged (or cinnamon) teal, spotted sandpiper, red-tailed hawk, harrier, belted kingfisher, magpie, flicker, sage thrasher, American goldfinch, and white-crowned sparrow. Sage grouse, mourning dove, horned lark, and vesper sparrow occur in the grasslands, along with antelope and mule deer.

The U.S. Geological Survey 1:24000 topographic maps — *Lone Haystack Mountain* and *Sinclair* — are not required, though the latter may be of some value in the portion off the paved road. Maps 30 and 31 in this volume should suffice.

Detailed Trail data are:

Upon reaching the paved Seminoe Road, turn right and follow it south across gently rising grasslands. A jeep trail turns left at 0.6, and one joins from the right as the Trail levels out at 1.0. Elk Mountain is prominent to the southeast, Ferris Mountain and Bradley Peak to the northwest. Cross a cattle guard at 1.6. Dip and then go over a small rise at 2.4. Sagebrush, shadscale, rabbitbrush, Russian thistle, resinweed, bracted vervain, and yellow sweetclover are typical members of the roadside plant community.

A jeep road leads off to the right at 3.6. The Trail continues on paved surface, starting a course that follows the east slope of Lone Haystack Mountain for a couple of miles. An inoperable windmill is 0.3 mile to the left of the Trail, by jeep track, at 3.9. A jeep road to the left at 5.6 leads half a mile or so to another windmill, presumably also not working. After the cattle guard at 7.4, bend right and descend. Do not bother looking for the spring (shown on the topo map) down the road that turns sharply to the left at 7.6.

Reach a steep embankment over the North Platte River at 8.0. The cottonwood clump by the water, through the gate to the left at 8.1, is on posted land. Check the draw at 8.2, where there is likely to be a flow of good creek water. Follow the road through steep-walled canyon.

Come to a scenic campsite at 8.9 as the road makes a big

North Platte River, at the Lower Dugway.

sweep to the left; there is a wide flat area by the river as it narrows to a single 100-foot channel at a gravel bar. The Lower Dugway, as the next stretch is known, is a canyon lined on the right bank with impressively steep stratified cliffs 200 to 300 feet high. Angle slightly away from the river to shortcut another bend. A cable stretches across the stream at the gauging station at 10.2.

Leave the paved road at 10.8 as it curves, to the right, far from the river; take the first dirt road, immediately passing a possible campsite and proceed up the left (west) bank. More dirt roads join from the right at 10.9. Keep straight as side roads lead over to the water. Walk along the edge of the river at 11.2. The road to the left at 11.4 goes to good campsites in a grove of narrowleaf cottonwoods at a ford.

Angle away from the river so as to take the higher route over the low ridge at 11.6. Go through a barbed wire gate on the far

183

side and drop back to the valley. Avoid the side trail that bears left to the river at 11.7. Stick to the river route at the junction in cottonwoods at 12.0 where another jeep road turns sharply back to the right.

The abandoned homestead at 12.3 is a pleasant spot. Beyond it, zigzag beneath utility wires. Take the indistinct left fork at 12.7 by the river's edge, crossing beneath wires again and negotiating two fences before passing a high water channel of the river at 12.8. There's another barbed wire gate at 13.1. Follow the river's edge, passing another dry channel at 13.4 and an island at 13.5. Keep straight in a scrubby area at 14.2 where a road turns right and goes under the wires and, again, when another road joins from the right at 14.4. Use a wooden bridge to cross the discolored and unappealing water of Sugar Creek at 14.6. Bend right, away from the river.

Reaching paved road at 14.9, turn to the right. (To the left it is 0.4 mile to a pumping station, where good drinking water is available; beyond it is a public park, with golf course and dining room.) Stay on the pavement, passing a jeep road from the left at 15.1. From the top of a rise at 16.2, look straight ahead to the refinery in Sinclair; on the left, and somewhat to the rear, is the Snowy Range, including nearby Elk Mountain and 12,000-foot Medicine Bow Peak. Disregard side roads and keep heading for the refinery.

Dip to the refinery's outlet lagoon and curve right at 18.3. (The former road, as shown on the topo map, goes straight; it is now barricaded.) Bend left at 19.2, pass black oil sumps, and come to the Seminoe Road (Carbon County route 351) at a power substation at 19.7. Follow the road toward the far end of the refinery, bearing left on a secondary street at 20.1. Bear left again at the next intersection and walk along the fence on the refinery's west edge. Follow tree-lined Sixth Street south, past private homes, to Lincoln Avenue at 20.6, where the Section ends. The center of Sinclair is the town square one block to the left.

Distances and elevations are:

0.0	Junction	6650
1.0	Junction	6750

2.2	Dip	6650
2.4	Rise	6700
3.6	Junction	6650
5.1		6550
5.6	Junction	6600
7.4	Cattle guard	6500
8.0	North Platte River	6400
8.9	Campsite	6400
10.0	Enter Sinclair Quadrangle	6450
10.8	Junction	6400
11.6	Ridge	6450
12.3	Homestead	6400
13.5	Island	6400
14.6	Sugar Creek	6450
14.9	Paved road	6450
16.2	Rise	6550
18.3	Curve	6550
19.7	Seminoe Road	6600
20.6	Sinclair	6600

EAST RIM SEGMENT
Section 7
Sinclair to Rawlins
Distance 6.9 Miles

The Trail is on paved road, parallel to railroad tracks and interstate highway. Some birdwatching opportunities provide the only attraction.

The route uses the old Lincoln Highway, former U.S. 30, all the way from Sinclair to Rawlins. The lightly-traveled road has been relocated slightly at the I-80 crossings at 0.3 and 4.7, but is otherwise as shown on the topographic maps.

Rawlins, with a population of about 10,000, is readily accessible by train and bus, on AMTRAK and Greyhound and Trailways trunk lines. Also, there are flights to the airport from Denver.

Modest accommodations are available in the center of town at the old Ferris Hotel, a couple of blocks from the post office (ZIP 82301). Other services were found to be quite scattered and rather inconveniently located — laundromats to the west of the city, the Bureau of Land Management (Rawlins District) two miles to the north, and principal outdoors supply store to the east.

There are no recommended campsites in this Section, so find lodging in Sinclair or Rawlins. Good drinking water is unavailable along the road, but beer and pop could be purchased at the gas station at 2.8.

The Section is shown on Map 31. The U.S.G.S. 1:24000 *Sinclair* and *Rawlins* topographic maps are not needed.

Detailed Trail data are:

The streets of Sinclair are shaded by cottonwoods that provide shelter for yellow warblers, house finches, robins, and other birds. The ornate Spanish-style hotel at the plaza in the town center retains some charm, if not its former elegance.

Start the Section one block west of the plaza, at the corner of Lincoln Ave. and 6th Street. Head west on Lincoln Ave. (old U.S. 30) for two blocks. Turn left at the gas station and walk a block on 8th Street. Turn right on Union Avenue and continue parallel to the Union Pacific tracks. Ferris Mountain is still visible far to the north.

The roadside is lined with yellow sweetclover, locoweed, and other pretty flowering plants. Among the birds that may be encountered in the sandy grassland over the next few miles are Say's phoebe, tree swallow, western meadowlark, nighthawk, lark bunting, loggerhead shrike, mourning dove, and Brewer's blackbird. The sloughs in the middle of the Section provide habitat for yellow-headed blackbirds, mallards, pintails, and blue-winged teal; they may also attract killdeer. Ground squirrels are very abundant.

Go through the underpass beneath Interstate 80 at 0.3. Hike on paved road between the tracks and the interstate highway. Cross the concrete culvert over polluted Sugar Creek at 1.5. After a small rise, pass under power lines at 2.0. A gas station is to the right at 2.8. Look for the ducks in the wet spots beyond the tracks at 3.2.

Follow the pavement as it swings right toward I-80. Turn left at the stop sign at 4.5 and pass beneath the I-80 underpass at 4.7. Continue straight toward Rawlins, passing the side road leading to the airport at 5.2. Keep on the main highway at 5.4 where Bypass U.S. 287 turns right. Gibson's, to the left, is a large dry goods store, with a reasonable selection of backpacking foods and outdoor equipment. The Holiday Inn and other motels and restaurants are clustered beyond the intersection. From 5.9, pass gas stations, motels, etc. continuously.

Enter the center of Rawlins at the intersection with 3rd Street (Wyoming Highway 789) at the bus station at 6.7. Walk west on Cedar Street. At 4th Street, it is one block right to the Ferris Hotel, one block left to the railroad depot. The Section ends at the post office at 6.9 (the intersection of Cedar and 6th Streets).

Distances and elevations are:

0.0	Sinclair	6600
0.3	Interstate 80	6600
0.5	Enter Rawlins Quadrangle	6600
1.5	Sugar Creek	6600
2.8	Gas station	6650
4.7	Interstate 80	6700
5.4	Bypass U.S. 287	6700
6.7	Rawlins (bus station)	6750
6.9	Rawlins (post office)	6750

South Buffalo Fork, in the Teton Wilderness.

Background
Information

Pingora Peak, in the Cirque of the Towers.

The Continental Divide Trail

America is gradually developing a network of trails for the use and enjoyment of the public. The charter for this effort is the National Trails System Act of 1968 (P.L. 90-543). A principal aim of this law is the establishment of national scenic trails, which are defined as "extended trails so located as to provide for maximum outdoor recreation potential and for conservation and enjoyment of the nationally significant scenic, historic, natural, or cultural qualities of the areas through which such trails may pass."

Congress determined in 1968 that the existing Appalachian Trail and the Pacific Crest Trail measured up to the standard and designated them as national scenic trails. Both had been laid out as a result of epic volunteer efforts, which in the case of the Appalachian Trail stretched back nearly 50 years.

Congress also recognized the potential of several other routes, with the Continental Divide Trail placed at the top of the list. These routes were to be studied, with the findings then to be submitted for legislative review.

The report on the Continental Divide Trail, completed in 1976, endorsed formal designation. Among the findings were these:

- Spectacular scenery of the quality and magnitude along the proposed CDT route is not available anywhere in the continental United States other than in the North Cascades area along the Pacific Crest Trail or in the Yellowstone-Teton area of Wyoming.
- The areas through which the trail would pass are also rich in the heritage and life of the Rocky Mountains and the southwestern United States.
- The hiker of the proposed route of the CDT would encounter a great variety of terrain, geology, climate, and plant and animal life. This would include the unique and unusual character of Glacier, Yellowstone, and Rocky Mountain National Parks and the back-country solitude of 16 National Forest wilderness and primitive areas, as well as the living quality of the Red Desert in Wyoming.

After hearings, the Continental Divide Trail was officially designated a national scenic trail on November 10, 1978, when the National Parks and Recreation Act of 1978 (P.L. 95-625) was signed into law. The responsibility for proceeding with development is entrusted to the Secretary of Agriculture (the overseer of the Forest Service) with the assistance of an advisory council representing public and private interest groups.

The Trail, as conceived by the authors of the study report, would be a simple facility for the hiker and horseman. There would be no significant alteration of the land or vegetation. Limited vehicle use would be permitted on certain existing primitive roads (primarily in the Great Divide Basin of Wyoming). The Trail would be as close to the Continental Divide as circumstances permit, but as far away as necessary to provide a safe trail which could be environmentally and economically justified and which would possess a general recreation appeal; established trails would be used whenever appropriate. Much of the route described in this series would be excellent for permanent selection, but deviations will and should be considered for many reasons, especially when a different location will enhance the enjoyment of users.

The Environment

Weather

From Yellowstone south through the Bridger Wilderness, the Trail is in the mountains — with cool weather and plenty of moisture. At places, precipitation averages up to about 60 inches a year, mostly as snow (with 300 inches or more not uncommon). Hence, high country in the Wind Rivers doesn't open up until July. Snow can fall at any time, although in summer it will burn off quickly; beyond September, don't count on being able to hike at the higher elevations unless you are prepared for winter conditions. During midsummer, temperatures in the mountains often get down to freezing at night, with daytime highs in the 70's; rains are usually brief showers, but occasionally a drenching downpour can last for hours. Surface water supplies are generally excellent, except on the porous soil in the Old Faithful Segment; during maximum runoff, in June and July, streams can become difficult, or impossible at times, to cross safely.

The climate of the lands around the Great Divide Basin stands in marked contrast to that of the mountains. Precipitation is only 10 inches or so per year, little of it in July or August. In July, the hottest month, expect average daytime highs in the 80's and nighttime lows about 50; May, June, and September should be the most pleasant times for your trip in the Sweetwater River, Green Mountains, and East Rim Segments. Surface waters are scarce. A major factor in choosing the route described here is the availability of water; if you find any of the creeks or springs dry at any time, which you may, please let the Society know of your experience.

The combination of rain and cool temperatures is dangerous. Everyone should thoroughly understand the risks of exposure and know how to avoid hypothermia (lowering of body temperature). Eating carbohydrates will help. But, more important, try at all times of maintain an insulating air layer next to the skin.

192

Set up a tent and get into warm dry clothing and sleeping bag if you find yourself out in wet weather with the shivers. Some hot food and hot drink and you should feel fine again.

Geology

The oldest rocks along the Trail date back two billion years or more. For aeons after their formation they lay buried by younger, now vanished, rocks. Subjected to enormous heat and pressure, they gradually metamorphosed from the primordial mudstone into crystalline gneiss and schist. Sometimes they actually melted and, upon solidification, took the form of granite. From Upper Green River Lake southward, the mountains of the Wind River Range are composed entirely of these ancient rocks.

The sedimentary rocks, which may be thousands of feet deep, are as much as 600,000,000 years old. These are primarily mudstones and sandstones that were deposited in shallow waters. Limestone, formed from marine sediments, occurs less abundantly.

A major upheaval, sometimes called the Laramide Revolution, occurred about 60 to 70 million years ago. What happened was that enormous forces in the earth's crust caused the fracturing and buckling of the surface. The general uplifting during this period resulted in the building of the Rocky Mountains. The turmoil in the crust left the old horizontal layers tilted in every direction, so that even the most ancient rocks were once again exposed. Sometimes the strata were turned on edge or upside down. At Ferris Mountain, for example, vertical limestone flatirons, free of softer adjacent rocks that have eroded away, run conspicuously for miles along the edge of the Great Divide Basin.

Relatively recent volcanic action has also left its mark, especially in the Yellowstone region. Prodigious quantities of lava and ash were spewed out in the eruptions of the Absarokas that began nearly 50,000,000 years ago. Some of this material is found in the northern part of the Teton Wilderness and also in the Togwotee Pass-Lava Mountain area. Much later eruptions — over the last two million years — created the rocks that now cover much of Yellowstone Park itself.

Changes continue to occur. Erosion wears down the mountains and fills in the valleys. Wind, water, and ice — glaciers, some of which persist in shrunken form in the Wind Rivers — all have done their part in sculpting the landscape that we see today. But the most vivid reminder that the earth's crust is dynamic comes at Yellowstone, where every hour Old Faithful testifies to the presence of molten rock only a few thousand feet below.

Birds

The diversity of habitats along the Trail in Wyoming offers the hiker an opportunity to identify birds of many a feather. A complete description in a few pages is impossible, but typical species can be noted briefly. For the most part, the ones described here are mentioned at some point in the text of the trail guide. Refer to one of the standard guides — Robbins' *Birds of North America* or Peterson's *Field Guide to Western Birds* — for more detail. A good checklist is available for Yellowstone National Park.

BIRDS ASSOCIATED WITH LAKES AND PONDS

A first group consists of diving birds. Probably the most common, in the lakes of the northern Rockies, is *Barrow's goldeneye*. It is short-billed, with dark head sharply contrasting with light breast; in the male, there is a white patch in front of the eye. The *common merganser* is similarly marked, but is larger and has a long narrow bill. (In the light-flanked *bufflehead*, found in Yellowstone, the conspicuous white patch is behind the eye; the *ruddy duck* has a large light patch on the lower cheeks, with a dark crown.) The *lesser scaup* is dark (in the male, purple-black) on both head and breast. (Others, less likely to be observed, include the whitewater-loving *harlequin duck*, and the *redhead* and *canvasback* which, in the male, have chestnut head and black breast). The *eared grebe* is a dark, notably small, diver with golden ear patches. The chicken-like *American coot* is nearly entirely black except for its stubby white bill.

Dabbling ducks, which may be difficult to distinguish in their plain summer plumage, are typically found on small ponds. *Mallards* are widespread, the males easy to spot because of their completely green head. The *American wigeon* can be made out, in flight, by the large white patch on the fore edge of the wing. Smaller ducks, with conspicuous pale blue patches on the front of the wing are the closely-related *blue-winged teal* and *cinnamon teal*. The *green-winged teal* has a trailing wing edge of vivid green, but no bright patch on the front upper surface. (Others, such as *pintail* and *gadwall*, are less readily identifiable.)

White-headed gulls in Yellowstone are most likely to be *California gulls*, but there and further south one might also find the very similar *ring-billed gull*, which is distinguishable by the black ring encircling the tip of its bill.

Canada geese, marked with a black neck and white face patch, and stately all-white *trumpeter swans* are the largest of the waterfowl. The swan, which was once almost extinct, now has a small range in and around Yellowstone.

HAWKS

The largest representatives of this order — the completely dark *golden eagle* and the fish-eating *osprey*, with a white belly, fly with wings outstretched (not raised in a V).

Other large hawks, birds that soar almost continuously on upswept wings, include the white-rumped *harrier* (usually seen quartering close to the ground) and the *red-tailed hawk* and *Swainson's hawk*. The typical adults of the latter two species can be distinguished by the rusty tail of the red-tailed and the unusual wing pattern of the Swainson's (undersurface light on front edge, dark on trailing edge).

The *American kestrel* is about the size of a robin, boldly patterned on the face, and rusty on back and tail.

GROUSE

Coveys of *sage grouse* are found, along with antelope, in the sagebrush country of central Wyoming. They are the largest members of their family, yet are rarely seen until flushed. The large black belly patch is diagnostic.

The *blue grouse* and *ruffed grouse* occur in the mountains, the latter in more densely forested situations. Look at the tail. The blue's is black, with gray tip; the ruffed's is brown, with broad black stripe at the tip.

OTHER BIRDS OF OPEN COUNTRY

The highest elevations are reserved for the dark sparrow-like *black rosy finch*.

A conspicuous open-country bird found in the mountains around timberline is *Clark's nutcracker*, a noisy member of the crow family. It is mostly gray, with a contrasting black and white pattern on wings and tail. The black *common raven* (crowlike, but with a harsh croak instead of a caw) may also be found quite high.

Extensive grasslands are home for the *horned lark*. It resembles a sparrow, but can be told by a black band across the breast as well as a complex facial pattern. Above treeline, the same habitat may be used by the *water pipit*, which one can repeatedly flush without ever seeing very well. It is also sparrow-like except for its thin bill; it bobs its tail, which is edged with white feathers.

The *vesper sparrow*, like the pipit, has a streaked breast and white outer tail feathers; it occurs at somewhat lower elevations, not at the pipit's alpine heights. The plain-breasted *white-crowned sparrow*, boldly marked with black and white stripes on the head, is the most readily identified member of its family. The sparrow-like *American goldfinch*, small and with a stout bill, is bright yellow on breast and back.

Swallows are gracefully acrobatic flyers, ordinarily observed in fast flight over water. The ones likely to be seen most often are iridescently green or dark blue on the back. The *violet-green swallow*, which is definitely green above, is very similar to the *tree swallow* (which is generally at lower elevations); the *barn swallow*, with its long forked tail, and the rusty-rumped *cliff swallow* can be expected in the valleys, especially near bridges. Entirely unrelated to swallows, but also distinctive for its erratic flight, is the *common nighthawk;* it is a larger, brown bird with slender pointed wings.

Shorebirds breeding in open lands along the Trail in Wyoming include the noisy *killdeer,* immediately recognizable by its two black necklaces. The needle-like bill of the small, approachable *Wilson's phalarope* will help to identify this puddle-loving species. The stockier, short-legged *common snipe* with a long stout bill, may be flushed unexpectedly from wet grasslands.

Also associated with wet places, especially marshes, are the well-named *yellow-headed blackbird* and the *redwing,* a blackbird with red epaulets. (Brewer's blackbird, which is entirely purplish-black, occurs in dryer locations, especially near roads and towns.)

The largest of the open country birds is the gray *sandhill crane,* which is most likely to be seen in rich meadows in Yellowstone. (The *great blue heron,* also tall, occurs in swamps and marshes.)

The *mountain bluebird,* blue on breast as well as back, breeds in extensive grasslands, including the mountains. (The *pinyon jay* is similarly marked, but larger, and would only be found where junipers are available for nesting.)

The remaining members of this group are restricted to middle and lower elevations, commonly where sagebrush predominates. There is no mistaking the showy *black-billed magpie,* black and white with an exceptionally long tail. It is related to the *common crow,* but occurs only at lower elevations. The *western meadowlark* has a golden breast with a dark chevron, and its short tail is edged with white. It is fairly widespread, as is the sparrow-sized *rock wren,* a slender-billed species found on rocky slopes. A few specialties — probably restricted to central and southern Wyoming portions of the Trail — are *loggerhead shrike* (gray and white, with black wings and tail); *sage thrasher* (perched in sagebrush in an upright posture, brown with heavily-streaked breast); *green-tailed towhee* (a ground-feeding green bird, with white throat, found where there is shrubby cover — similar to the dark-backed *rufous-sided towhee,* which prefers denser undergrowth); *Say's phoebe* (a black-tailed dusky flycatcher suffused with rust in the belly, often near buildings); and *lark bunting* (a sparrow-like bird, the male black with white wing patches).

The *common flicker, mourning dove,* and *western kingbird,* discussed below, might also have been treated as birds of open country.

BIRDS OF THE FOREST

Birds that may readily be observed along mountain streams include the *spotted sandpiper,* the *dipper (water ouzel),* and *belted kingfisher.* The sandpiper's constant bobbing motion and conspicuous brown spots on its white breast distinguish it. The chunky all-gray dipper, which also bobs up and down, dives into cascades and rapids to feed off the streambed. The kingfisher, larger than a robin, is blue-backed with a white breast; its loud rattling call is distinctive.

The woodpeckers and sapsuckers are recognizable as a group, but species identification can be difficult. The largest, and most evident, representative, the *common flicker,* is often found on the ground. Basically brown, its hallmark is the showy white rump that flashes in flight. Robin-sized brown woodpeckers are the very similar female *Williamson's sapsucker* and *yellow-bellied sapsucker.* The male sapsuckers also resemble one another closely, being predominantly black and white with a complex facial pattern and conspicuous white wing patch; Williamson's has a black breast, the yellow-bellied a white breast with narrow black necklace. The *hairy woodpecker* and *northern three-toed woodpecker* are about the size of the sapsuckers, also black and white, but their wings are solid black or merely speckled with white. The hairy has a pure white stripe down the back, the three-toed a barred back.

Jays are conspicuous because of their size and bold behavior. These include the *Steller's jay* (blue, with black crest) and the *gray jay,* or camprobber, which is gray, with black on the nape. The gray jay lacks the black and white tail markings of Clark's nutcracker, which prefers more open country.

Flycatchers, typically, are olive-colored birds that perch in a vertical posture, occasionally venturing off to dart after an insect. The *western wood pewee* and *olive-sided flycatcher,* which are probably the most common, lack conspicuous field marks. The pewee has a descending burry call; the olive-sided's call is three pips, its song a loud whistle descending on the last of the three notes. The breast of the olive-sided displays a narrow white line between the dusky sides. The slightly larger *western kingbird,* almost robin-sized, occurs in areas of scattered trees, especially near streams; the black tail, with the outer feathers white, distinguish it.

Grosbeaks and finches are characterized by their short, stubby seed-cracking bills. Grosbeaks are almost as large as robins. The male *black-headed grosbeak,* except for the short

197

bill and white patches in its wings, is reminiscent of the robin. The male *evening grosbeak* is bright yellow, with black tail and wings, with large white wing patches. By far the most common is the *pine grosbeak*, the male red above. (The females of these species are less showy, yet readily recognizable as grosbeaks by their size and bill shape). Smaller birds that could be mistaken for the male pine grosbeak are the male *Cassin's finch* and the male *red crossbill* (with offset curved mandibles and solid black wings). The male *house finch*, also largely red, occurs around human settlements, not in mountain forests.

The most abundant of the smaller stout-billed birds is the unstreaked *dark-eyed junco*, easily spotted by its conspicuous white outer tail feathers. Another common species, which is also plain-breasted, is the *chipping sparrow;* its bright rusty crown is a distinctive field mark. Forest birds of this group with streaked breasts are most likely to be *pine siskins* (which display characteristic flashes of yellow in wings and tail and are generally observed in flocks).

A few remaining species may be divided by size, arbitrarily, into two groups — the larger ones about the size of a robin, the smaller ones chickadee-sized. The *American robin* itself, an abundant thrush, needs no description; its close relative, the *hermit thrush*, is a shy resident of deep forest, positively identified only by its reddish tail and spotted breast. The *mourning dove* is a drab brown bird, with a long pointed tail fringed with white. The *western tanager* is yellow and black, the male immediately recognizable by its bright red head.

The characteristic small thin-billed forest bird is the blue-backed *mountain chickadee*, with a black cap and throat, and a white stripe over the eye. The *red-breasted nuthatch*, more frequently heard than seen, is similar except that it has a white throat (and rusty belly). The *brown creeper*, which spirals up tree trunks in search of insects, belongs in this group; its unusual climbing habits and brown color are distinctive. The warblers are also small and thin-billed, but have at least a bit of yellow coloration. In the *yellow-rumped warbler*, the yellow is restricted to spots, including the rump and throat. Of the predominantly yellow species found in thickets, *MacGillivray's warbler* can be made out by its gray head and throat and the male *Wilson's warbler* can be identified by its tidy black cap. The female Wilson's, of the mountains, is quite similar to the female *yellow warbler*, which is usually found in thickets or deciduous trees at lower elevations. (The male yellow warbler has thin red streaks on breast and belly.)

Mammals

The backpacker observes few of the mammals that live along the Trail. Many are nocturnal, and others have learned to be inconspicuous in the presence of man or natural predators. The following brief description points out the more commonly seen species.

Carnivores. Two bears occur in mountainous portions of the Trail, both in small numbers. The more widespread is the *black bear*, which has a nearly straight facial profile and high rump (as high as the shoulders), and lacks long claws on the front feet. The *grizzly bear*, a larger animal, occurs in the vicinity of Yellowstone National Park. The face has a "dished-in" look, and the humped shoulders are higher than the rump. (Bears, and especially the grizzly, represent a potential hazard to the hiker. To minimize the risks, observe the precautions summarized in free Park Service brochures — for example, carry bells and sleep away from cooksites.)

Coyotes, the most common wild dogs along the Trail, are most likely to be seen (or heard howling at night) in open spaces. (The smaller *red fox* has a white-tipped tail.)

The *badger*, a member of the weasel family, is distinguished by the white stripe extending down the front of its face. Its habitat is open sagebrush country.

Ungulates. *Wild horses* roam in the Great Divide Basin, but are not common along the Trail.

Pronghorn (antelope) are abundant on the plains, especially around Green and Ferris Mountains. The white rump and dark bands on the throat distinguish it from the *mule deer* (which has a rope-like black-tipped tail and bounding gait) and the less common *white-tailed deer* (bushier tail lacking a black tip, with a gait more like a horse's gallop).

The two large members of the deer family are *moose* (dark brown or blackish, in moist places from Yellowstone south to Sweetwater Canyon) and *elk*. The latter is dark on the neck, lighter on the body, with a conspicuous light rump patch. During summer, elk are found in semi-open forest and mountain meadows.

Bison occur in small numbers in Yellowstone Park, notably in the Hayden Valley between the Grand Canyon and Yellowstone Lake. The summer range of *mountain sheep*, which are not often observed, is mostly high grassland, generally above timberline in the more rugged mountain areas.

Rodents. The presence of *beaver* is revealed more frequently by the dams and lodges it has constructed than by direct observation. It is likely to be confused, if at all, with *muskrat*, which is another aquatic lodge-building rodent. The muskrat is much the smaller species, its length (excluding tail) only about 12 inches; its tail is narrow and flattened vertically.

The *yellow-bellied marmot* is by far the largest reperesentative of the squirrel family. It is readily seen near its burrows in rocky areas. The slender *red squirrel* lives in dense coniferous forests; its noisy scolding chatter is often the first sign of its presence. *Chipmunks*, most often observed near forest edges or openings, are small rodents with stripes along the side that extend through the face. (Some of the ground squirrels also have stripes, but not on the face.) *Richardson's ground squirrel* is an abundant resident of sagebrush country; it has neither stripes nor spots and resembles its larger cousin, the extremely colonial, mound-building, *black-tailed prairie dog*.

Porcupines, unmistakable because of their quills, may occasionally be seen in forests along the Trail.

Hares and rabbits. The largest member of this family, the *white-tailed jackrabbit*, may be found in open country throughout the state. Its long ears, up to 6 inches, are a good field mark. When surprised, it speeds off in flight. (*Cottontails* are much smaller, with shorter ears, and tend to hide when surprised.) The *pika*, a tailless rabbit with short round ears, is seen exclusively at the rockslides which shelter its nests; it is superficially quite similar to a rodent in appearance.

Fish and Game

The trout fisherman will find plenty of opportunity along the Trail, at least as far south as the Sweetwater River. A Wyoming fishing license is required, except in Yellowstone National Park. For current fees, and a free Wyoming Fishing Guide, contact the Wyoming Game and Fish Department, Communications Branch, Cheyenne, Wyoming 82002. A short-term fishing license, available at reduced charge, allows the holder to fish most of the waters of the state — but some spots along the Trail may be closed to this class of permittee. Open season varies by area, but from Memorial Day through October few restrictions can be expected. Limits should be more than sufficient for a hiker's needs.

A non-fee fishing permit is required for fishing in Yellowstone National Park. A few places are closed, or posted with catch-and-release requirements, but backcountry sites are open to fly fishing. Daily limits are relatively low (typically two trout). Permits are issued at ranger stations throughout the Park.

Hunting is prohibited in Yellowstone Park. Under Wyoming laws, which apply elsewhere along the Trail, coyotes, porcupines, and jackrabbits may be taken without license throughout the year. The principal season for game animals extends from September to December, with wide variations for species and area; black bear are also hunted in the spring. Opening dates for sage grouse are in late August, with other bird seasons following in the fall. A hiker is most likely to run into hunters in the antelope country around the Great Divide Basin, where seasons begin in the latter part of September or October.

Wildflowers

Perhaps it would be best to skip wildflowers altogether — there are just too many of them. Some are showy, others shy; there are giants and there are dwarfs; we have flowers that blanket meadows and flowers that sparkle on gray summits. We can enjoy them all, with or without names; and, after all, "a rose by any other name would smell as sweet."

But one of the joys of travel is getting to know the land and learning how the pieces fit together. To do this we need labels. The following key therefore aims to provide many of the labels that a hiker may want, particularly in midsummer.

Although the key is selective, most flowers seen along the Trail in July or August should be identifiable at least as to genus. (This is especially so in the mountains, above 8000 feet elevation.) With few exceptions, shrubs and aquatic plants are excluded.

Several factors account for the species identified in the margin — their abundance, mention by name in the text, the presence of critical characteristics needed for distinguishing members of the genus, or ease of positive identification. Descriptions, particularly in the case of species, are sometimes deliberately narrowed so as to prevent misidentification with similar unlisted plants.

The key sticks as much as possible to obvious flower and leaf characteristics. A glossary at the end of the key defines some essential terms. Scientific names and classification are taken from C.L. Hitchcock and A. Cronquist, *Flora of the Pacific Northwest* (1973), except for the exceptional species not included, for geographic reasons, in that text. Several other references were also consulted, and they are the source of many of the vernacular names.

Flower families are included in the key, using the following abbreviations:

Ast	Aster (Composite)	Lly	Lily
Blz	Blazingstar (Loasa)	Mad	Madder (Bedstraw)
Bor	Borage (Forget-me-not)	Mal	Mallow
But	Buttercup	Min	Mint
Dog	Dogbane	Orc	Orchid
E-P	Evening-primrose	Par	Parsley (Carrot)
Fig	Figwort	Pea	Pea (Bean)
Flx	Flax	Phx	Phlox
Gen	Gentian	Pnk	Pink
Ger	Geranium	Prm	Primrose
Hbl	Harebell (Bluebell)	Pur	Purslane (Portulaca)
Hea	Heath (Shinleaf)	Ros	Rose
Hon	Honeysuckle	San	Sandalwood
Irs	Iris	Sax	Saxifrage

201

Stc	Stonecrop (Live-forever)	Vio	Violet
Stj	St. Johnswort	Vvn	Vervain
Val	Valerian	Wat	Waterleaf

I. **Monocotyledons** (flower parts in 3's or 6's, not 4-parted or 5-parted; leaves simple and entire, with veins parallel rather than branched).
  - A. Flowers radially symmetric.
    1. Flowers blue, one or few, not tightly clustered. **(Irs)**
       a. Flower showy, an iris. *Iris.*
       b. 3 petals and 3 sepals indistinguishable, yellow at base; leaves grasslike, only ¼" wide. *Sisyrinchium.* (BLUE-EYED GRASS)
    2. Flowers not as above. **(Lly)**
       a. 3 whitish petals, blotched or hairy near base, and 3 green sepals; leaves long and narrow. *Calochortus.*
       b. 3 petals and 3 sepals indistinguishable in shape and color.
          (1) Flowers axillary, one per stalk, bell-shaped, *Streptopus.*
          (2) Flowers terminal.
              (a) Flowers solitary or few.
                  (i) Flowers showy, yellow, on leafless stalk; broad basal leaves. *Erythronium.*
                  (ii) Flowers white , leaves linear. *Lloydia.*
              (b) Flowers, not individually showy, in clusters of 5 or more (usually many more).
                  (i) Flowers in head or umbel, typically bluish or reddish; petals and sepals distinct, not partially fused. *Allium.*
                  (ii) Flowers, in raceme or panicle, white, cream or green.
                      - Tall plants (over 3').
                        * Narrow leaves (less than 1" wide); flowers cream-colored. *Xerophyllum.*

Iris missouriensis. ROCKY MOUNTAIN FLAG.
Calochortus gunnisonii. GUNNISON'S MARIPOSA. Base of petal marked with transverse hairy gland and thin purple band just beyond it, these forming concentric rings; outer rim of petal rounded, lacking a small pointed tip.
Streptopus amplexifolius. CLASPING-LEAVED TWISTEDSTALK. Sharply-bent flower stalks.
Erythronium grandiflorum. GLACIER LILY.
Lloydia serotina. ALPLILY. At high, rocky places.
Allium cernuum. NODDING ONION. Flowers long-stalked, in an umbel that bends downward.
Allium schoenoprasum. CHIVES. Flowers bluish, in compact head; leaves round and hollow.
Xerophyllum tenax. BEARGRASS.

            * Broad leaves; flowers in panicle.
              Veratrum.
       - Lower plants (to 3').
            * Many broad leaves on stem,
              petals white. *Smilacina.*
            * Principal leaves at base of plant;
              flowers saucer-shaped.
              † Petals and sepals marked with
                conspicuous spot near the
                base. *Zigadenus.*
              † Petals and sepals unmarked.
                Tolfieldia.

B. Flowers bilaterally symmetric. (Orc)
  1. Plants with green leaves.
    a. Lower petal a spurred pouch, not spotted; plants
      slender, usually over 1', with numerous white or
      green flowers not arranged in spiral ranks.
      Habeneria.
    b. Lower petal lacking spur; typically 1' or less.
      (1) Numerous whitish flowers arranged in spiral;
         leaves lance-shaped, alternate. *Spiranthes.*
      (2) Flowers greenish or yellow; a pair of broad
         leaves midway on stem. *Listera.*
         (TWAYBLADE)
  2. Plants lacking green color, with reddish spots or stripes
    on the lip. *Corallorhiza.* (CORALROOT)
II. Dicotyledons (plants various, but not as above).
A. Aster Family. Flowers densely clustered in heads, in the
  manner of daisies, dandelions, and thistles, usually with
  green involucre (small leaf-like bracts surrounding the base
  of the head). (Ast)
  1. Plants with evident rayflowers (flattened corolla parts,
    as in daisies and dandelions).
    a. Daisy-like flowers (with a ring of rays encircling a
      center of tubular flowers).
      (1) Rays yellow or orange.
         (a) All leaves (or at least the lowest ones on
            stem) opposite, none lobed or divided.

Veratrum californicum. CALIFORNIA FALSE-HELLEBORE. Flowers
    white, panicle branches spreading or ascending (not drooping).
Smilacina racemosa. FALSE SOLOMONSEAL. Flowers very numerous,
    in a panicle.
Zigadenus elegans. MOUNTAIN DEATHCAMAS. Petals and sepals nearly
    ½" long; flowers well-separated, not compactly clustered.
Tolfieldia glutinosa. FALSE ASPHODEL.
Habenaria dilatata. WHITE BOG-ORCHID. Flowers white, not at all
    greenish; leaves narrow, with several on lower part of stem, not
    just at base.
Spiranthes romanzoffiana. HOODED LADIES-TRESSES.

      (i)   Rays 1" or more, bright yellow; upper leaves sometimes alternate; leaves often rough to the touch. *Helianthus, Helianthella.* (SUNFLOWER)

      (ii)   Rays ½"-1"; all leaves opposite; stems to 3'; generally, in moist woods or meadows, or alpine. *Arnica.*

(b)   Stem leaves, if present, all alternate; otherwise, leaves all basal.

      (i)   Heads large, one or few per stem.

        -   Rays 3-lobed at tip.

           * Leaves divided into narrow segments; alpine. *Hymenoxys.*

           * Leaves variable, but not as above. *Gaillardia.*

        -   Rays rounded at tip. *Balsamorhiza.*

      (ii)   Heads smaller, less than 2" across.

        -   Heads very numerous; rays short (¼" or less), 7 or more per head; plant not shrubby. *Solidago.*

        -   Heads fewer, rays medium (¼"-1").

           * Involucre very sticky, with bracts curving outward. *Grindelia.*

           * Involucre not sticky; bracts not curved backward.

              † Bracts in one ring, all of equal length (sometimes with a few much smaller ones near the stem); rays fewer than 20. *Senecio.*

Arnica cordifolia. HEARTLEAF ARNICA. Stem 8"-24", with 2-4 pairs of leaves on stem; also basal leaves, which are always strongly lobed (heart-shaped) at the base of the blade.

Arnica fulgens. ORANGE ARNICA. Stem 8"-24", with 2-6 pairs of leaves on stem, the lower ones woolly in the axils; basal leaves larger, lance-shaped; one head per stem; montane open places.

Hymenoxys grandiflora. OLD-MAN-OF-THE-MOUNTAIN.

Gaillardia aristata. BLANKETFLOWER. Rays often purplish at base.

Balsamorhiza sagittata. ARROWLEAF BALSAMROOT. Leaves arrow-shaped, basal, very large; flowers in early summer.

Solidago canadensis. MEADOW GOLDENROD. Stems tall, often over 30", the upper half downy; leaves lance-shaped, toothed, gradually becoming smaller higher on stem; flowers in pyramid-shaped panicle, with heads in a rank on panicle branches; montane.

Grindelia squarrosa. CURLYCUP GUMWEED or RESINWEED.

Senecio canus. WOOLLY GROUNDSEL. Plant densely woolly; stem 4"-12"; entire or tooothed stem leaves few and markedly smaller than the long-stalked basal leaves; heads several, not nodding.

Senecio crassulus. THICKLEAF GROUNDSEL. Stem leaves lance-shaped, margins neither lobed nor sharp-toothed, upper ones (some over 3" long and clasping) nearly as large as lower ones; stem 8"-24".

Senecio triangularis. ARROWLEAF GROUNDSEL. Stem 2'-5'; stem leaves, especially lower ones, coarsely toothed (not lobed) and triangular (not tapering gradually to base), often over 2" wide.

       † Bracts of involucre overlap-
ping like shingles.
- + Plants hairy, not shrubby
or mat-forming; leaves no
more than 2" long.
Chrysopsis.
(GOLDASTER)
- + Plants sometimes shrubby
or mat-forming; leaves gen-
erally long and narrow.
Haplopappus.
(GOLDENWEED)

(2) Rays white, blue, purple, or pink; leaves various,
but not spiny-tipped.
- (a) Leaves fernlike; heads numerous and small,
each with 3-5 very short rays. *Achillea.*
- (b) Leaves not deeply lobed or divided (except
in some daisies of high elevations).
- (i) Bracts of involucre overlapping like
shingles.
- - Plants to 12"; leaves entire, often
all at base; base of individual flowers
with rigid bristles. *Townsendia.*
- - Plants often taller; leafy stems;
leaves entire or toothed; base of individual flowers with long hairs;
fewer than 40 rays. *Aster.*
- (ii) Bracts of involucre about equal in
length; heads solitary or few; rays
usually over 40. *Erigeron.*

Achillea millefolium. COMMON YARROW. Abundant.

Aster conspicuus. SHOWY ASTER. 12-35 purplish, ½", rays; leaves
sharply toothed, broad, some 4" or longer; stem over 12"; heads
in a loose flat-topped cluster at top of stem; involucre somewhat
greasy.

Aster engelmannii. ENGELMANN ASTER. Rays white, 8-13, to 1" long;
stem 2'-5'; leaves lance-shaped, 2"-4" long.

Aster foliaceus. LEAFY ASTER. Highly variable. Typically, 1'-3' tall;
rays purplish, ½", 15-35; heads relatively few and large; involucre
not at all greasy; bracts more nearly equal than in other asters; stem
leaves broadly lance-shaped or elliptic (some 5" or longer), entire,
not hairy on flat surfaces.

Erigeron compositus. CUTLEAF DAISY. Leaves divided, near their tips,
into 3 narrow lobes (which may again be divided into 3 narrow
lobes). In the similar *E. pinnatisectus,* the leaves have more than 3
primary divisions.

Erigeron peregrinus. SUBALPINE DAISY. Aster-like, with 30-80 bluish
and broad (1/8" wide) rays, but with bracts of about equal length;
heads 1-3 per stem.

Erigeron simplex. ALPINE DAISY. Stem to 8", bearing a solitary head;
involucre covered with white wool; 50-125 bluish rays, less than ½"
long; base of stem green, not purple.

b. Dandelion-like flowers (the head consisting of flat rays only, not encircling a disk; stems with milky juice).
   (1) Flowers yellow or orange, head solitary, leaves all strictly basal.
       (a) Leaves divided or strongly lobed pinnately (less so in alpine species). *Taraxacum.*
       (b) Leaves long and slender, entire or with a few distant teeth or very shallow lobes (yellow-flowered species not alpine).
           (i) Flowers yellow; bracts of involucre conspicuously black-dotted. *Microseris.*
           (ii) Flowers yellow or orange (but if yellow, bracts green). *Agoseris.*
   (2) Flowers yellow or white; stem leaves or multiple heads, or both, present; leaves various, but not prickly-edged.
       (a) Plants with grasslike leaves sheathing the lower stem; bracts of involucre sharp-pointed, longer than rays; flowers yellow. *Tragopogon.* (SALSIFY)
       (b) Leaves broadly lance-shaped or ovate in outline, though sometimes cleft into very narrow linear segments; montane and above.
           (i) Rays white or yellow; slender stems, 4"-48"; leaves entire or with small teeth. *Hieracium.*
           (ii) Rays yellow; plants, if over 4" tall, with leaves having large teeth or deep incisions. *Crepis.* (HAWKSBEARD)
2. Thistles, pussytoes, and others lacking flat rays.
   a. Head black, like the disk of a black-eyed susan, but much elongated. *Rudbeckia.*
   b. Heads other than as above.

Taraxacum officinale. COMMON DANDELION. Plant robust; outer bracts widely spreading or bent back; the end-lobe of the leaf larger then inner segments.
Microseris nigrescens. BLACK-HAIRY MICROSERIS.
Agoseris aurantiaca. ORANGE FALSE-DANDELION. Flowers orange.
Agoseris glauca. PALE FALSE-DANDELION. Flowers yellow.
Hieracium albiflorum. WHITE HAWKWEED. Rays white, stem 12"-30".
Hieracium gracile. SLENDER HAWKWEED. Rays yellow; stem 4"-12"; leaves hairless, or nearly so, to 4" long.
Rudbeckia occidentalis. RAYLESS CONEFLOWER or BLACKHEAD. 1½'-6'; leaves ovate, up to 10" long.

(1) Thistles. Leaf margins, and bracts of involucre, spiny-tipped; flowers white or purplish; leaf bases not forming wings on stem. *Cirsium.*
(2) Bracts and leaves not spiny.
  (a) Leaves divided pinnately into narrow lobes. *Chaenactis.* (FALSE-YARROW)
  (b) Leaves entire; heads small, numerous, compactly clustered; involucral bracts chaffy, not green.
    (i) Plant with a tuft of leaves at base of stem. *Antennaria.*
    (ii) Plant with well-developed (3"-5") stem leaves, but no tuft at base; leaves white-hairy below, green above; involucre not sticky. *Anaphalis.*

B. Other Dicotyledons.
  1. Flowers radially symmetric, with sepals and/or petals.
    a. Flowers with sepals that are generally showy (petal-like), but no true petals.
      (1) Individual flowers small, clustered; leaves entire.
        (a) Stem, 1' or less, with many alternate leaves; flower cluster compact, not elongated. *Comandra.* (San)
        (b) Stem with few leaves, or none at all. (Bkw)
          (i) Flowers yellow or white, in umbels or heads. *Eriogonum.*
          (ii) Flowers in raceme or panicle.
            - Leaves kidney-shaped, plant 6"-12"; flowers green or reddish. *Oxyria.*

Cirsium flodmanii. FLODMAN'S THISTLE. Corollas purple; involucre no taller than 1"; lower leaf surface matted with woolly hair; heads on definite stalks; moist places.

Cirsium scariosum. ELK THISTLE. Corollas pale, usually whitish; stemless, or with stem to 40"; heads tightly congested; bracts of involucre only sparingly hairy.

Cirsium undulatum. WAVYLEAF THISTLE. Like *C.flodmanii,* except involucre is about 1½" tall and this occurs in dry habitats.

(*Salsola kali.* RUSSIAN THISTLE, or TUMBLEWEED, is an intricately branched, spiny weed that is not related to the true thistles.)

Antennaria microphylla. ROSY PUSSYTOES. Individual heads less than ¼" long, the chaffy bracts (including their tips) white or pink; stem 2"-16"; basal leaves, woolly above and below, less than 1" long; leafy surface runners between stems.

Anaphalis margaritacea. COMMON PEARLY-EVERLASTING. 1'-2' tall.

Comandra umbellata. BASTARD TOADFLAX. 5 sepals and 5 stamens; often with sagebrush.

Eriogonum umbellatum var. *subalpinum.* UMBRELLA PLANT. Flowers cream or pale yellow, in umbels; stem (4"-12"), leafless except for whorl of bracts where umbel rays fork at tip of stem; sepals not at all hairy; flower clusters surrounded by involucres with lobes bent back.

Oxyria digyna. ALPINE MOUNTAIN-SORREL. This is especially conspicuous when the very numerous flowers have been replaced by dry, red, winged seeds.

- Leaves lance-shaped.
  - * Flowers white or pale pink, in raceme. *Polygonum.*
  - * Flowers strongly pigmented, in panicle. *Rumex.*
- (2) Individual flowers larger, solitary or few. (But)
  - (a) Leaves toothed, but not lobed or divided; flower with 5-12 white sepals, usually solitary. *Caltha.*
  - (b) Leaves deeply lobed, or divided, palmately; flowers with 5 (or more) showy sepals.
    - (i) Stem leaf or leaves alternate. *Trollius.*
    - (ii) Stem leaves paired or whorled. *Anemone.*
- b. Flowers with petals as well as sepals (but sepals sometimes scarcely detectable, as in *Galium* and *Valeriana*).
  - (1) Petals separated to the base, not fused.
    - (a) Petals only 4.
      - (i) Petals rounded (or very shallowly notched), no longer than ½"; sepals 4; stamens 6 or fewer. (Mus)
        - Plant aquatic; petals white; leaves pinnately compound. *Rorippa.*
        - Plant terrestrial (key limited to plants of subalpine meadows or streambanks, or alpine).
          - * Seedpods lance-shaped or broader, flattened; leaves entire or toothed (not cleft or compound).
            - † Outer tip of seedpod blunt or notched; flowers white. *Thlaspi.*

Polygonum bistortoides. WESTERN BISTORT. Plant 4"-28"; abundant in high meadows; raceme broad (length less than three times breadth), with flowers densely crowded.

Polygonum viviparum. ALPINE BISTORT. Plant 4"-12"; raceme much more elongated than in western bistort.

Rumex paucifolius. ALPINE DOCK. Plant 8"-20", with simple, unbranched stem; leaves tapered at both ends; in subalpine meadows. (Other docks are mostly taller, more leafy on stem.)

Caltha leptosepala. ELKSLIP MARSHMARIGOLD. Wet places. Leaf blades decidedly longer than broad.

Trollius laxus. GLOBEFLOWER. Wet places.

Anemone parviflora. NORTHERN ANEMONE. Stem to 8", with a single pair of unstalked leaves; basal leaves less than 2" wide; flower solitary, with white sepals.

Rorippa nasturtium-aquaticum. WATERCRESS.

Thlaspi fendleri. MOUNTAIN CANDYTUFT. Stem to 10", with leaves clasping the stem.

   † Seedpods elongated and tapered at tip; flowers white or
   yellow. *Draba* (in part).
  * Seedpods linear.
   † Flowers yellow, petals less
   than ¼"; seedpods flattened
   (sometimes twisted), not 4-
   angled. *Draba* (in part).
   † Flowers white, pink, or purplish.
    + Leaves heart-shaped; stem
    12"-30"; petals white.
    Cardamine.
    + Leaves not heart-shaped.
    -- Seedpod about ½";
    leaves pinnately lobed;
    low cushion-forming
    plant. *Smelowskia.*
    -- Seedpod well over ½";
    leaves entire or toothed,
    not lobed. *Arabis.*
(ii) Petals often notched, sepals 4, stamens
 8. (E-P)
 - Petals about ½" or more, shallowly
 notched, leaves alternate or in basal
 rosette; montane or below.
 Oenothera.

Draba crassifolia. THICKLEAF DRABA. Flowers pale yellow; leaves all
 basal (sometimes 1 on a stem); plant to 8".
Draba lanceolata. LANCELEAF DRABA. Flowers white, petals notched
 at tip; stem 3"-10", with alternate stem leaves.
Cardamine cordifolia. BROOKCRESS.
Smelowskia calycina. ALPINE SMELOWSKIA.
Arabis lemmonii. LEMMON'S ROCKCRESS. Seedpods about horizontal
 or drooping slightly; basal leaves finely hairy, like felt, with rounded
 tip; raceme with up to 10 purplish flowers on one side of stem; alpine.
Oenothera caespitosa. ROCK-ROSE. Petals white or pink, at least 1"
 long; all leaves basal.
Oenothera coronopifolia. CUTLEAF EVENING-PRIMROSE. Petals
 white or pink, about ½" long; stems to 10", bearing stem leaves
 with narrow pinnate lobes.
Oenothera strigosa. COMMON EVENING-PRIMROSE. Petals yellow,
 ½"-1" long; stems 12"-40", with many lance-shaped stem leaves;
 stigma divided into 4 threadlike lobes.

- Petals mostly small and distinctly notched, not yellow; but if rounded, then ½" or more, with reddish flowers in terminal raceme. *Epilobium.*

(b) Petals 5 (petals over 5 under (c) below).
  (i) Individual flowers small, in compound umbels. (Par)
    - Flowers yellow.
      * All leaves simple. *Bupleurum.*
      * All leaves compound (and with leaflets also lobed or divided).
        † Tuft-forming plants of alpine tundra; umbel stalks few (6 or less) and short (½" or less); leaves strictly basal. *Oreoxis.*
        † Plants of sunny places, subalpine or below, not at all tuft-forming; umbel stalks more numerous and longer than preceding; leaves close to ground, though not necessarily strictly basal; no more than one umbel per stem. *Lomatium.*
    - Flowers white, all leaves compound; leafy-stemmed plants mostly above 8000' elevation (lower in *Perideridia).*
      * Leaves divided only once, the leaflets well-defined (lance-shaped or broader).
        † Leaves with 3 large leaflets, lobed but not divided; tall, robust plant. *Heracleum.*

Epilobium alpinum. ALPINE WILLOWHERB. Petals white or pink, about ¼"; leaves opposite, some over ¼" broad (ovate or broadly lance-shaped).

Epilobium angustifolium. FIREWEED. Petals reddish-purple, rounded, about ½"; stem 3'-7', with numerous lance-shaped leaves.

Epilobium latifolium. RED WILLOWHERB or RIVERBEAUTY. Petals similar to fireweed; stem to 20"; subalpine or above, especially on streambanks.

Bupleurum americanum. THOROUGHWAX. Basal leaves linear.

Oreoxis alpina. ALPINE PARSLEY. Stem 7" or less.

Lomatium cous. COUS BISCUITROOT. Leaves smooth, not hairy, the ultimate divisions being very short (under ¼") lobes; stems to 12"; northern Wyoming.

Lomatium dissectum. FERNLEAF LOMATIUM. Leaves much-divided; stems, clustered, 20"-60".

Lomatium triternatum. NINELEAF LOMATIUM. Leaflets divided into relatively few, long and linear, divisions; stems downy, to 20".

Heracleum lanatum. COW PARSNIP. Often much over 3' tall.

† Leaves with 7-9 toothed (but not lobed) leaflets, not over 2" long. *Oxypolis.*

* Leaves not as above; 10 or more umbel stalks.

† Leaves much-divided, fern-like, with a broad sheath clasping the stem; stem 20"-40", lacking leafy branches. *Conioselinum.*

† Leaves not at all fernlike.

+ Leaves divided twice, the divisions relatively large and broad. *Angelica.*

+ Leaves divided once or twice, the ultimate divisions linear. *Perideridia.*

(ii) Flowers not in compound umbels (rarely in simple umbel).

- 10 or fewer stamens; leaves simple.

* Leaves deeply lobed palmately; white or reddish rounded petals, dark-veined , ½"-1"; stamens 10. *Geranium.* (Ger)

* Leaves entire or toothed (or with shallow lobes, similar to leaves of maples or currants).

† Stem leaves crowded, succulent, small and stalkless; flowers densely clustered at top of short (to 15") stem. *Sedum.* (Stc)

Oxypolis fendleri. COWBANE. Subalpine, along streams; stem 20"-40".

Conioselinum scopulorum. HEMLOCK PARSLEY. Plant single-stemmed (not clumped); stem often with only 1 or 2 leaves; ultimate leaf-segments small, but not threadlike.

Angelica arguta. SHARPTOOTH ANGELICA. Plant tall, 2'-5', in wet places of northern Wyoming.

Perideridia gairdneri. GAIRDNER'S YAMPA. Leaf divisions 1"-6" long.

Geranium caespitosum. COMMON WILD GERANIUM. Stems numerous, forming tufts, to 20"; petals pink or rose.

Geranium richardsonii. WHITE GERANIUM. Stems, single or very few, 1'-3' tall; petals white, purple-veined; flowers always in pairs.

Geranium viscosissimum. STICKY PURPLE GERANIUM. Stems single, 1'-3' tall; petals pink or rose, flowers sometimes in 3's or 4's.

Sedum lanceolatum. STONECROP. Flowers yellow; stem leaves may fall before plant blossoms.

Sedum rhodanthum, ROSECROWN. Flowers pink; stamens not longer than petals; moist places at high elevations.

Sedum rosea. KINGSCROWN. Flowers dark rose, with stamens projecting beyond petals; moist or rocky places at high elevations.

   † Stem leaves, if present,
not succulent.
    + Stem leaves present, oppo-
site or whorled.
     – Sepals 5; flowers white
or reddish.
      ** Petals cleft, or with
at least a distinct
notch, at tip. (Pnk)
       †† Sepals fused
for most of
their length;
in mountains.
Lychnis, Silene.
(CAMPION)
       †† Sepals distinct.
*Cerastium,
Stellaria.*
(CHICKWEED)
      ** Petals rounded or
barely notched,
white.
       †† Leaves paired,
linear; low
matted plants
with small
flowers. *Aren-
aria,* (SAND-
WORT), *Sag-
ina.* (PEARL-
WORT). (Pnk)
       †† Leaves whorl-
ed, lance-
shaped or
broader; flow-
ers sometimes
in simple um-
bel. *Chima-
phila.* (Hea)

Silene acaulis. MOSS CAMPION. Flowers pink to purplish; plants with
densely crowded, linear, leaves; in low mats; alpine.
Cerastium arvense. FIELD CHICKWEED. Petals conspicuous, about ½",
projecting well beyond sepals; leaves linear, averaging 1"; montane
and subalpine; styles 5 (styles 3 in *Stellaria*).
Chimaphila umbellata. PIPSISSEWA. Stem to 12", with 4 or more pink
flowers; deep shade.

-- Sepals 2; plants with a single pair of stem leaves. *Claytonia.* (Pur)

+ Leaves on stem alternate, or all leaves basal.

    -- Flowers, solitary or in raceme, drooping, with prominently protruding style; leaves in basal rosette (or some only slightly offset near the ground). *Pyrola.* (Hea)

    ∸ Flowers lacking protruding style.

- - - - - - - - - - - - - - - -

** Flowers blue; leaves linear. *Linum.* (Flx)

** Flower never blue. (Sax)

    †† Flower solitary, on naked stalk, or bearing only one stem leaf. *Parnassia.*

    †† Flowers several to many.

        ++ Petals divided into 3 or more segments.

        --- Petals divided into threadlike segments; leaves basal. *Mitella.*

        --- Petals divided, palmately, into broader segments; plant leafy-stemmed. *Lithophragma.* (FRINGECUP)

Claytonia lanceolata. LANCELEAF SPRINGBEAUTY. Subalpine, about 6" tall.

Claytonia megarhiza. ALPINE SPRINGBEAUTY. Alpine, with prominent basal rosette; stems to 4", the stem leaves only 1" or less.

Pyrola secunda. SIDEBELLS PYROLA. 6-20 white or greenish-white flowers, with straight style, in one-sided raceme; in shade.

Pyrola uniflora. WOODNYMPH. Stem to 6", with solitary white flower.

Linum perenne. WILD BLUE FLAX. In well-drained mountain grasslands.

Parnassia fimbriata. FRINGED GRASS-OF-PARNASSUS. Lower half of the white petals finely fringed; subalpine wet places.

Mitalla pentandra. COMMON MITREWORT; Petals greenish, divided pinnately into about 7-9 segments.

++ Petals rounded.
--- Petals reddish-
purple; 1 or 2
stem leaves.
Telesonix.
--- Petals white to
greenish-yellow;
leaves usually ba-
sal, never leathery.
*** Petals con-
spicuous,
though ¼" or
less; stamens
10. *Saxifraga.*
*** Petals narrow,
inconspicuous;
leaves round,
shallowly lo-
bed and tooth-
ed, all basal;
stamens 5.
Heuchera.
(ALUMROOT)

- -

- More than 10 stamens or leaves
compound or (except as noted)
both.
* Flowers with 5 small sepal-like
bracts alternating with sepals;
leaves compound. (Ros)
† Flowers white; leaves 3-part-
ed; running stems on surface
of the ground. *Fragaria.*
(STRAWBERRY)
† Plants not as above (flowers
usually yellow; basal leaves
usually divided into more
than 3 parts).

Telesonix jamesii. JAMES SAXIFRAGE. Low plant (to 8") of talus and
rock crevices.
Saxifraga arguta. BROOK SAXIFRAGE. Leaves round, large-toothed,
all basal; flowers in open panicle.
Saxifraga bronchialis. SPOTTED SAXIFRAGE. White petals dotted with
purple or yellow; narrow entire leaves on stem as well as at matted
base.
Saxifraga rhomboidea. DIAMONDLEAF SAXIFRAGE. Stem less than
1'; flowers in single congested cluster; leaves basal, to 3", narrowing
to winged stalk.

214

+ Basal leaves pinnate, either
as described for footnoted
species or with the terminal
leaflet clearly larger than
the others; petals yellow
or reddish; no running
stems. *Geum.*

+ Basal leaves generally palmate (but some species, subalpine or below, with pinnate leaves with 5-11
about-equal leaflets or
with running stems);
flowers saucer-shaped, stamens occasionally 10 or
fewer; petals yellow,
cream, or deep red.

   -- Leaflets 3; petals much
shorter than sepals; 5
stamens. *Sibbaldia.*

   -- Leaflets (on basal
leaves) generally 5 or
more; petals about as
long as (or longer than)
sepals; stamens usually
more than 10. *Potentilla.*

* Plants lacking bracts between
sepals.

   † Leaves opposite, simple.
Hypericum. (Stj)

   † Leaves alternate, or all basal.

     + Flowers reddish, leaves
simple (but palmately
lobed). (Mal)

Geum rossii. ALPINE AVENS. Flowers deep yellow, petals about ½",
sepals purple-tinged; stem to 12"; basal leaves with numerous (up
to 33) lobed leaflets; alpine.

Geum triflorum. PRAIRIESMOKE AVENS. Stem 8"-16", bearing about
1-3 nodding vase-shaped blossoms with reddish sepals; basal leaves
with 9-19 leaflets.

Sibbaldia procumbens. CREEPING SIBBALDIA. A mat-forming alpine,
with stems to 4".

Potentilla anserina. SILVERWEED CINQUEFOIL. Basal leaves pinnate,
with 15-29 leaflets; petals yellow; prominent running stems.

Potentilla concinna. EARLY CINQUEFOIL. Similar to *P. diversifolia*,
except that this has leaves shorter, white-woolly beneath; stem 8"
or less.

Potentilla diversifolia. VARILEAF CINQUEFOIL. Basal leaves palmate,
with 5-7 leaflets, greenish above and below (not white-woolly on
undersurface), the central leaflet no longer than 2"; stem 6"-18";
petals deep yellow; montane to alpine.

Potentilla gracilis. NORTHWEST CINQUEFOIL. Basal leaves palmate,
with 7-9 leaflets, sometimes pale or woolly on undersurface, the
central leaflet over 2" long; stem 16"-32"; petals deep yellow.

Hypericum formosum. WESTERN ST. JOHNSWORT. Petals yellow,
about ½", with black dots along edges.

-- Leaves maple-like;
stem 2'-6'; petals pink,
about 1". *Iliamna.*
-- Leaves very deeply
lobed, almost com-
pound; stem under 12".
Sphaeralcea.
+ Flowers yellowish or blue
(white in *Actaea).*
-- Columbines (long-
spurred blossoms and
much-divided leaves).
Aquilegia. (But)
-- Flowers not spurred.
†† Flowers white, in-
conspicuous;
leaves much div-
ided, the final di-
visions ovate (or
lobed) and sharply-
toothed. *Actaea.*
(But)
†† Flowers yellow.
++ Buttercups;
leaves smooth
to touch.
Ranunculus.
(But)

Iliamna rivularis. STREAMBANK GLOBEMALLOW. (MOUNTAIN
HOLLYHOCK)
Sphaeralcea coccinea. SCARLET GLOBEMALLOW.
Aquilegia coerulea. COLORADO COLUMBINE. Sepals blue; spur about
1" or longer.
Aquilegia flavescens. YELLOW COLUMBINE. Sepals yellow; spur
about ½".
Actaea rubra. WESTERN RED BANEBERRY. Showy clusters of toxic
red (sometimes white) berries; in moist woods.
Ranunculus adoneus. SNOW BUTTERCUP. Petals 5, about ½"; basal
leaves divided several times, the final divisions threadlike; alpine
(to 8"), especially near snowbanks.
Ranunculus alismaefolius var. *alismellus.* DWARF PLANTAINLEAF
BUTTERCUP. All leaves entire, not at all hairy, the basal ones ovate
and long-stalked; stem 12" or less.
Ranunculus eschscholtzii. SUBALPINE BUTTERCUP. Petals 5, ¼"-½";
stem 4"-10", not at all hairy; basal leaves deeply cleft into 3 principal parts; subalpine, in meadows and talus.

++ Leaves sand-papery, tooth-ed or pin-nately cleft; plants of lower elevations. *Mentzelia.* (BLAZING-STAR) **(Blz)**

   (c) Petals more than 5.
      (i) Plants keyed above, sometimes with over 5 yellow petals. *Ranunculus, Mentzelia.*
      (ii) Other plants; petals white or pink.
         - Petals white; leaves with rounded teeth; an alpine shrub. *Dryas.* **(Ros)**
         - Petals pink, leaves untoothed. *Lewisia.* **(Pur)**
 (2) Petals fused at least near their base.
   (a) Corolla with 4 lobes (sometimes 3 in *Galium*).
      (i) Flowers white or greenish-white; leaves in whorls along stem.
         - Flowers small, white. *Galium.* **(Mad)**
         - Flowers large, greenish-white, on robust plants. *Frasera.* **(Gen)**
      (ii) Flowers deep blue; corolla tubular or bottle-shaped. *Gentiana* (in part) **(Gen)**
   (b) Corolla with 5 lobes.
      (i) Leafy-stemmed plants with many-flowered clusters.
         - Flowers small, white or pale pink; stem leaves opposite.
            * At least some leaves divided or lobed; calyx inconspicuous. *Valeriana.* **(Val)**

Dryas octopetala. WHITE DRYAD. Flower solitary, on leafless (to 6") stem; petals 8-10.

Lewisia pygmaea. PYGMY BITTERROOT. Stem to 3", with solitary flower; 6-8 petals; sepals 2.

Lewisia rediviva. BITTERROOT. Stem to 3", with solitary flower; 12-18 petals, about 1" long; sepals 5-9.

Galium boreale. NORTHERN BEDSTRAW. Leaves in whorls of 4; flowers, with 4 lobes, extremely numerous; stem erect, 1'-2'.

Frasera speciosa. GREEN GENTIAN. Stem about 3'-5'; corolla lobes to 1" long.

Gentiana detonsa. WESTERN FRINGED GENTIAN. Stem 6"-16"; corolla (one per stem or branch) 1"-1½", with 4 finely fringed lobes.

Valeriana occidentalis. WESTERN VALERIAN. Stem 16"-36"; flowers in compact cluster, not an elongated panicle; corolla saucer-shaped or bell-shaped, only 1/8" long; lateral lobes or leaflets on stem leaves relatively broad (some to ½").

               * Leaves simple, entire; plants with milky juice; corolla bell-shaped. *Apocynum.* (Dog)

        - Flowers purplish or white, with stamens extending out far beyond corolla; leaves alternate, usually pinnately cleft or divided. (Wat)

               * Flowers in globular head. *Hydrophyllum.*

               * Flowers in elongated terminal cluster. *Phacelia.*

  (ii) Plants not as above

        - Leaves (generally simple and entire) opposite or all basal.

               * Leaves all basal. (Prm)

                  † Flowers purplish, with lobes bent far backward toward the stalk. *Dodecatheon.* (SHOOTING STAR)

                  † Flowers with lobes spreading, not bent backward.

                     + Flowers showy, red or purple. *Primula.*

                     + Flowers white, corolla no more than ¼" long. *Androsace.* (ROCKJASMINE)

               * Plants with leaves on stem, at least the lower ones opposite.

                  † Leaves simple, entire or few-toothed.

                     + Flowers pink, nodding, in pairs on short stem. *Linnaea.* (Hon)

Apocynum androsaemifolium. SPREADING DOGBANE. Flowers pinkish, leaves drooping toward ground.

Hydrophyllum capitatum. BALLHEAD WATERLEAF. Leaves rise above the flower clusters; leaflets entire, or lobed only at tip.

Phacelia sericea. SILKY PHACELIA. Stem hairy but not sticky, to 2'; flowers, with deep blue or purple ¼" corolla, in dense terminal raceme; all leaves pinnately lobed or compound.

Primula parryi. PARRY'S PRIMROSE. Leaves, growing nearly vertically, 4"-10" long; handsome flower of subalpine and alpine moist places.

Linnaea borealis. WESTERN TWINFLOWER.

+ Flowers blue, violet, or white.
  -- Leaves lance-shaped, not especially crowded; corolla tube generally broad. *Gentiana* (in part). (Gen)
  -- Plants, mostly densely cushioned, with crowded narrow (generally linear) leaves; narrow corolla tube flared at right angles to showy (about ¼") round lobes. *Phlox.* (Phx)
† Leaves cleft palmately into deep lobes, thus appearing whorled. *Linanthastrum.* (Phx)
- Stem leaves all alternate, simple or compound; corolla (or at least its lobes) bluish or reddish.
  * Leaves pinnately compound or cleft into linear segments. (Phx)
    † Corolla lobes blue; leaves pinnately compound with many (9 or more) distinct leaflets. *Polemonium.*
    † Corolla bright red, with long (often over 1") narrow tube; leaves with threadlike divisions, but not distinct leaflets. *Gilia.*
  * Leaves neither compound nor lobed.
    † Corolla lobes spreading at right angles from yellow-throated corolla tube. (Bor)
      + Stem 1½'-4'; corolla about ¼" diameter (or up to ½" in some species). *Hackelia.* (STICKSEED)

Gentiana affinis. PLEATED GENTIAN. Stem 4"-12", with several large (1" or more) blue flowers in terminal cluster; the upper leaves lance-shaped (at least twice as long as broad).

Phlox pulvinata. TUFTED PHLOX. An alpine cushion-forming plant with white or pale blue flowers; leaves about ¼"-½" long, linear (1/16" wide).

Linanthastrum nuttallii. FRAGRANT GILIA. Aromatic; stem to 12".

Polemonium viscosum. SKY PILOT. A low (less than 12") plant of high elevations, with small leaflets whorled (not merely paired) around the axis of the leaf.

Gilia aggregata. SCARLET GILIA. Common in open woods.

+ Stem 1' or less; plants of high mountains.
    -- Plant erect, in moist places. *Myosotis.*
    -- Plant low, cushion-forming. *Eritrichium.*
† Corolla, or its outer part, in bell shape; undisturbed places in mountains.
    + Outer corolla flaring abruptly from tube; corolla pink at first, then blue. *Mertensia.* (Bor)
    + Entire corolla bell-shaped. *Campanula.* (Hbl)
2. Flowers bilaterally symmetric.
    a. Petals (or some of them) separate to the base.
        (1) Leaves simple, not deeply cleft; petals 5; sepals green. *Viola.* (Vio)
        (2) Leaves compound, or at least deeply cleft.
            (a) Sepals petal-like, petals small; leaves palmately lobed or divided. (But)
                (i) Upper sepal long-spurred, blue or purple; petals 4. *Delphinium.*
                (ii) Upper sepal arched, forming a hood that conceals the petals. *Aconitum.*

Myosotis sylvatica. WOOD FORGET-ME-NOT.

Eritrichium nanum. PALE ALPINE FORGET-ME-NOT. Leaves only about ¼" long, covered with long soft hairs; exposed rocky places above timberline.

Mertensia ciliata. BROADLEAF BLUEBELLS. Stem 1½'-4'; conspicuous along subalpine streams.

Campanula rotundifolia. ROUNDLEAF HAREBELL. Several flowers per stem; leaves on stem narrow, those at base (if present) ovate to round; stem 6" or taller.

Campanula uniflora. ARCTIC HAREBELL. Flower solitary; stem to 5"; rocky places at high elevations.

Viola adunca var. *bellidifolia.* SUBALPINE BLUE VIOLET. Dwarf plant, about 2" tall; petals purplish (not whitish), the side petals hairy; moist subalpine places.

Viola biflora. ALPINE YELLOW VIOLET. Plant leafy-stemmed, 2"-8" tall; flowers, usually 2 to a stem, yellow with dark streaks; leaves round or kidney-shaped (not triangular or ovate); moist subalpine or alpine places.

Viola nuttallii var. *linguaefolia.* TONGUELEAF VIOLET. Flowers yellow (not purplish on back); stem 4"-10"; leaves (sometimes all basal) lance-shaped, entire or nearly so, some over 2" long; subalpine or below, often in some shade.

Delphinium barbeyi. SUBALPINE LARKSPUR. Stem over 20"; sepals dark purple; moist subalpine places.

Delphinium nuttallianum. UPLAND LARKSPUR. Stem less than 20"; upper petal white; lower petals, white or purple, deeply notched.

Aconitum columbianum. MONKSHOOD. Flowers usually bluish-purple, occasionally yellow.

(b) Sepals not petal-like; corolla consisting of prominent upper petal (banner) separated from side petals (wings) and fused lower petals (keel); leaves once-compound (leaflets not cleft or divided). **(Pea)**

    (i) Leaves 3-parted; flowers ¼"or more.
- Flowers in dense heads, not blue; leaflets toothed. *Trifolium.*
- Flowers in racemes of about 10 or more flowers spaced out along the stalk.
  * Flowers white or yellow, about ¼"; leaflets toothed. *Melilotus.*
  * Flowers showy, yellow, ½" or more, leaflets untoothed. *Thermopsis.*

    (ii) Leaves many-parted, flowers in racemes.
- Leaves divided palmately into 7 or more leaflets, flowers bluish. *Lupinus.*
- Leaves pinnately divided.
  * Leaves terminating in tendrils; leaflets 8 or more; flowers purplish. *Vicia.*
  * Leaves lacking tendrils.
    † Keel enlarged and extending beyond other petals. *Hedysarum.*
    † Keel not enlarged.
      + Keel terminating in a sharp point; leaves all or mostly at base of stem. *Oxytropis.* (CRAZYWEED)

Trifolium longipes. LONGSTALK CLOVER. Flowers white (in var. *reflexum*); leaflets, some over 1" long, narrow, pointed at tip, and sharply toothed.

Melilotus officinalis. YELLOW SWEETCLOVER. Flowers yellow; tall roadside weed.

Thermopsis montana. MOUNTAIN GOLDENPEA. Stem 18" or taller; seedpods straight and erect, not spreading out from stem.

Lupinus argenteus. COMMON LUPINE. Stem 12"-28"; leaflets, no longer then 2", smooth (not silky or hairy) on upper surface; plains to subalpine in various forms, but with dark red-purple stems in sagebrush desert.

Vicia americana. AMERICAN VETCH. Raceme consisting of up to 10 (about ¾") flowers.

Hedysarum sulphurescens. YELLOW SWEETVETCH. Flowers yellow-white.

+ Keel not sharp-pointed;
plants usually leafy-
stemmed; leaflets 5 or
more.
-- Leaflets sharp-pointed;
leafy-stemmed tall (12"
-40") plants with num-
erous ½" yellowish-
white flowers in a dense
raceme. *Glycyrrhiza.*
-- Leaflets usually not
sharp-pointed; stems
usually 12" or less.
Astragalus. (LOCO-
WEED, MILKVETCH)

b. Petals fused at least near the base of the corolla.
(1) Leaves opposite, stem square; flowers (not
yellow) compactly clustered at the end of the
stem.
(a) Corolla only slightly irregular, with 5 lobes;
leaves often lobed. *Verbena.* (Vvn)
(b) Corolla evidently bilaterally symmetric;
leaves often toothed, but not lobed. (Min)
(i) Corolla at least 1"; the upper lip of
the lavender corolla long and narrow.
Monarda.
(ii) Corolla about ½".
- Plant robust, 3'-6'; leaves toothed,
broad; stamens 4, clearly extending
out beyond corolla. *Agastache.*
- Stem less than 2'; leaves entire or
obscurely toothed; flowers in dense
raceme completely concealing
naked stem without interruption.
Prunella.
(2) Stem not square. (Fig)
(a) Stamens only 2; stem 16" or less; leaves entire or toothed, but not deeply cleft.

Glycyrrhiza lepidota. WILD LICORICE. Weedy plant of lower elevations.

Astragalus kentrophyta. THISTLE MILKVETCH. Leaflets 5-11, sharp-
pointed, not sharply separated from leaf axis; only 1-3 flowers, only
about ¼", per stalk — in all the foregoing respects uncharacteristic
of this complex genus; flowers purplish; plants typically matted,
with flowers not rising above the mat, montane and above.

Verbena bracteata. BRACTED VERVAIN. Weak-stemmed plants with
purplish flowers, which are much shorter than the leaflike bracts
among them; a weed of lower elevations.

Monarda fistulosa; HORSEMINT.

Agastache urticifolia. NETTLELEAF GIANT-HYSSOP. Flowers light
purplish; leaf undersurfaces green, not white-woolly.

Prunella vulgaris. COMMON SELFHEAL.

    (i)   Corolla barely irregular, small, saucer-shaped, blue-violet; leafy-stemmed plants with at least the lower leaves opposite. *Veronica.*

    (ii) Corolla decidedly irregular (or absent), with conspicuously projecting stamens; flowers in a dense raceme. *Besseya.*

(b) Stamens 4 or 5; corolla strongly irregular or funnel-shaped.

    (i)   At least some alternate stem leaves present; terminal raceme of 8 or more flowers.

- True flowers accompanied by brightly colored bracts; upper lip of corolla much longer than lower lip. *Castilleja.* (INDIAN PAINTBRUSH)

- Flowers lacking reddish or yellowish bracts, upper lip of corolla hooded or beaked.

    * Leaves fernlike (or merely toothed). *Pedicularis.*

    * Leaves entire or with 3 entire lobes. *Orthocarpus.*

Veronica wormskjoldii. ALPINE VERONICA. Flowers crowded in a short terminal raceme; stem long-hairy, erect (not creeping at base).

Besseya alpina. ALPINE KITTENTAILS. Corolla purplish; stem, with a few alternate leaves, 6" or less; alpine.

Besseya wyomingensis. WYOMING KITTENTAILS. Corolla absent, stamens conspicuously purplish.

Castilleja miniata. SCARLET PAINTBRUSH. Flowers and deeply-cleft bracts bright red; stems about 12"-24"; moist and shady places in the mountains.

Castilleja nivea. SNOW PAINTBRUSH. Bracts yellowish; bracts and upper lip of corolla conspicuously woolly or hairy; stem 2"-6"; alpine.

Castilleja rhexifolia. ROSY PAINTBRUSH. Bracts rose-purple, entire or shallowly lobed; stem unbranched, about 6"-12"; subalpine and alpine meadows.

Castilleja sulphurea. SULFUR PAINTBRUSH. Flowers and bracts yellow; stem 12"-20"; meadows and moist slopes in the mountains.

Pedicularis bracteosa var. *paysoniana.* BRACTED LOUSEWORT. Plant 1½'-3'; corolla yellow, less than 1" long, the upper lip not pointed at tip; leaves fernlike, the ones on stem not much smaller than ones at base.

Pedicularis groenlandica. ELEPHANTSHEAD. Beak of reddish corolla curved upward like the trunk of an elephant; wet meadows.

Pedicularis parryi. PARRY'S LOUSEWORT. Plant 12" or less; corolla white or yellow, less than 1" long, the upper lip with a short straight pointed tip; leaves pinnately cleft, but lacking distinct leaflets.

Pedicularis racemosa. PARROTSBEAK. Stem 1'-2', with toothed but otherwise undivided leaves; corolla white, the upper lip arched down in a slender beak.

Orthocarpus luteus. YELLOW OWLCLOVER. Flowers about ½", golden yellow, in leafy-bracted raceme.

BACKGROUND INFORMATION

(ii) All stem leaves opposite.
- Flowers red or yellow, with 4 stamens,borne (usually singly) on long axillary stalks. *Mimulus.*
- Flowers blue or purplish with 5 stamens, one of which is sterile; flowers near end of stem, often in several whorls or all on one side of stem. *Penstemon.*

Mimulus guttatus. YELLOW MONKEY FLOWER. Flowers yellow, the corolla 1" or more and strongly two-lipped; stem about 1'-2', generally bearing 6 or more flowers; montane and subalpine.
Mimulus lewisii. RED MONKEYFLOWER. Flowers red, the corolla about 2"; stem 1'-3'; streamsides in mountains.
Penstemon procerus. SMALL-FLOWERED PENSTEMON. Corolla blue, not hairy on outside, ¼"-½"; stem usually 8"-16"; leaves entire, lance-shaped or broader; open places, typically subalpine meadows.

GLOSSARY

Alpine. Above timberline.
Alternate. Occurring singly, as in the arrangement of leaves on a stem — that is, not in pairs or whorls.
Axil. The angle between a leaf and the stem to which it is attached.
Basal. With reference to leaves, joining the stem at ground level.
Bilaterally symmetric. Symmetric with respect to one axis only. (Compare *radially symmetric.*)
Bract. A structure, usually small and leaflike, where a flower or its stalk is attached to the stem; also, a similar structure forming part of an involucre.
Calyx. A structure enveloping the flower, lying outside the corolla (if present); collectively, the sepals of a flower. (Compare *corolla.*)
Cleft. With deep divisions, but not separated into completely distinct parts.
Compound. Divided into completely distinct parts, as the leaflets of a compound leaf or small umbellate clusters in a compound umbel.
Corolla. In a flower with two floral structures surrounding the reproductive organs, the inner and usually showy structure; collectively, the petals of a flower, especially (in this key) when they are fused.
Entire. Not at all toothed, notched, lobed, or divided.
Head. A dense and compact cluster of flowers, not one that is elongated along a stem.
Involucre. A ring (or rings) of bracts at the base of a head.
Irregular. Bilaterally symmetric.
Keel. The fused lower petals of a flower in the Pea Family.

Lance-shaped. Fairly narrow but broadened at some point, usually tapered at the ends.

Leaflet. One of the divisions of a compound leaf.

Linear. Grasslike or needle-like, not at all broadened.

Montane. In the lower forested zone of the mountains, where lodgepole pines predominate.

Opposite. Paired or whorled, as in the arrangement of leaves on a stem.

Ovate. Egg-shaped, nearly as broad as long.

Palmate. Divided from a common point, like fingers on a hand.

Panicle. An elongated flower cluster, with branches of several flowers each forking off from the axis of the cluster.

Petal. A floral structure, usually colored, part of the corolla.

Pinnate. Divided (like a feather) into lobes, leaflets, or other structures perpendicular to a central axis. (Compare *palmate.*)

Pistil. The female organ at the center of the flower.

Raceme. An elongated flower cluster, with flowers attached singly to the axis of the cluster.

Radially symmetric. Arranged like spokes of a wheel, thus symmetric around any of several axes.

Ray. In the Aster Family, a strap-shaped corolla (for example, the white "petal" of a common daisy.)

Rosette. A ring of basal leaves.

Runner. A prostrate above-ground stem which takes root at several places.

Sepal. A floral structure, usually green, part of the calyx.

Simple. Not compound (though sometimes lobed or cleft).

Solitary. Just one (flower or head) per stem.

Stamens. Long-stalked organs, generally pollen-bearing, surrounding the pistil of a flower.

Stigma. The pollen-receiving organ at the tip of a style.

Style. A stalk-like portion of the pistil; in flowers with several styles and stamens, the styles arise from the very center and are surrounded by stamens.

Subalpine. In the upper forested zone of the mountains, where spruces and firs predominate.

Tendril. A slender, coiling structure extending from the tip of a leaf.

Terminal. At the end of a stem or branch.

Umbel. An umbrella-like flower cluster, with stalks from a common point leading to individual flowers or subclusters.

Trees and Shrubs

The following key should help to identify most of the woody plants along the Trail. A few technical terms, defined in the Wildflowers section, are also used here.

BACKGROUND INFORMATION

Conifers (including juniper): trees, except as indicated.

A. With needles.
    1. Needles in bundles.
        a. 2 needles per bundle. *P. contorta.* LODGEPOLE PINE.
        b. 5 needles per bundle. (The references to these two species in the text are apt to be erroneous.)
            (1) Cones purple, about 3'' long. *P. albicaulis.* WHITEBARK PINE.
            (2) Cones brownish, usually longer than 3''. *P. flexilis.* LIMBER PINE.
    2. Needles attached singly.
        a. Needles flat.
            (1) Bark smooth, grayish; cones disintegrate on tree. *Abies lasiocarpa.* SUBALPINE FIR.
            (2) Bark deeply furrowed; cones commonly on ground, with sharp-pointed bracts between scales. *Pseudotsuga menziesii.* DOUGLAS FIR.
        b. Needles more-or-less square or round.
            (1) Tree. *Picea engelmannii.* ENGELMANN SPRUCE.
            (2) Shrub, with berry-like fruit. *Juniperus communis.* COMMON JUNIPER.
B. With scale-like leaves (berry-like fruit on female plants).
    1. Tree.
        a. Berries blue, usually with 2 seeds. *Juniperus scopulorum.* ROCKY MOUNTAIN JUNIPER.
        b. Berries reddish-brown, usually with 1 seed. *Juniperus osteosperma.* UTAH JUNIPER.
    2. Sprawling shrub. *Juniperus horizontalis.* CREEPING JUNIPER.

Broadleaf Plants

A. Trees and tall shrubs.
    1. Leaves opposite, deeply lobed. *Acer glabrum.* ROCKY MOUNTAIN MAPLE.
    2. Leaves alternate.
        a. Trees about 20' or taller, leaves toothed. *Populus.*
            (1) Bark white. *P. tremuloides.* QUAKING ASPEN.
            (2) Bark in mature trees thick and furrowed; leaves long and very narrow; along streams. *P. angustifolia.* NARROWLEAF COTTONWOOD.
        b. Trees or tall shrubs typically about 10' tall.
            (1) Leaves pinnately compound. *Sorbus scopulina.* WESTERN MOUNTAIN-ASH.
            (2) Leaves simple.
                (a) Branches with stout thorns. *Crataegus.* HAWTHORN.

    (b) Thornless.
        (i) Leaves untoothed, smooth and shiny above; narrowly lance-shaped. *Cercocarpus*. CURLLEAF MOUNTAIN-MAHOGANY.
        (ii) Leaves toothed.
           - Teeth at broad outer end of leaf only. *Amelanchier*. SERVICE-BERRY.
           - Teeth extending to lower half of leaf.
              * Leaves ovate to round, under 2" long; along streams. *Betula occidentalis*. WATER BIRCH.
              * Leaves over 2" long.
                † Leaves double-toothed (prominent teeth with finer teeth); along streams. *Alnus incana*. MOUNTAIN ALDER.
                † Leaves with small, regular teeth; in rich, moist soil; trees growing individually, not in thickets. *Prunus virginiana*. COMMON CHOKECHERRY.

B. Low woody-stemmed shrubs (typically about 5' or less).
    1. Stems with thorns or prickles; leaves alternate.
        a. Leaves compound.
           (1) 5 or more leaflets, arranged pinnately. *Rosa*. ROSE.
           (2) 3 leaflets (on most leaves). *Rubus* (in part). RASPBERRY.
        b. Leaves simple, but deeply lobed (maple-like). *Ribes* (in part). GOOSEBERRY.
    2. Stems lacking thorns or prickles.
        a. Leaves opposite.
           (1) Leaves pinnately compound, with finely-toothed leaflets. *Sambucus*. ELDERBERRY.
           (2) Leaves simple.
               (a) Margins entire (except as noted).
                  (i) Locally abundant in saline ground at lower elevations. *Atriplex canescens*. SHADSCALE.
                  (ii) Plants of mountains, or near streams.
                      - Leaf undersurface silvery, with small brown scales. *Shepherdia candadensis*. CANADA BUFFALOBERRY.
                      - Leaf undersurface lacking brown scales.
                        * Flowers mostly in leaf axils

(margins variable, but not sharply toothed).

† Axillary stalks with two flowers (or red or black berries). *Lonicera.* HONEYSUCKLE.

† Axillary stalks with 1-several flowers (or white berries). *Symphoricarpos.* SNOWBERRY.

* Flowers in terminal clusters.

† Many-stemmed shrub; leaves strongly veined. *Cornus stolonifera.* RED-OSIER DOGWOOD.

† Low evergreen shrub; subalpine wet places. *Kalmia microphylla.* ALPINE LAUREL.

(b) Margins sharply toothed.

(i) Leaves with three lobes (maple-like). *Viburnum edule.* HIGHBUSH CRANBERRY.

(ii) Leaves unlobed.

- Plant low, under 18"; evergreen. *Pachistima myrsinites.* MOUNTAIN LOVER.

- Plant taller, to 6'; leaves pale below. *Jamesia americana.* WAXFLOWER.

b. Leaves alternate.

(1) Leaves compound or palmately lobed (maple-like).

(a) Leaves pinnately compound; typical yellow cinquefoil flowers. *Potentilla fruticosa.* SHRUBBY CINQUEFOIL.

(b) Leaves palmately lobed (maple-like).

(i) Smooth bark; fruit fleshy.

- Leaves broad (usually over 4"). *Rubus parviflorus.* THIMBLEBERRY.

- Leaves smaller (rarely over 3" wide). *Ribes* (in part). CURRANT.

(ii) Peeling bark; fruit dry, not fleshy. *Physocarpus.* NINEBARK.

(2) Leaves simple, not palmately lobed. (6 families) Aster Family. Abundant shrubs of open, usually arid, country of lower and middle elevations.

(i) SAGEBRUSH. *Artemisia.* (Leaves with three rounded teeth at tip in the abundant *A. tridentata.*)

228

    (ii) RABBITBRUSH. *Chrysothamnus.* Leaves linear, entire; also known as false goldenrod because of the numerous heads of bright yellow flowers, but these lack rays; bracts overlapping like shingles.

Heath Family. Flowers with urn-shaped or bell-shaped corolla of fused petals; leaves entire except as noted.

    (i) Leaves crowded, linear; high elevations. *Phyllodoce.* MOUNTAIN-HEATH.

    (ii) Leaves ovate, only ½" long; a low ground cover. *Vaccinium scoparium.* GROUSE WHORTLEBERRY. (Also, several related plants. These include HUCKLEBERRY, WINTERGREEN, KINNIKINNICK, etc., with somewhat larger, entire or toothed, leaves; and in Yellowstone Park, the much taller, 3'-6', RUSTY MENZIESIA.)

Birch Family. Flowers in catkins; twigs warty; leaves small, toothed, almost round. *Betula glandulosa.* BOG BIRCH.

Willow Family. Flowers in catkins; thicket-forming plants, along streams or on mountain slopes; leaves usually long and narrow. *Salix.* WILLOW.

Buckthorn Family. Flowers in axillary clusters; leaves ovate or broader.

    (i) Leaves glossy on upper surface, fragrant; flowers in dense panicle. *Ceanothus velutinus.* MOUNTAIN BALM.

    (ii) Leaves prominently veined; flowers few, petals small or absent. *Rhamnus alnifolia.* ALDER BUCKTHORN.

Rose Family.

    (i) Prostrate shrub, on exposed rocks; dense raceme. *Petrophytum caespitosum.* ROCKY MOUNTAIN ROCKMAT.

    (ii) Erect shrubs; leaves toothed.

       - Leaves with wedge-shaped base, 3-toothed at tip. *Purshia tridentata.* ANTELOPE BRUSH.

       - Leaves relatively broad, teeth not restricted as above.

          * Flowers in axils, not numerous (forming a long feathery fruit). *Cercocarpus montanus.* BIRCH-LEAF MOUNTAIN-MAHOGANY.

BACKGROUND INFORMATION

> * Flowers in dense terminal
> clusters.
> † Pyramid-like panicle. *Holo-
> discus.* OCEANSPRAY.
> † Flat-topped cluster. *Spiraea
> betulifolia.* SHINYLEAF
> SPIREA.

History

EARLY INDIAN SETTLEMENT

Man is a newcomer to the Americas. His migration from Asia, by way of a great ice bridge across the Bering Strait, occurred as recently as the last ice age — between 40,000 and 10,000 years ago. Some of the bands traveled down the west coast, eventually continuing to the farthest tip of South America, while others spread out on the plains and into the forests closer to the Atlantic.

Early settlement began in Wyoming about 10,000 years ago, but it was interrupted by a long dry period. With improving conditions, starting about 2500 B.C., a new population moved in. The people were foragers at first, but gradually evolved a culture and economy based upon the buffalo as a source of food, hide, and many other wants.

Western Wyoming was part of the ancestral lands of the Shoshones, a tribe related to the Aztecs of Mexico, while much of the territory east of the Continental Divide was Crow (Absaroka) country. White colonization had a ripple effect, resulting in a general westward movement of Indian tribes. From Minnesota came the Arapahos, of Algonquian origin, and other Plains tribes. The contact of these groups set the stage for years of warfare and raids, with complex and changing alliances.

EXPLORATION

The interior of the continent remained largely unexplored by white men during the eighteenth century, though the possibilities of fur trading and the discovery of a Northwest Passage had stimulated some tentative probing — notably the Verendrye expeditions between 1728 and 1743. No one approached the Continental Divide in Wyoming during the period, however.

The bulk of Wyoming east of the Divide became part of the United States by virtue of the Louisiana Purchase of 1803. From 1804 to 1806, Lewis and Clark led a successful expedition through the acquired lands, from St. Louis to the Pacific and back, but their route was to the north, never entering Wyoming.

An important consequence of the Lewis and Clark journey was the stimulation of fur trading in the northwest. With the full support of President Jefferson, who wished to secure American claims along the Pacific, John Jacob Astor sent out a party to reconnoiter locations for a string of trading posts across the country. Some trappers were already working the mountains, mostly east of the Continental Divide; but one of their number, John Colter, who had been with Lewis and Clark, discovered and later described the natural marvels of Yellowstone. On more than one occasion, Colter found himself at odds with the Blackfoot Indians, a tribe of warriors from Montana. Indeed, he was captured by them, but after making an escape, without clothes or arms, managed to walk nearly 300 miles barefoot to safety at a fort on the lower Yellowstone River.

Colter's experiences, together with Lewis' encounters with the Blackfeet, persuaded Astor's party, under the leadership of Wilson Price Hunt, to choose a southerly route across the Rockies. The expedition's path took them over Union Pass (in the Gros Ventre Segment of the Trail) in 1811. Although Hunt's half-starved group eventually reached Astoria at the mouth of the Columbia River, the route through Union Pass (which Colter had previously traveled) has never assumed great commercial importance.

The next year a small party from Astoria, under Robert Stuart, returned to the East through South Pass. Almost caught by early snows, they were groping around in the Gros Ventres until they met up with a band of Shoshones who directed them to travel south to get through the mountains. They made the easy crossing of the Continental Divide at South Pass on October 22, 1812 and continued down the Atlantic slope along the Sweetwater River, blazing a way for the 300,000 emigrants who traveled the Oregon Trail between 1840 and 1869.

The trapping era in Wyoming was brief. It began in earnest after Major Andrew Henry returned from the upper Yellowstone in 1822 with two boatloads of beaver pelts. The next few years were profitable ones for the trappers, initially under the leadership of Gen. William Ashley. Tom Fitzpatrick and Jedediah Smith, working for Ashley, rediscovered South Pass — Stuart's report having been forgotten or ignored. Water travel along the Sweetwater and Platte proved to be impractical, but by 1827, when settlement rights for United States citizens in the Northwest were confirmed by treaty, the possibility of wagon travel across the Rocky Mountains had already been demonstrated.

Jackson Hole was one of the places where beaver were particularly sought. (The valley was named for David Jackson, one of Ashley's associates. The Indians of the area were the Sheepeaters, a Shoshone people adept at hunting mountain sheep with bow and arrow, and the Gros Ventres, a band of Arapahos.) Most of the famous mountain men, including the young Jim

Bridger and Kit Carson, trapped in the area.

As active trapping continued for the next decade, wagon travel became more common. One such expedition, led by William Sublette, worked the eastern side of the Wind Rivers in 1829 and another, under Capt. Benjamin Bonneville, visited the western slope of the range in 1832. Trading with the hundreds of trappers and the Indians centered about temporary encampments; not until 1834, when Fort Laramie was built on the North Platte, was there any permanent trading post or garrison.

The mountains were explored thoroughly from the time of Colter onward. One of the notable pioneers was Bonneville, who made a complete circuit of the Wind Rivers in the 1830's. Then in 1842, with Carson as guide, Lt. John Fremont (the Pathfinder) headed an exploring expedition that penetrated the heart of the range. He managed a climb to the summit of one of the major peaks, perhaps Mt. Woodrow Wilson, which he erroneously believed to be the highest mountain in the range, and included a full report of his exploits in a widely-read volume published in 1845.

EMIGRATION

The imaginative writings of Hall J. Kelley, who founded the American Society for Encouraging the Settlement of the Oregon Territory, prompted the Pacific-bound expeditions of Nat Wyeth in 1832 and 1834. Although Wyeth failed to make his anticipated profit carrying trade goods by pack train overland to the trappers, he twice reached the lower Columbia and demonstrated the feasibility of travel on what was to become the Oregon Trail. A large party, using wagons, transited Wyoming in 1836; included in the caravan were the Spaldings and Whitmans, two missionary couples, Eliza Spalding and Narcissa Whitman being the first white women to cross the country. With the passage of more wagon parties, a rutted trail to Portland was well established by 1839.

The nation's attention focused upon the West, with the annexation of Texas (including southeastern Wyoming) in 1845 and then the settlement of the Oregon Boundary, giving the United States sole rights to the lands west of the Continental Divide from the 42nd to the 49th parallels, in 1846. Boundary disputes led to war with Mexico, the outcome being the cession of the American Southwest (including a corner of Wyoming) in 1848.

The westward flow of emigrants steadily grew. 1846 saw the passage of the ill-fated Donner Party, destined to become snowbound in the Sierra Nevadas on their way to California. Brigham Young followed the next year, leading the first expedition of Mormons to take up settlement by Salt Lake. And with the discovery of gold in California in 1848, traffic westward became a stampede. Among the best of the accounts, with acute observations and thorough scientific descriptions, was written by Capt. Howard Stansbury of the Army Engineers after his 1849-50 expedition to Utah. (See the Sweetwater River Segment for his report on the Sweetwater Canyon.) Stansbury's eastward return journey was guided by Jim Bridger, the explorer-extraordinary of Wyoming; Bridger's 49 years of roaming took him from Yellowstone to Colorado, and the settlement he founded in 1842 in southwestern Wyoming was the first permanent outpost in the state west of the Rockies.

Although the travelers were only transients, occasional skirmishes with Indians forebode future troubles. The government called an assembly at Fort Laramie in 1851 and negotiated a treaty which gave the United States the right to secure roads and military and other posts in the region; the treaty also fixed tribal boundaries (with the Shoshones west of the Rockies, the Crows, Arapahos, and Cheyennes on the eastern slope), guaranteed protection against depredations by U.S. citizens, and provided financial compensation. The next years were difficult ones for the Indians — decimated by smallpox introduced by the white man, occasionally the victim of massacres stemming from misunderstandings or arrogance on the part of the army, embroiled in battles of their own such as those that forced the Crows northwest to Montana.

Despite the friction between white and red man, punctuated by more treacherous and bloody army raids, travel routes across Wyoming continued to be improved. Stagecoaches went into regular service on the Oregon Trail in the 1850's, and the Pony Express followed in 1860 — only to be discontinued as a telegraph line across the country went into service the next year. In 1862 another stage route, the Overland Trail through Bridger Pass, was developed as a southern Wyoming alternate for westbound travel.

COLONIZATION AND DEVELOPMENT

Gold and the Union Pacific were magnets for the first settlements in Wyoming. Cheyenne sprang up overnight in 1867 as the railroad approached — not along the Oregon Trail, but further south where coal deposits provided a ready source of fuel. Rawlins and other towns developed along the tracks. While the railroad was pushing its way westward to its 1869 meeting with the Central Pacific from California, there was a simultaneous rush to prospect for gold in rich placer deposits discovered near South Pass. Several boom towns dotted the landscape. South Pass City, served by a stagecoach connection to Point of Rocks on the new railroad, reached a population of 4000 by 1870, but within a few years had been virtually abandoned.

BACKGROUND INFORMATION

The venerable Chief Washakie's Shoshones, traditionally friendly with the whites, bowed to the inevitable and agreed in 1868 to accept a reservation in the Popo Agie Valley on the east side of the Wind Rivers. (The boundaries of the Wind River Reservation were reduced in 1872, 1896, and 1904.) The Indians' rights to northeast Wyoming were violated during the army campaigns of 1876 and 1877; as a result, remnant Arapahos were settled, over Washakie's protests, with their old enemies, the Shoshones. There they remain today still — two tribes on a single reservation.

With amazing speed, the settlers of Cheyenne secured the approval of the Dakota Legislature and Congress, in 1868, to the organization of the Wyoming Territory. Controversial laws were enacted — allowing gambling, prohibiting racial intermarriage, and providing (for the first time in the United States) that women should have full rights to vote and hold office. Wyoming's nickname, the Equality State, commemorates this initiative. And in 1872, after the Washburn-Langford Expedition's report on the wonders of Yellowstone, the northwest corner of the territory was set aside as the world's first national park.

Livestock production was one of the earliest economic activities in the newly settled region. Violence was common, with cattle raisers warring among themselves, setting up vigilante committees to track down thieving rustlers, and feuding with sheepmen. Overgrazing, a practice not yet eradicated, hurt the range; but it was a bitter winter and lack of water that caused the first cattle boom to burst.

The great gold mining days of the South Pass area were over before the granting of statehood in 1890. Yet minerals have remained important. Coal, originally recovered to power the Union Pacific locomotives, is now being developed as a national fuel resource. Oil, a curiosity when reported by Bonneville in 1832, is refined at several places, including Sinclair on the Trail's route. A spur rail line at South Pass City leads to a modern taconite (iron) mine near Atlantic City. Uranium mining, milling, and prospecting are important activities; the Trail passes the Western Nuclear mining operations near Jeffrey City. Gemstone jades are recovered in the same vicinity.

The turn of the century also marked the establishment of forest reserves that form the basis of present-day national forests. Large tracts — now the Bridger Wilderness and the Teton Wilderness — were classified as primitive areas in 1931 and 1934, respectively, and obtained permanent protection under the Wilderness Act of 1964. But while these areas, along with Yellowstone National Park, are already well-known and often visited, the remainder of the Trail offers the traveler a different, and also rewarding, view of Wyoming. So the history of the state may soon record the marking of a Continental Divide National Scenic Trail all the way from Yellowstone to Colorado.

Addresses

Government Agencies

U.S. GEOLOGICAL SURVEY

Distribution Section, U.S. Geological Survey, Federal Center, Denver, Colorado 80225.

FOREST SERVICE

Regional Forester, Rocky Mountain Region, P.O. Box 25127, Denver, Colorado 80225 (for information regarding the Continental Divide Trail as a whole).

Targhee National Forest
Supervisor, Targhee National Forest, 420 N. Bridge St., St. Anthony, Idaho 83445.
District Ranger, Island Park Ranger District, Island Park, Idaho 83429.

Bridger-Teton National Forest
Supervisor, Bridger-Teton National Forest, P.O. Box 1888, Jackson, Wyoming 83001.
District Ranger, Buffalo Ranger District, P.O. Box 278, Moran, Wyoming 83013.
District Ranger, Gros Ventre Ranger District, P.O. Box 1888, Jackson, Wyoming 83001.
District Ranger, Pinedale Ranger District, Pinedale, Wyoming 82941.

Shoshone National Forest
Supervisor, Shoshone National Forest, P.O. Box 961, Cody, Wyoming 82414.
District Ranger, Wind River Ranger District, Dubois, Wyoming 82513.
District Ranger, Lander Ranger District, P.O. Box FF, Lander, Wyoming 82520.

NATIONAL PARK SERVICE

Superintendent, Yellowstone National Park, Wyoming 82190.

BUREAU OF LAND MANAGEMENT

District Manager, Rock Springs District, Bureau of Land Management, P.O. Box 1869, Rock Springs, Wyoming 82901 (north of South Pass City).

BACKGROUND INFORMATION

Area Manager, Lander Resource Area (Rawlins District), Bureau of Land Management, P.O. Box 589, Lander, Wyoming 82520 (South Pass City to Muddy Gap).

District Manager, Rawlins District, Bureau of Land Management, P.O. Box 670, Rawlins, Wyoming 82301 (Muddy Gap to Rawlins).

STATE AGENCIES

Wyoming Game and Fish Department, Communications Branch, Cheyenne, Wyoming 82002.

Superintendent, South Pass Historic Site, South Pass City, Wyoming 82520.

Transportation

AMTRAK. Use toll-free phone for information. Check local directory for listing. (Rail service to Rawlins and Rock Springs.)

Grand Teton Lodge Co., Moran, Wyoming 83013. (Bus service between Jackson and Jackson Lake Lodge.)

Greyhound. (Transcontinental services through Rawlins and Rock Springs and also, in Montana, through Billings, Livingston, and Bozeman; also, from Salt Lake City to West Yellowstone via Idaho Falls and Macks Inn.)

Jackson-Rock Springs Stages, Inc., 514 Lewis Street, Rock Springs, Wyoming 82901. (Rock Springs to Jackson via Boulder and Pinedale.)

Trailways. (Transcontinental service through Rawlins and Rock Springs.)

Yellowstone Park Lines, Inc., Yellowstone National Park, Wyoming 82190. (Throughout Yellowstone Park; also, to West Yellowstone, Bozeman, Livingston, and Billings, Montana and to Jackson Lake Lodge.)

Zanetti Bus and Fast Express, Inc., 1002 Pilot Butte Ave., Rock Springs, Wyoming 82901. (Daily service from Rawlins to Lander via Muddy Gap, Jeffrey City, and Sweetwater Station; once-a-week service from Rock Springs to Lander via South Pass City.)

References

Some useful references are noted above in the descriptions of the wildflowers and the birds along the Trail. In addition to the Hitchcock & Cronquist work referred to in the text, the flower key relies heavily upon H.D. Harrington's *Manual of the Plants of Colorado*, 2nd ed., Swallow, 1964, as well as several more popular books. Among these, H.W. Rickett's massive

236

Wild Flowers of the United States, vol. 6, covering the Central Mountains and Plains. (McGraw-Hill, 1973), is particularly valuable.

The *Weather Atlas of the United States,* U.S. Dept. of Commerce, Washington, 1968, available at public libraries, provides an overview of important climatological data.

For a general history, refer to T.A. Larson's *History of Wyoming,* Univ. of Nebraska, 1965. The mountain fur trade is the focus of Bernard DeVoto in *Across the Wide Missouri,* Houghton Mifflin, 1947. The beginnings of the Oregon Trail are recounted in *Westward Vision,* by David Lavender, McGraw-Hill, 1973; the Oregon Trail's later history, along with that of the other routes of commerce, is told in Ralph Moody's *Stagecoach West,* Promontory Press, 1967. Some interesting historical sidelights are found in Mae Urbanek's *Wyoming Place Names,* Johnson Publishing Co., 1974. Early accounts worth consulting include J.C. Fremont's *Report of the Exploring Expedition to the Rocky Mountains* (1845) and Howard Stansbury's *Expedition to the Valley of the Great Salt Lake* (1855).

Yellowstone, by Ann and Myron Sutton, Macmillan, 1972, is a handsome and comprehensive treatment of its subject. Bryce S. Walker explores the Continental Divide in Montana, Wyoming, and Colorado in *The Great Divide,* Time-Life Books, 1973. In *The Ultimate Journey,* Chronicle Books, 1973, backpacker Eric Ryback describes a one-summer trip through the Rockies from Canada to Mexico; it is a colorful adventure story, but it is not always reliable. The *Guide to the Wyoming Mountains and Wilderness Areas,* 3rd ed., Swallow, 1974, by Orin H. and Lorraine Bonney, is a valuable source for technical climbers. *Roadside Geology of Wyoming,* Mountain Press (in press), should provide much-needed nontechnical coverage of the state's geology.

The *Continental Divide Trail Study Report,* prepared by the Bureau of Outdoor Recreation, U.S. Dept. of the Interior, September 1976, describes a possible location for the Trail. The Bureau's Final Environmental Impact Statement, FES 77-11, addresses concerns raised by public officials and private citizens.

Several other environmental impact statements and environmental assessments provide information in depth about various portions of the Trail. See, especially, the following:

Island Park Geothermal Area (Forest Service/BLM, 1979)
Dunoir Special Management Unit (Forest Service, 1978)
Union Pass Planning Unit (Forest Service, 1976)
Bridger Wilderness Management Plan (Forest Service, 1975)
Sandy Grazing (BLM, 1978)
Wild and Scenic River Study: Sweetwater River (NPS, 1979)
Bison Basin Project (Nuclear Regulatory Commission, 1980)
Split Rock Uranium Mill (NRC, 1978)
Sweetwater Uranium Project (NRC, 1977)
Coal Leasing: Carbon Basin Area (BLM, 1979)

About the Author

Jim Wolf has traveled throughout the United States in pursuit of his interests as a backpacker and naturalist. He particularly enjoys long-distance walking, a fervor that stems from his Georgia-Maine hike on the Appalachian Trail in 1971.

Since 1973, he has scouted the Continental Divide from the Canadian border southward to southern New Mexico. He was active in the successful campaign to have Congress designate the route as a national scenic trail. He is now continuing his efforts on behalf of the Trail — both as Director of the Continental Divide Trail Society and as a member of the Continental Divide National Scenic Trail Advisory Council. This guidebook series records his observations and suggestions concerning the present status and future development of the Trail.

The author served as president of the Audubon Society of Western Pennsylvania for two years, and he has held other offices with the Environmental Planning and Information Center of Pennsylvania, the Pittsburgh Climbers, and the Explorers Club of Pittsburgh. He is also a member of numerous conservation and trails organizations.

He is an attorney by profession and is currently on the legal staff of the United States Nuclear Regulatory Commission.

About the Society

The Continental Divide Trail Society is dedicated to the planning, development, and maintenance of the Continental Divide Trail as a silent trail — one laid out with appreciation of its natural environment and sensitivity to yearnings for a sense of contact with the wilderness. It stresses each person's responsibility to be a good steward, with respect for fellow travelers, for proprietors of the land, and for the creatures of the earth.

To further these objectives, the Society:

● Scouts the terrain, identifies possible Trail locations, and — through its publications — describes existing feasible routes.

● Collects bibliographic and photographic materials related to the Continental Divide corridor.

● Monitors land use actions of governmental agencies and participates in administrative review procedures. Typical projects have involved wilderness and scenic river studies, and proposals to construct railroads and power transmission lines through scenic areas along the Trail.

● Cooperates with local and regional organizations and encourages volunteer efforts, by individuals and groups, on behalf of the Trail.

● Serves as a clearinghouse for the suggestions of Trail users and other interested persons.

The Society publishes DIVIDEnds, a semiannual newsletter on matters of current interest. DIVIDEnds is distributed to members of the Society and, on an exchange basis, to other organizations with similar interests.

The *Guide to the Continental Divide Trail* is the Society's major publication. The series so far includes:

Vol. 1: Northern Montana (Canada to Rogers Pass, 268.0 miles).
Vol. 2: Southern Montana and Idaho (Rogers Pass to Macks Inn, 537.2 miles).
Vol. 3: Wyoming (Macks Inn to Rawlins, 496.8 miles).

Additional titles, covering Colorado and New Mexico, are in preparation.

Inquiries and suggestions are welcome and will be greatly appreciated.

Acknowledgments

My first thanks are to the landowners, some of them unknown to me, whose lands I crossed while scouting this route. I sincerely hope that my visit, and my descriptions here, will not be a cause of concern to any of them. As indicated in the text, the Society solicits the landowners' cooperation and wants to work with them in the planning for the Trail over the coming years. I do wish to apologize, however, to the extent I may have offended.

I should also like to express my gratitude to the numerous officials who gave me advice in planning my hikes or who read over the manuscript or otherwise assisted in putting this book together. I cannot begin to list them all; but, whether they were representing the National Park Service, the Forest Service, the Bureau of Land Management, or the Wyoming Recreation Commission, they made my task much easier. I believe that most of them share my enthusiasm for the Continental Divide Trail and will join in maximizing its recreational appeal.

These guidebooks can be improved by the incorporation of observations of other hikers. This volume includes two such contributions. Dave James, a friend whose acquaintance I made while on the Trail, provided some needed information on the route near Little Sandy Lake. As mentioned in a footnote in the text, Dave Clarendon, hiking from Mexico to Canada in 1980, recommends a route along Buck Creek near the ford of the South Fork of Fish Creek in the Gros Ventre Segment. He also chose to cross Shannon and Hat Passes in the northern part of the Bridger Wilderness; although details are lacking, his report suggests that his route there may be preferable, except in early season, to the Trail described in this book. My thanks to both Daves and, once again, an invitation to other hikers to share their experiences with the Society.

Finally, I am greatly encouraged by the initial actions of the Continental Divide National Scenic Trail Advisory Council, under the helm of its chairman, Regional Forester Craig Rupp. Although the present text was completed before organization of the Council, I am confident that its views will provide valuable guidance in the preparation of future volumes.

South Fork Falls, in the Teton Wilderness.

Maps
Legend

Map Number	6
Continental Divide	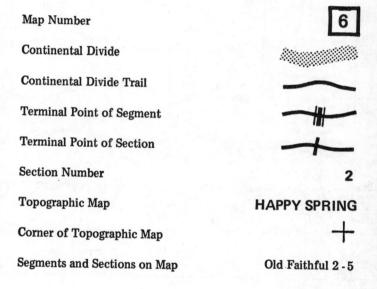
Continental Divide Trail	
Terminal Point of Segment	
Terminal Point of Section	
Section Number	2
Topographic Map	HAPPY SPRING
Corner of Topographic Map	+
Segments and Sections on Map	Old Faithful 2 - 5

Scale of Miles
(½" = 1 mile)

0   1   2   3

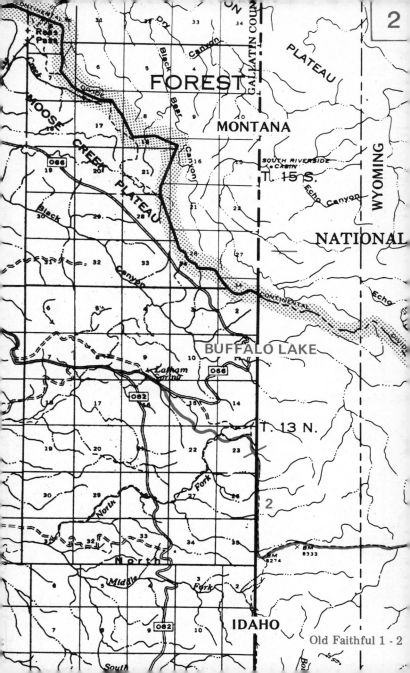

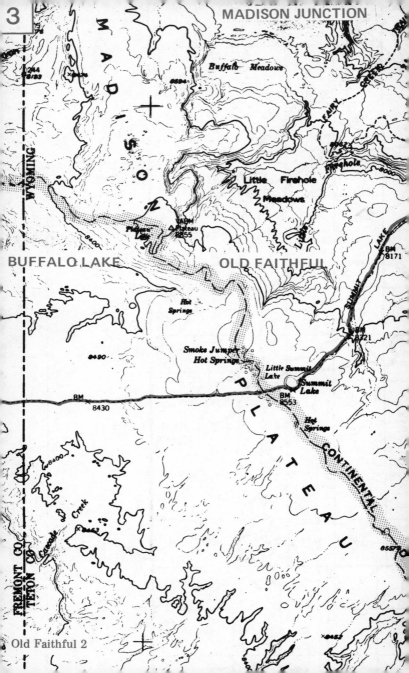

MADISON JUNCTION

M
A
D
I
S
O
N

Buffalo Meadows

7244
78/83

WYOMING

Little Firehole
Meadows

Firehole

Plateau
Hill

BM
Plateau
8855

BUFFALO LAKE

OLD FAITHFUL

LAKE

BM
8171

Hot
Springs

BM
8221

8490

Smoke Jumper
Hot Springs

Little Summit
Lake

P
L
A
T
E
A
U

SUMMIT

BM
8430

Summit
Lake

BM
8553

Hot
Springs

C
O
N
T
I
N
E
N
T
A
L

8400

Cascade Creek

FREMONT CO.
TETON CO.

8557

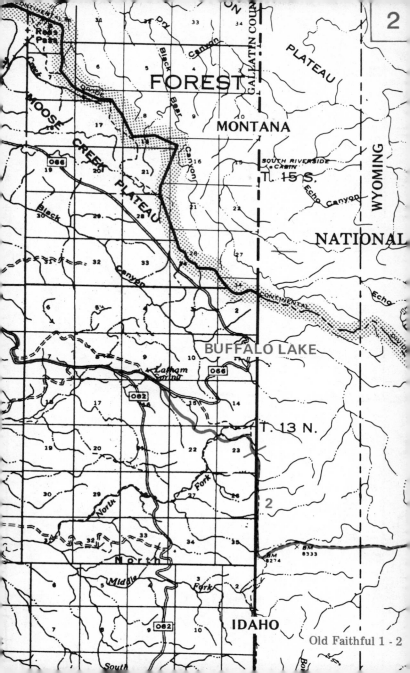

2

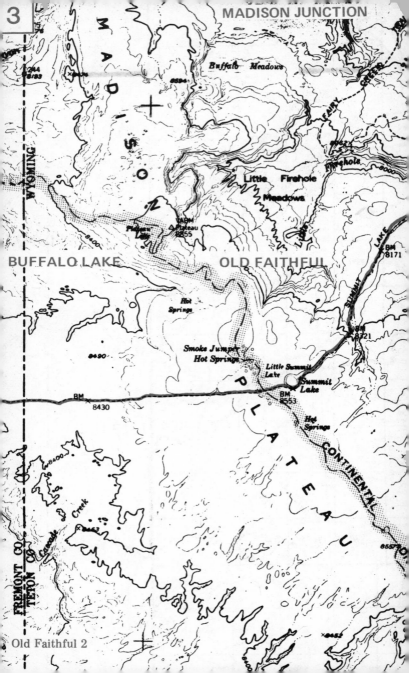

M A D I S O N

Buffalo Meadows

WYOMING

Buffalo Meadows

1244
08/83

+

Little Firehole

Meadows

FAIRY CREEK

Firehole

Plateau
Hill

VABM
Plateau
8255

BUFFALO LAKE

OLD FAITHFUL

BM
8171

SUMMIT LAKE

Hot
Springs

Smoke Jumper
Hot Springs

8490

Little Summit
Lake

BM
8721

P L A T E A U

BM
8430

BM
8553

Summit
Lake

Hot
Springs

CONTINENTAL

8400

Cascade Creek

8657

FREMONT CO.
TETON CO.

Old Faithful 2

OLD FAITHFUL

2

TRAIL

BM
8171

Fairy
Falls

Spring
Creek

Crater
Hills

Rabbit

Mystic
Falls

Sapphire
Pool

Biscuit
Basin

Upper

Morning Glory Geyser
Pool

Ghost
Geyser

Geyser
Basin

Castle
Geyser

Observation Point

Old Faithful Inn

Old Faithful

BM
8721

Fern
Cascades

SUMMIT LAKE

First
Cascades

4

BM
7583

Kepler
Cascades

ROAD

LOG

Spring
Lake

BM
7920

×8536

Mallard
Lake

Tent
Lake

Hot Springs

OBSERVATION TRAIL

Lone Star
Geyser

Hot Springs

Firehole

Grand
Spring

Shoshone

Cement

Hills

Pocket
Lake

Creek

×8557

DIVIDE

CONTINENTAL

Madison
Lake

VABM
Madison
8600

Trischman
Knob

8670

Pocket Basin
Shoshone
Geyser Basin

Old Park Bdy
Base Mon

5

SHOSHONE

SHOS

WEST THUMB

SHOSHONE LAKE

LEWIS LAKE

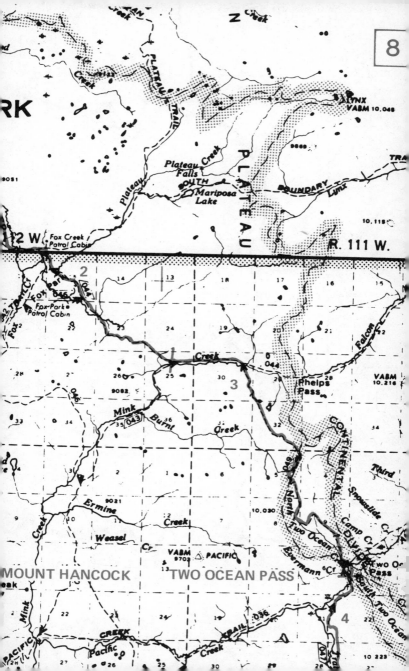

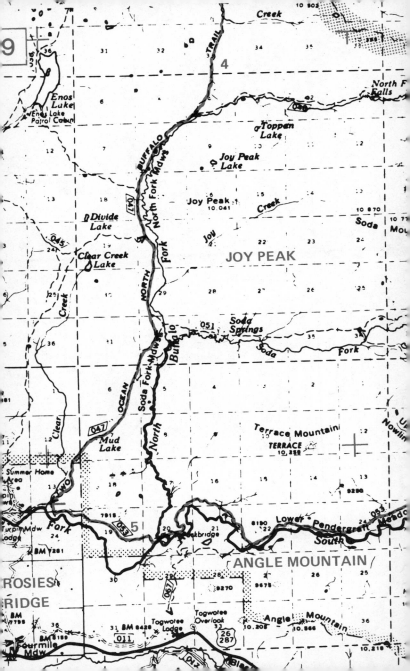

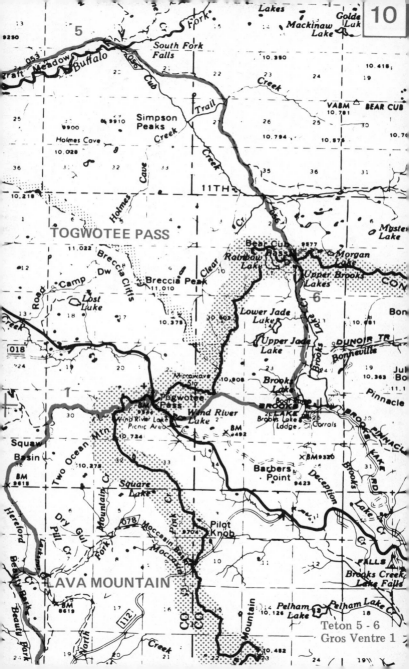

Lakes
Golde
Luk

Mackinaw
Lake

5

Fork
Fork

053
Buffalo
raft Meadow
South Fork
Falls

9250

056
Cub

South Fork
Falls

10.380

10.416

10.76

25

9900

9910

Simpson
Peaks
Creek

Trail

10.781
VABM
BEAR CUB

Holmes Cave
10.028

Creek

24

19

26

25

30

36

32

Holmes

Cave

Creek

10.794

10.875

10.218

11TH

Cr

056

6

Myste
Lake

1

TOGWOTEE PASS

Bear Cub
9577

Morgan
Lake

Rainbow
Lake

CON

11.022

Breccia

Dw

Breccia Peak
11.010

Clear

Upper Brooks
Lakes

12

Road

Camp
Cliffs

6

Lost
Luke

Lower Jade
Lake

10.403

Brooks

13

18

17

10.379

10.981

Bon

Creek

018

Upper Jade
Lake

DUNOIR TR

Bonneville

24

Microwave
Sta

10.808

Brooks
Lake

Ju
Bo

10.363

11.1

1

Togwotee
Pass

Wind River
Lake

BROOK

Pinnacle

30

BM

Wind River Lake
Picnic Area

BROOKS LAKE
Brooks Lake
Lodge

Corrals

PINNACL

Squaw
Basin

Two Ocean Mtn

10.724

BM
9492

RD

10.278

14

X BM9320

31

BM
9615

Square
Lake

Barbers
Point
9423

Deception

Hereford

Dry Gul

Mountain Cr

078

Moccasin Fall

Pilot
Knob
9704

Brooks
Lake

Cr

Pill Cr

Fork

Moccasin

10

FALLS

Beauty Park

LAVA MOUNTAIN

11

12

Brooks Creek
Lake Falls

BM
9615

112

17

16

CO

CO

Mountain

Pelham
Lake
10.126

Pelham Lake

Cr

18

Beauty Park

Forth

Creek

19

20

21

10.482

23

24

19

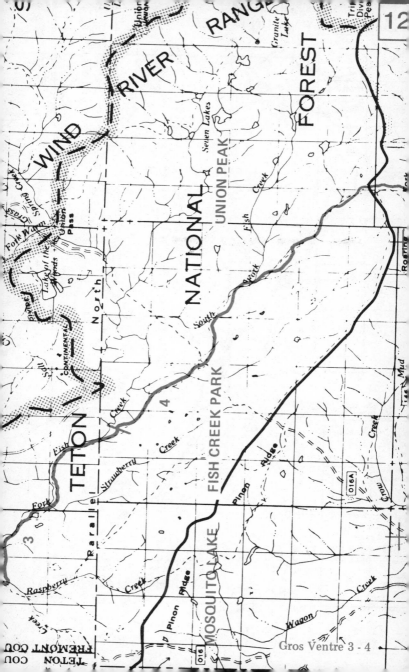

Gros Ventre 3 - 4

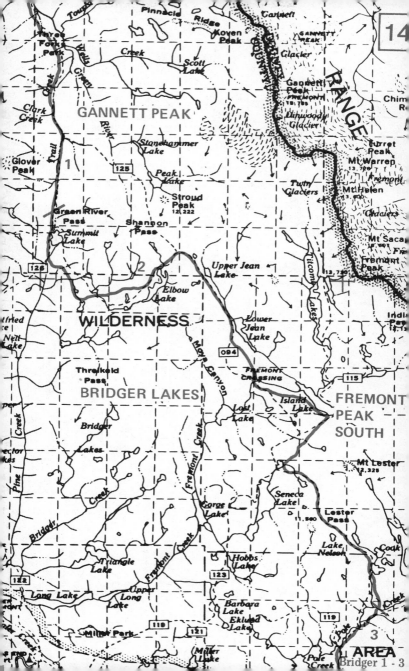

RIVER

Lake

Ridge

MOUNT BONNEVILLE

Milky

Milky Lakes

Milky

Creek

CONTINENTAL

Medina Mountain

Lake Prue

Bridgestone Lakes

Europe Canyon

Mt Victor
12,254

141

Lake Victor

Medina Lake

Lake Winaga

DENTS AZIMUTH PEAK
11,255

North Fork Peak

North Fork

Round Top Mountain

118

FREMONT PEAK SOUTH

Mt Baldy
11,755

Rinico Lake

Hay Pass

Macs Lake

Edmond Lake

HORSESHOE LAKE

Lake Sequa

Lake George

Falls Creek

Bald Mountain Basin

Baldy Lake

098

Barren Lake

120

Falls

117

Hopkins Lake

04

New Fork Peak
11,898

Spruce Lake

Chain Lakes

Hidden Lake

AREA

3

Junction Lake

Baldy Lake

Belford Lake

119

Pole Creek Lakes

Spruce Creek

Little Brown Point

Black Lake

Lake Surprise

117

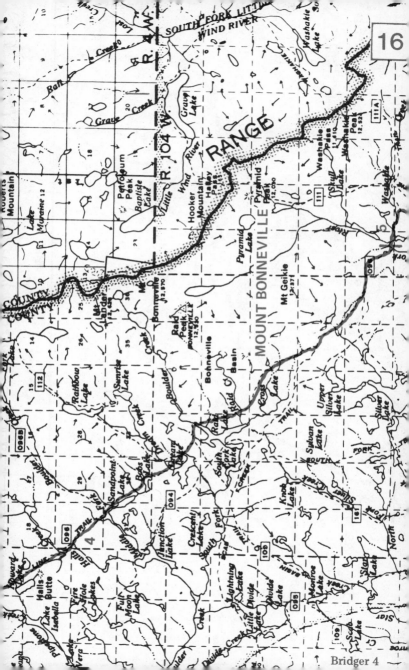

16

SOUTH FORK LITTLE
WIND RIVER

Washakie
Lake

Ban Creek

Grave
Lake

Creek

Grave Creek

RANGE

Washakie
Peak
12,52

R. 104 W.

Washakie Pass
11,610

111A

18

Petroleum
Peak

Roberts
Mountain

Little Wind River

Baptiste
Lake

Moraine 12
Lake

Hooker
Mountain

Pyramid
Peak
12,030

Lizard

Skull
Lake

Hailey
Pass
11,161

111

109

Mt Geikie
12,378

Pyramid Lake

MOUNT BONNEVILLE

COUNTY
COUNTY

25

26

Mt
Lander
12,623

35

Mt
Bonneville
13,570

Bald Peak
Bonneville
12,580

Bonneville
Basin

Bonneville Creek

Raid
Lake

Raid Cr

Cross Lake

Upper
Silver
Lake

Silver
Lake

112

Rainbow
Lake

15

28

Sunrise
Lake

Boulder Creek

Boulder Creek

South Fork
Lake

TRAIL

Sylvan
Lake

SOUTH

FORK

29

Boss Lake

Sandpoint
Lake

Dream Lake

094

South Fork

Raid Cr

Knob
Lake

101

096

TRAIL

Halls

Junction
Lake

Crescent
Lake

Seas Trail

South Fork

108

Monroe
Lake

Howard
Lake

Halls
Butte

Fire
Hole
Lakes

Full
Moon
Lakes

Lightning
Lake

Little Divide

Divide
Lake

098

Lake
Isabella

Lake
Vera

Divide Creek

Bolder Creek

Slide
Lake

Scab
Lake

Bridger 4

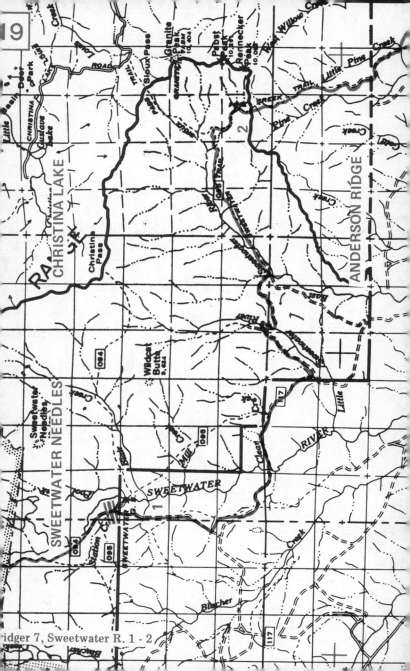

Little Basin Dvr.

CHRISTINA LAKE

Christina Park

Gustave Lake

RA

CHRISTINA LAKE

Christina Pass

Long Creek

Cat Lous

ROAD

TRAIL

Sioux Pass

Granite Peak

GRANITE PEAK

Pt. Post
10.554

Reinecker Peak
10.361

Reinecker Peak
10.065

Red Willow Creek

Little Pine Creek

Pine Creek

BREEK TRAIL

Pine Creek

Creek

Creek

Creek

ANDERSON RIDGE

084

Wildcat Butte
9,684

SWEETWATER NEEDLES

Sweetwater Needles

Creek

River

River

Stonywash

Little

River

17

095

Clean Creek

Mill Creek

084

SWEETWATER

1

Station Creek

SWEETWATER

095

RIVER

Creek

Blacher

117

Blacher

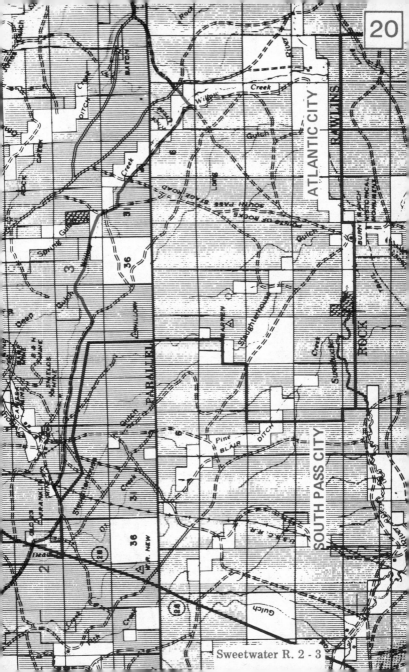

ATLANTIC CITY

RAWLINS

ROCK

SOUTH PASS CITY

Willow Creek

Gulch

POINT OF ROCKS SOUTH PASS ROUTE

BURN RANCH

S. PARALLEL

Pine BLAIR DITCH

Gulch

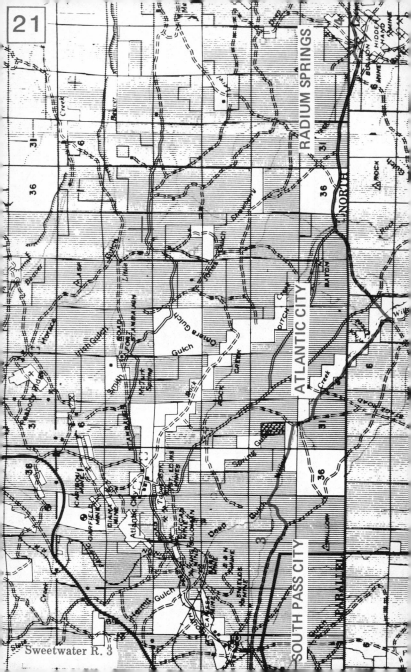

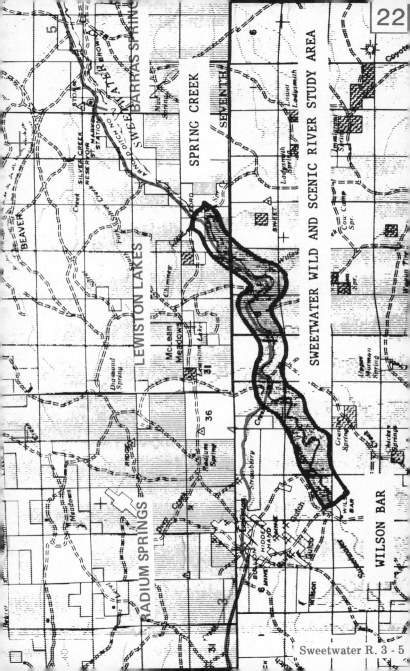

SWEETWATER WILD AND SCENIC RIVER STUDY AREA

SPRING CREEK

LEWISTON LAKES

RADIUM SPRINGS

WILSON BAR

SEVENTH

BARRAS SPRINGS

SWEETWATER CREEK

SILVER CREEK

BEAVER

McLean Meadows

Lewiston Lakes

△ 36

31

5

6

Sweetwater R. 3 - 5

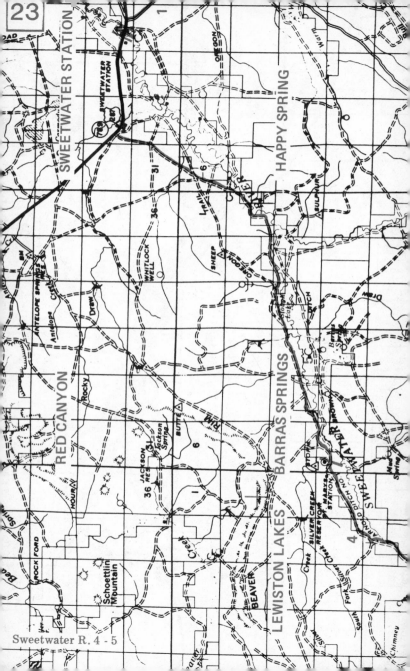

23

SWEETWATER STATION

HAPPY SPRING

RED CANYON

BARRAS SPRINGS

LEWISTON LAKES

BEAVER

Sweetwater R. 4 - 5

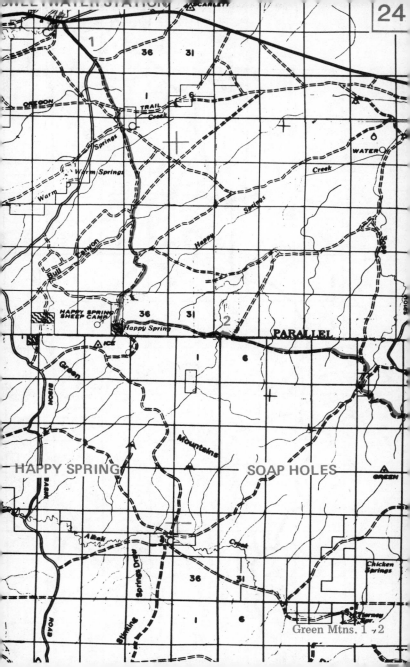

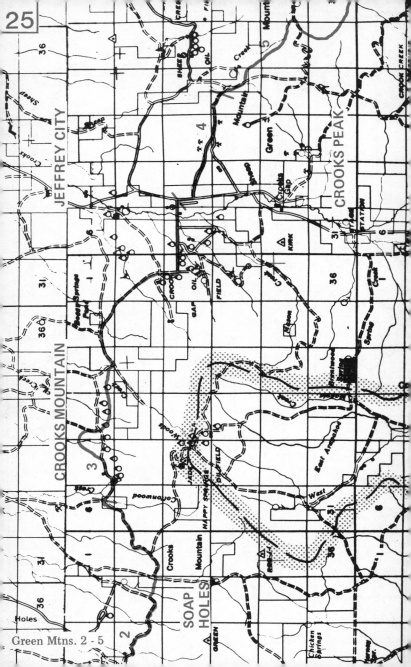

25

Green Mtns. 2 - 5

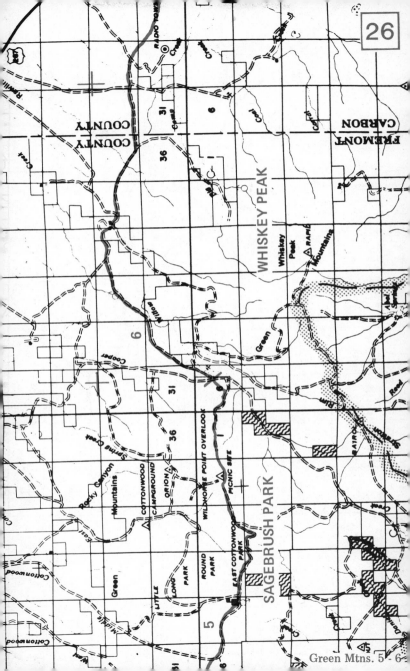

FREMONT CARBON

WHISKEY PEAK

Whiskey Peak

Rattle Mountains

SAGEBRUSH PARK

COUNTY COUNTY

RADIO TOWER

Coal Creek

Green

Bairoil Road

WILDHORSE POINT OVERLOOK

PICNIC SITE

COTTONWOOD CAMPGROUND

ORION

Rocky Canyon

Mountains

Spring Creek

Cooper

East Green

Little

Long Park

Round Park

EAST COTTONWOOD PARK

West Cottonwood

Middle Cottonwood

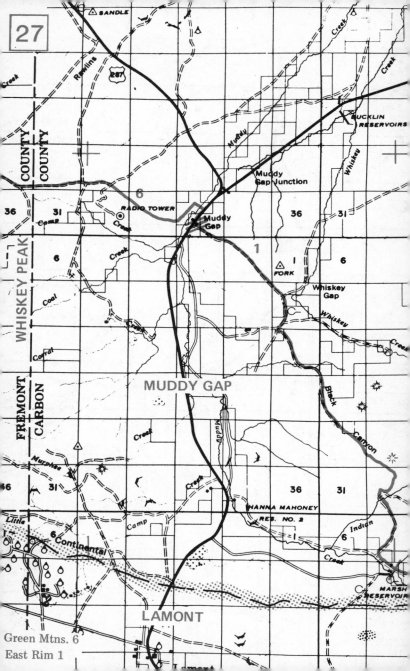

YOUNGS PASS

FERRIS

LAMONT NE

East Rim 2

Spanish Mine

Cave

Sand Springs

Larsen Place

Youngs Pass

Mountains

Creek

Well

Ferris

Canoe

Muddy

Mahoney Dome Oil Field

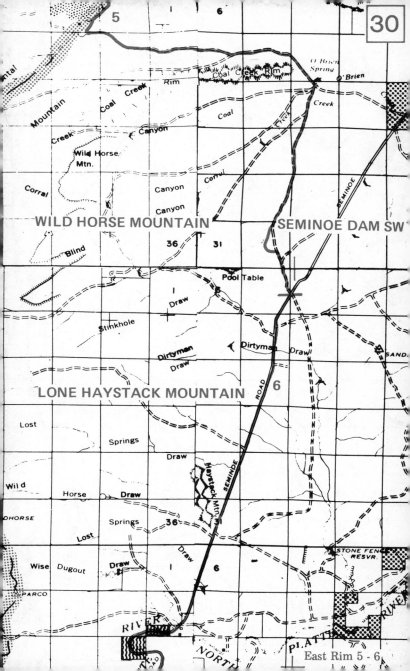

5 | 6

O'Brien
Spring

Coal Creek Rim
Rim
O'Brien

Coal
Creek
Creek

Coal

Mountain
Creek

Coal
Creek
Creek
Canyon

Wild Horse
Mtn.
Creek

Corral
Canyon
Corral

Canyon
SEMINOE

WILD HORSE MOUNTAIN
Canyon
SEMINOE DAM SW

Blind
36 | 31

Pool Table

Draw
6

Stinkhole

Dirtyman
Draw
Dirtyman Draw
SAND

LONE HAYSTACK MOUNTAIN
ROAD 6

Lost

Springs

Draw
SEMINOE

Wild
Horse Draw

Haystack Mtn.

OHORSE
Springs
36 | 31

Lost

Draw

Wise Dugout Draw
1 | 6
STONE FENCE
RESVR.

PARCO

RIVER
PLATTE

NORTH

East Rim 6 - 7